INTERNATIONAL POLICY FORMATION IN THE USSR

Yugoslavia after Tito (Boulder, Colorado, Westwood, 1977)
The Evolution of the Soviet Use of Surrogates in Military Relations with the Third World (Rand Paper P-6420)
"Cyprus, 1974 to 1978" (in *Ethnic Resurgence*, Elmsford, N.Y., Pergamon, 1980)
"Surrogate Forces and Power Projection" (in *Projection of Power*, Hamden, Connecticut, Archon Books, 1982)

INTERNATIONAL POLICY FORMATION IN THE USSR

Factional "Debates" during the Zhdanovschina

Gavriel D. Ra'anan

With a Foreword by
Robert Conquest

Archon Books
1983

© 1983 Gavriel D. Ra'anan. All rights reserved.
First published 1983 as an Archon Book,
an imprint of The Shoe String Press, Inc.,
Hamden, Connecticut 06514
Printed in the United States of America

Library of Congress Cataloging in Publication Data
Ra'anan, Gavriel D.
    International policy formation in the USSR.

    Bibliography: p.
    Includes index.
    1. Soviet Union—Foreign relations—
1945–   . 2. Soviet Union—Foreign
relations Yugoslavia. 3. Yugoslavia—
Foreign relations—Soviet Union. 4. Zhdanov,
Andrei Aleksandrovich, 1896–1948. I. Title.
II. Title. Zhdanovshchina.
DK267.R28 1983   327.47   83-6064
ISBN 0-208-01976-6

65864

The paper in this book meets the guidelines for
permanence and durability of the Committee on Production
Guidelines for Book Longevity of the Council on Library Resources.

For my lovely wife, Holly;
my parents, for their efforts;
and for Michael, my brother and my friend

CONTENTS

FOREWORD

Dr. Ra'anan's investigation into the factional struggle in the Soviet Communist Party during the late 1940s brings us to grips with the true nature of Soviet politics, and the way in which policy is thrashed out. It therefore has profound implications not merely for the period it covers, but also for the events of a later epoch.

It is a difficult and laborious task to unravel the detail of the struggle, and above all to interpret the position of particular personalities. Yet this is vital work, for political life in the USSR, then as now, was confined to a few hundred people, with only a few dozen playing any important role. Much of this sort of work is interpretative, and cannot claim finality; I find myself in disagreement on certain points, as is inevitable in such studies. For example, I feel that Dr. Ra'anan's listings in chapter three give, not so much in themselves as by cumulative effect, an impression of the overwhelming ascendancy of the Zhdanov faction, which slightly overstates the case. And on individuals, I do not agree with his characterization of Patolichev as owing allegiance to Zhdanov. But these are minor points, and the general sweep of the story, and the evidence brought together, gives us a splendid general picture of the time.

In saying that the study is directly relevant to present-day matters, I do not wish to give the impression that this is a question of simple immediacy. To unravel any major section of the Soviet past, still kept so obscure and secret in official sources, is itself necessary to a clear understanding of the whole Soviet experience, and so required for any proper view of the USSR past and present. Nevertheless, these events of the 1940s still have a direct connection with Andropov, and in the most striking fashion. For Andropov was made second secretary of the Central Committee of the Communist Party of the Karelian Soviet Socialist Republic in 1947, and this republic was always regarded as an appanage of Zhdanovite Leningrad. In 1949, when the Leningrad Case purge struck the Zhdanov apparatus in the city, Karelia too suffered. The local First Secretary G.N. Kupryanov was arrested, tortured, and sent to prison; and his successor, A.A. Kondakov, was almost at once also removed (and shot). That Andropov survived, and was indeed short-ly afterwards brought to Moscow to serve as one of Stalin's new

"inspectors" of the Central Committee, a highly trusted group designed
to implement the new planned purge of the dictator's last days, indicates
that he himself was directly involved (as of course he must have been
in his capacity as organizational secretary), and gave satisfaction, in the
events recounted in this book. Thus they are part of the present Soviet
background in a very intimate sense.

This is a striking illustration of the value of the study of Soviet
political history in the sense of Dr. Ra'anan's valuable contribution to
our knowledge—of which it might also be said that to increase our
understanding of the Soviet leadership and its motivations is in our
present circumstances a true public service.

ROBERT CONQUEST

Preface

Research for this book began in the mid-1970s when I was a graduate student at The Fletcher School of Law and Diplomacy at Tufts University, which accepted my Ph.D. dissertation on the topic in 1980. My focus since that time has been on international relations and public policy, with particular emphasis on the USSR. My work on this subject has been enhanced considerably by the encouragement I received from my colleagues and employers at the Advanced International Studies Institute.

G.D.R.
Washington, D.C.,
February 1982

INTRODUCTION

Owing at least partly to the rapid sequence of dramatic events just preceding Stalin's demise and continuing through the succession struggle immediately following, Sovietologists became so preoccupied with study of the years between the nineteenth and twentieth congresses of the Communist Party of the Soviet Union (October 1952–February 1956) that little of their attention was left for the previous, formative period of Soviet postwar foreign and security policy, 1944–52.

Thus, most accounts dealing with Soviet attitudes of that time toward the rest of the world, and particularly toward the West, continue to emanate primarily from writers untrained in the methodologies essential for study of the USSR. As might be expected, these authors base their work overwhelmingly on American and other Western sources, rather than upon Soviet and other communist documentation. This one-dimensional approach, which has been typical both of "revisionist" and "traditionalist" historians, has failed to capture the essence of Soviet decision making. Presumably, it has been simpler for followers of both "schools" to read through the increasingly available U.S. postwar archival material than to analyze the voluminous, but esoteric, literature published by the CPSU and the "fraternal parties" then and subsequently. Yet, that material reveals the footprints of a Soviet "debate," in ideological terms, concerning the formulation of an appropriate international strategy.

This polemic, overlooked by so many scholars and analysts, who have tended curiously to view Soviet policy as primarily reactive to Western actions and declarations, was the outgrowth, it appears, of a factional power struggle between groups centered primarily upon Georgii M. Malenkov and Andreii A. Zhdanov. Significantly, it seems that the ideological dimension of the "debate," rather than being an end in itself, merely was a manifestation of the life-and-death contest between the two semifeudal alignments, each formed around one of Stalin's lieutenants. (As will be shown, such disputations, under Soviet conditions, bear only the most superficial resemblance to genuine debates.)

1

It was characteristic of the doctrinal style of this struggle that each of the protagonists all but ignored "objective reality," as reflected in Western actions and statements, while focusing their polemics upon each other's ideological shortcomings. Thus, the "leftist" Zhdanov-Voznesenskii group attacked its adversaries over such arcane matters as the alleged failure of the latter to realize the imminent approach of the "third stage in the general crisis of world capitalism," or their unwillingness to acknowledge the irreversibility of the subjection of the East European "new democracies" to Soviet control, or their insistence that the war had brought about a major political change in the relationship between the Western "imperialists" and their erstwhile colonies. Even the key issue of whether the United States or Great Britain was to be regarded now as "the primary adversary" was fought out over highly doctrinal socioeconomic propositions, with little reference to Western statements and policies, real or alleged.

While these topics had direct operational implications vis-à-vis the West, they were fought out in such a manner as to all but exclude a major Western input into the internecine conflict. It was clear that the immediate "primary antagonist" of each of the two predominant factions in Moscow was the other, with policy concerning the West a more long-term concern. Thus, the "revisionist" historians have little basis for their assumption that the West could have changed Moscow's hostility during this period, but for Washington's supposed sins of commission or omission; the "traditionalists," on their part, may have erred in believing that an appropriate U.S. response might have constrained sanguine expectations, if not attitudes, in the Kremlin. In fact, the West's role in influencing Soviet policy was relatively minor.

It does not follow, however, that because they were preoccupied with considerations of personal power, rather than with issues, the competing Soviet factions neglected to design their respective "platforms" in the most credible manner possible, that is, as coherent, lucid, consistent, and articulate propositions likely to prove persuasive. Conversely, one should not assume that because specific cliques advocated particular approaches to international affairs over protracted timespans and expressed themselves in a logical, plausible, and elegant manner it follows that these were primarily issue-oriented groups rather than "feudal" (chieftain-retainer) associations that exploited policy questions to score tactical points against one another. Were this not the case, it would be difficult to comprehend why, once its adversaries were clearly routed, the victorious faction generally showed no compunction about adopting and implementing the policies supported by its erstwhile antagonists. If issues really constituted a binding "glue" between individual members of a faction, then it is well-nigh inexplicable that, in any serious analysis of the composition of the "Leningrad" (Zhdanov) group, to take just one instance, such a central role should be played by biographical data (the Leninist "Who-Whom": who was appointed by and served with whom and where, and conversely, who "replaced" or helped to purge whose associates).

This study could affect qualitatively our concepts regarding the Soviet policy-making process, not only during that period, but at present (since instances of seemingly factional "debate" over policy issues continue to stud the Soviet landscape). Certain universal laws of power and politics appear to prevail during periods of succession struggle in closed societies; insight into these phenomena during Stalin's last years may provide useful analogies that add another dimension to investigations of current jostling for advantageous positions in the Kremlin.

Moreover, this analysis should help to shed additional light on the Soviet-Yugoslav rift, providing significant evidence that it, too, was an instance of fallout from the factional struggle in Moscow and that Tito was purged for his close links with the (losing) Zhdanov faction. Altogether, that episode reflects the highly significant role played by Tito and his associates throughout the period under consideration, in Soviet "domestic" affairs no less than in the context of the Kremlin's international policy, not merely with regard to the Balkans, but even the Middle East, South and Southeast Asia, Central Europe, and the West European Communist parties. The Zhdanov group, in fact, used its Yugoslav clients as surrogates in world affairs: that is why this work focuses repeatedly upon Titoist statements and operations.

The study is based upon detailed analysis of voluminous documentation from Soviet as well as other Communist Party sources; it utilizes also many firsthand accounts, some published and others constituting oral history, collected in the United States and in Europe, in many cases from Soviet and East European emigrés.

The Soviet policies analyzed are of truly global scope, affecting such key issues as the future of the Soviet occupation zone of Germany, the strategies of the French and Italian Communist parties, the proposed Balkan federation, Communist operations in the newly independent states of South and Southeast Asia, and the Soviet posture toward the Middle East. Moreover, these questions were intertwined with such "internal" matters as the direction of the Soviet economy, of Russian culture and science, of Communist Party management, etc., which must be addressed, therefore. "International" and "domestic" aspects of policy do not exist in watertight compartments, particularly for an elite habituated to view developments in terms derived from an all-embracing, "scientific" ideology.

Instrumental in triggering the questions that have motivated much of this study were the contributions of two outstanding Sovietologists of the immediate postwar period, Boris Nicolaevsky (particularly in his frequent articles for the *New Leader*) and Franz Borkenau (in his book *European Communism*). Their work reflected remarkable insight, but was limited severely at the time by a dearth of sources. Subsequently, it has been supplemented by various firsthand accounts, including the testimony of such witnesses as Eugenio Reale, Ernst Lemmer, Erich Gniffke, Vladimir Rudolf, Nikolai Grishin, N. S. Patolichev, and Wolfgang Leonhard. Moreover, a dissident Soviet historian, Anton Antonov-Ovseyenko, who for a brief period during the "thaw" had access to classified sources, initiated the publication in the West of valuable documentation supportive of the same general theme. While some of Nicolaevsky's and Borkenau's specific assertions have been questioned, no material has appeared to disprove their basic thesis (which, however, continues to be viewed by certain analysts as controversial, albeit without valid cause).

A. Ross Johnson, in *The Transformation of Communist Ideology: The Yugoslav Case, 1945–53*, specifically attacks one of the key assumptions of both Borkenau and Nicolaevsky, namely, that Zhdanov was allied closely with Tito and his Yugoslav C.P. However, he produces no new documentation to sustain that rebuttal. In a recent study by William O. McCagg, Jr. (*Stalin Embattled, 1943–1948*), there is some discussion of such links, but the book does not entirely transcend what is essentially the "bureaucratic-organizations" approach to Soviet foreign policy; it omits analysis of the projection beyond the Soviet frontiers of the personal, almost "feudal," struggle between the Zhdanov "clan" and its rival counterpart, led by Malenkov and Beria.

Many scholars have tackled the period without discussing the implications of the struggle between the two factions, which manifested itself in the form of an ideological "debate" on foreign affairs. Generally perceptive writers, such as Zbigniew Brzezinski, discuss East European foreign policies of the period at length without devoting a great deal of attention to the issue of the linkages between the competing groups that made "policy" within each party; numerous shifts in the policies of these parties cannot be explained primarily in terms of East-West relations or even of monolithic Soviet-client state interactions. Needless to say, all serious research on the present topic would be handicapped without the solid base created as a result of the pioneering work done in related areas by scholars of the caliber of Robert Conquest, Merle Fainsod, John Erickson, Leonard Schapiro, David Dallin, or Adam Ulam.

Given the very understandable preoccupation of analysts and historians with the seemingly all-encompassing dark shadow cast by the awesome reach and grim personality of Stalin, it is not surprising that somewhat less attention has been paid to developments just below that apex of power. Consequently, an implicit "single-actor model" came to be employed. It is questionable, however, just how realistic that model is, even for communist regimes. The dialectic seems to be at work here, too: the autocracies of classical antiquity lacked the technical means to impose a single will consistently over areas separated by travel time; their contemporary counterparts do possess such means, but technology has introduced complexities and a proliferation of sources and data beyond the capacity of a single mind to master, or even to follow.* The political process cannot be halted by fiat or "ukaz"; it simply assumes different, "factional," forms.

Theoretically, of course, "factions" were outlawed long ago, but cliques held together by mutual interest have continued to assert themselves, even if their missions seem less elevated when compared with the more issue-oriented groups of the "left" or "right" that characterized an earlier period. This study does not wish to give the impression that Stalin was the "unknown warrior" of the 1940s, a picture that would be a grotesque distortion; this caveat is necessary, since the focus on less-known developments in his entourage is bound to shift the spotlight from his own actions, of which any student of communist affairs is fully apprised by now. In fact, "factionalization" in the 1940s continued only in part *despite* Stalin, who was absent for prolonged periods from daily management of affairs because of ailments and infirmities discussed subsequently in this analysis. Rather, to a very significant extent, the phenomenon was due to Stalin's *deliberate* attempts to keep would-be successors at each other's throats by purposeful duplication of functions or through balancing moves, of the kind to which Khrushchev ascribed his transfer to Moscow, late in 1949, in order to neutralize Malenkov's growing power. In so acting, Stalin was following time-honored modalities for preventing rising stars from eclipsing the setting sun.

The "factional model" employed in this study is useful, not merely as a guide for interpretation of the Soviet decision-making process, but as an important clue to the relationships between various communist parties, both ruling and nonruling. Thus, the present analysis revolves around the following key issues:

1. The impact of factional struggles on the political process in closed societies. Traces of this continuing process are manifested in such

---

*Note, for instance, the very abundance of intelligence data, described by Roberta Wohlstetter, which contributed to the U.S. failure to anticipate Pearl Harbor.

phenomena as the appearance, often side by side, of public statements at variance with one another, reflecting not a change in the Party's "general line," but rather the ability of particular factions to "get their points across."

2. The ramifications of factional conflict within the "Motherland of Socialism" upon policies adopted by other communist parties and states. The reactions of the non-Soviet communist parties during the period under investigation appear to have varied quite significantly. In certain cases, it seems that communist parties were affiliated completely with one Kremlin group or another; some parties changed their policies or even leaderships to conform with what appeared to be the dominant faction in the USSR at the moment. Still others were a microcosm of the Soviet Union, with competing local factions (allied to their counterparts in Moscow) attempting to carry out mutually contradictory policies. In many instances, communist parties demonstrated considerable confusion, a perfectly reasonable reaction to the inconsistent messages emanating from Moscow. (This phenomenon began to manifest itself as early as the period of Ruth Fischer's *Stalin and German Communism*).

3. The degree to which Soviet decision making with regard to foreign policy took into account the statements and actions of Western leaders. This remains a crucial question, given the "origins of the Cold War" polemics associated with this period. In fact, Soviet and other communist-party "debates" on foreign policy reveal remarkably little consideration of what the West was or was not planning, saying, or even doing. Rather, these "debates" concentrated on abstract ideological considerations regarding the "objective" economic (and resultant political) changes likely to develop in the wake of World War II. "Debates," as was pointed out earlier, centered around the issue of the inevitability of the "third stage in the general crisis of world capitalism," the question of which Western power (the U.S. or Great Britain) now constituted the "primary antagonist," and the international implications of developments among and within the "New Democracies." (The tendency to ignore Western words and deeds was characteristic far less of the aging Stalin personally, who could remain above the "debates," for a protracted time, being content to manipulate the factions against one another; since he had no need to score debating points, he could afford, health permitting, to concern himself with genuine "concrete reality.")

Within the general context of this model, particular emphasis has to be placed upon an examination of the "Soviet-Yugoslav Rift," not only because of the dramatic steps taken by the Cominform in 1948 and 1949 against Tito, but, more importantly, because there is considerable evidence that most of the Yugoslav party leaders embraced political sentiments coinciding to a remarkable extent with the positions adopted by the Zhdanov-Voznesenskii group in the USSR.

A great deal has been published concerning the antecedents and causes of the Stalin-Tito break. Works by eminent Western scholars, as well as accounts by such important Yugoslav eyewitnesses as Milovan Djilas and Vladimir Dedijer, have stressed various aspects of this historic development:

Soviet economic exploitation of Yugoslavia during 1944–48, the treatment of Yugoslav Partisans, particularly women, by the "liberating" Red Army at the end of World War II, Yugoslav "ingratitude" (as viewed by the Kremlin) regarding the Russian role in freeing Belgrade, Moscow's refusal to let Tito develop an indigenous arms industry, infiltration of Soviet agents into Yugoslavia, and alleged Yugoslav attempts to form a Southeast European federation, centering on Belgrade, without Moscow's permission are among the most prominent factors mentioned.

However important their role in the dispute, these items present a picture lacking some essential dimensions, particularly with regard to the nature of the Soviet decision-making process, a focus of this study.

1 Soviet Factions and Decision Making The Modalities

Precisely during the period between the liberation of Belgrade in 1944 and Tito's expulsion from the Cominform in 1948, Stalin is reported by contemporaries to have suffered recurrent bouts of debilitating ill health, a factor that appears to have constrained significantly his ability to supervise policy implementation from day to day in a really detailed and sustained manner. At the same time, most probably as a result of this state of affairs, Stalin's younger associates, particularly A. A. Zhdanov and G. M. Malenkov, waged an almost overt struggle for power.

An understanding of these developments within the USSR is required not only as they pertain to Moscow-Belgrade relations; it should be borne in mind also that, during this very period, the "Cold War" began to take shape. Most revisionist accounts of the "Cold War," to the extent that they address themselves at all to the Soviet side of the picture, portray the Soviet leaders both as monolithic and essentially passive, "reacting" merely to Western moves and policies. The Soviet decision-making process, however, was contingent as much upon developments in factional struggles within the Soviet empire, as upon "objective" Soviet interests abroad.

Tentatively, at this stage, two main competing groups can be identified: a "leftist" faction, both in foreign and domestic affairs, led by Andreii A. Zhdanov and Nikolai A. Voznesenskii, which developed intimate ties to the Yugoslav, Bulgarian, Finnish, and, briefly, the Indian Communist parties; and a group advocating a less "forward," or militant, international policy, with a generally less dogmatic approach to domestic affairs and with apparent ties to the Czechoslovak, Hungarian, and Romanian Communist parties. (Among the so-called "new democracies," Poland appears to have remained outside the framework of Soviet factional alignments.)

Thus, as in so many other instances, Soviet "policy" concerning various communist parties largely seems to have been a function of the ebb and flow of factional conflict.

Generally, in the Soviet Union and in the communist movement, factions seem to coalesce and part ways kaleidoscopically, operating on the basis of personal struggles for power and influence, rather than on any particular, consistent ideological lines or specific issue-orientations. It appears that members of the Politburo focus their factional struggles on tactically advantageous issues, rather than the issues determining the factions. Thus, each coalition of Politburo members reflects the interests of the individuals concerned in preventing their personal adversaries from successfully promoting issues with which they have become strongly identified. The adoption of a policy linked to the name of one man or one group generally is perceived within the Soviet Union as reflecting an increase in that faction's influence and power vis-à-vis opponents.

Because real power reflects such perceptions, it is crucial to the political careers of Soviet leaders to ensure that no policies be adopted which might be regarded as issues backed by their opponents, lest that development be deemed to mark a shift in the internal Soviet balance of power. Thus, merely by virtue of their adversaries' support for a position, certain Politburo members may oppose it.[1] After the outcome of the factional struggle has been determined, it is safe for the victor to adopt the loser's platform, as happened, for example, when Stalin switched to a line of support for a five-year plan of intensive industrialization once Trotsky, the advocate of this approach, had been vanquished. Similarly, after Malenkov had been eliminated politically, Khrushchev reversed his earlier position and adopted Malenkov's more consumer-oriented economic policy.

A second, albeit subordinate, element in the Soviet decision-making process is the question of departmental interests. According to several sources, important Soviet cadres, at least to a certain degree, tend to be turned into "lobbyists" of the institutions with which they are associated. Since each leader's subordinates also constitute his power base, he must reflect their views to some extent if he is going to maintain his own power. As one author put it, "The Soviet political structure has a strongly 'feudal' pattern, with each top personality investing subordinates, whenever possible, with power and positions in return for personal 'fealty' and allegiance."[2]

Thus, the personal influence of individual Soviet political figures derives also from the ability of each to promote the interests of his loyal clients, thereby increasing his own power. Such accretion of influence can be evaluated both in concrete terms, since the implementation of the line one advocates is facilitated by the elevation of allied cadres, and through resort to perceptual criteria, since the promotion of cadres who are identified clearly with a particular faction indicates a trend that guides "neutrals" in whose interest it is to jump as quickly as possible on the bandwagon of whichever political group appears to be ascendant.

(Western writers with a penchant for "mirror-imaging" may object that the various ingredients of the recipe for gaining and maintaining power and for manipulating institutions are not unique to the USSR; perhaps not, but the peculiar "mix," as described in the preceding and subsequent pages, is characteristic of closed societies, especially those with a strong ideological flavor.)

Consequently, "ideological" positions adopted on important issues do not necessarily reflect personal ideological predilections, but rather the political obligations of various leaders to their subordinates and allies. In the case of "neutrals," such positions are likely to be functions of their interest in maintaining a delicate balance of power (or, at least, if one of the factions appears to be gaining the upper hand, of a concern not to be caught on the losing side). The scope of factional struggle may cover vast areas, including international affairs, military questions, economic policy, and even science and culture. Although orchestrated by means of "ideological debate," however, these battles are usually resolved on the basis of personal expediency.

There is no reason to doubt that the Soviet leaders, having spent decades in the party, and in many cases having been educated in party schools, are more or less dedicated Leninists — at least in their analytical precepts. Probably all of them approach international affairs with the same strategic goals in mind. It is "only" tactics upon which they disagree.

The explanation for the ideological flavor of these "debates" relates to the fundamental issue of legitimacy. In the absence of established, constitutional, time-honored rules and modalities for power transfer, known efforts to seize or reapportion power in the USSR to date may be categorized essentially as coups, attempted or successful, "administrative" or more flagrantly violent. In this connection, one need recall only Stalin's usurpation of the succession to Lenin; the manner in which he disposed of the more widely accepted "heirs;" the murder of one of his "crown princes," Kirov, and the forcible removal, as this study will demonstrate, of another, Zhdanov; the eventual displacement of Stalin's final "anointed" successor, Malenkov, by Khrushchev; the "execution" of the "co-heir," Beria; the temporarily successful coup against Khrushchev — and his countercoup — in 1957; the mysterious political disappearance of Khrushchev's "crown prince," Kirichenko; and the eventual "retirement" imposed upon Khrushchev by the last of his "heirs," Brezhnev. It appears to be a rule of politics, however, that the more arbitrary a regime's antecedents, the greater are its compulsions to seek legitimation.

In the case of the USSR, legitimacy may be conferred (if at all) by means of the ideology; that is, by establishing oneself as the only genuine and "orthodox" interpreter and executor of Leninism, which in turn, of course, carries with it the mantle of being the sole "scientific" interpreter of History, with an implicit claim to infallibility. Hence, the importance of having rivals and competitors "excommunicated" as deviationists or heretics, thus justifying not only their demotion, but also, if necessary, their "liquidation." It was "no accident" that one of Stalin's earliest acts, in grasping for the crown, was to swear his famous oaths on Lenin's bier. These, expanded into his "Foundations of Leninism" (1924), were intended to demonstrate that he alone fully comprehended, and would implement correctly, the creed upon which rested the regime as a whole.

2 THE ZHDANOV-MALENKOV STRUGGLE
Antecedents

Presumably, not too many observers today would still quarrel seriously with the contention first advanced three decades ago by Boris I. Nicolaevsky, Franz Borkenau, and a few others, that during the middle and late 1940s a bitter struggle was fought out between two factions, led by Andreii A. Zhdanov and Georgii M. Malenkov. One recent study by Jonathan Harris traces back the origins of this conflict as far as the March 1939 Eighteenth Party Congress of the CPSU, where sharp differences emerged between the conflicting concepts of these two secretaries of the Central Committee regarding administrative hierarchies in the field of production. Their approaches reflected primarily the respective bureaucratic functions, at the time, of these two relatively young competitors. (There were only four secretaries of the Central Committee in 1939, Stalin and A. A. Andreyev being the two others.)[1] Stalin himself placed varying degrees of stress upon "economic work," a fairly straightforward functional approach to production, and "party-political work," which concerned the "recruitment, placement, and education of personnel, the development of effective party organization, improved intra-party communication, and monitoring performance of other party members" in the field of production.

Zhdanov had been Stalin's implicitly recognized expert on Party history since January 1936; two years later, he became responsible for Marxist-Leninist education and, in 1939, soon after the Party congress, he was appointed director of Agitprop, with responsibility for supervision of the press and Party education.[2] Also immediately subsequent to the congress, Malenkov became the director of the new Cadres Directorate of the Secretariat, with responsibilities for supervision of industry and personnel management.[3]* He also became involved personally in the inspection of industries.[6] Given their antithetical institutional responsi-

---

*In fact, Malenkov is believed to have been Yezhov's deputy, since 1936, in charge of the department that was superseded by the Cadres Directorate, and to have succeeded Yezhov, both in that post and as editor of the Central Committee journal, *Partinoe Stroitel'stvo.*[4] (In the latter capacity, Malenkov became associated with one of Zhdanov's assistants, G.F. Aleksandrov, a relationship that was to prove significant.) Thus, Malenkov's role in supervising production personnel antedated the congress and explains his rivalry with Agitprop representatives attempting to implement the same task from an "ideological" point of departure. Moreover, his earlier post must have brought him into

bilities, it was hardly surprising that the two rising Apparatchiki would espouse divergent approaches.

At the Eighteenth Congress, Malenkov stressed the role of the Secretariat in providing industry with "concrete guidance" and sought to bring about a restoration of the "production branch" departments of the Sovnarkom (Council of People's Commissars), which had been eliminated recently. These code phrases symbolized an "expert," "technocratic," and "economic" approach toward Soviet industry. At the same congress, Zhdanov announced that Primary Party Organizations (PPO) in the various localities, concerned with ensuring ideological orthodoxy, would enjoy the right to monitor the performance of factory managers. Malenkov refrained notably from endorsing this "red" (versus "expert") approach to management. Zhdanov's formulations proved victorious at the congress, since the need to raise political consciousness was stressed in its proceedings, as was the "mastery of the fundamentals of Marxism-Leninism." Perhaps more important, Zhdanovite operational preferences were endorsed at the gathering. The industrial and transport departments of the Secretariat were abolished, and PPO control in individual enterprises was extended considerably.[7]

The controversy between the two factions was to intensify after this opening salvo. Malenkov's position was championed by his own journal, *Partinoe Stroitel'stvo*, whereas *Bol'shevik*, the theoretical organ of the Central Committee and subject to the directives of that body's "ideological expert," not surprisingly backed Zhdanov's line.* The degree of support for either position extended by *Pravda* (under the guidance of Lev Z. Mekhlis), as well as the phrasing of the Central Committee and Politburo resolutions, generally served as a barometer of the backing attracted within the leadership by the two contending secretaries.[8] Zhdanov's political fortunes (as reflected in part by Politburo support for his position on "Party-political" work) were determined to a considerable extent by the successes or failures of international ventures that he supported. (Zhdanov had been appointed chairman of the Supreme Soviet's Foreign Affairs Committee in 1938, symbolizing his interest in, and identification with, international issues.)[9]

It is believed that, as leader of the Leningrad Party organization since 1934, replacing Kirov (and purging Kirov's supporters), Zhdanov enthusiastically backed the invasion of neighboring Finland late in 1939.

close contact with Lavrentii P. Beria, who in 1938 became another of Yezhov's assistants, except that Beria was detailed to cover N.K.V.D.-internal security-affairs.[5] (see Appendix A for information on Zhdanov's tie to Yezhov.)

*This may have been the cause of the condemnation by the CPSU Central Committee of *Bol'shevik*'s editorial board in July 1949, when the Zhdanovites were being purged. See pp. 164–65.

In fact, he did so quite overtly, appearing at the signing of the December 1939 "treaty" between the USSR and Otto Kuusinen's Communist-dominated Finnish "government in exile"; the final peace treaty of March 12, 1940, ending the Winter War and enlarging the Soviet coastline north of Leningrad, carried Zhdanov's signature.[10] It should be noted that the troops employed in the Soviet assault on Finland came primarily from Zhdanov's Leningrad military district.[11] As a member of the Supreme Naval Council, Zhdanov could not but be concerned that the Leningrad base of the Soviet Baltic fleet could be blockaded through hostile control of the Finnish and Estonian coasts; as early as the December 1936 Eighth All-Union Congress of Soviets, Zhdanov had threatened Finland and the Baltic States publicly with resort to force, if necessary, to enlarge Russia's "much too small window to Europe."[12] The Soviet demand for key positions on the Finnish coast, at Vipuri and Hankö, precipitated the Finnish Winter War.

During the period that followed, as the Soviet offensive stalled, the Malenkovist line gained the upper hand.* Zhdanov's star, however, resumed its ascendency after the end of the Finnish War. It may be assumed that he continued to derive prestige from having served as an architect of the Ribbentrop-Molotov Pact,† which seemed beneficial in 1939–40 from the Soviet viewpoint, although its advantages were to prove ephemeral. Not only had Zhdanov supported the pact, at least

---

*Moreover, in other symbolic moves, Zhdanov was replaced as the Party's main spokesman on ideological matters by A. S. Shcherbakov—later linked to Zhdanov in death as an alleged covictim of the "Doctors' Plot." The significance of Shcherbakov's seeming adversary role should not be exaggerated, however; he was Zhdanov's brother-in-law and his ally. In the 1920s, he served with Zhdanov in the Gorkii party organization and joined him again, in 1936–37, to aid in the purge of Leningrad Kirovites. When Shcherbakov died in 1945, he was replaced as head of the Chief Political Directorate of the Red Army by another Zhdanovite, Col.-Gen. I. V. Shikin (see p. 88). Zhdanov was not included in a December 1939 Central Committee publication of essays by Stalin's "closest comrades in arms," nor was he present among various important political figures, including Malenkov, who gathered for a public commemoration of the anniversary of Lenin's death in January 1940.[13]

†Zhdanov's incentives for obtaining this pact are not difficult to deduce. As Party chief of Leningrad, he was concerned directly with control of the Baltic region and stood to gain from an extension of Soviet power to the Baltic States (as stipulated in the secret Protocol of the Pact). Moreover, as Stalin's personal representative on the Supreme Naval Council during this period, he had developed an obvious interest in projecting Soviet naval power abroad. Like his protégé, Admiral Nikolai G. Kuznetsov, he realized the military implications of securing the maritime egress from Leningrad, primarily by establishing Soviet sea and air bases in Estonia, Latvia, and Finland. It is noteworthy that Zhdanov supported *naval* preparations for war while otherwise deprecating the chances of a conflict in the spring of 1940. His plans were vetoed at the Supreme Military Council by Malenkov, among others, who stated, perhaps sarcastically, that he opposed programs "conceived as if we were going to be at war tomorrow."[14] Malenkov's jibe may have been aimed at Zhdanov's willingness to contradict himself on the war issue when it suited his factional interests.

implicitly, as early as June 1939, when he published a key article in *Pravda* attacking British and French plans (and in effect ruling out these two countries as potential allies),* but he continued to defend the relationship with Berlin, even after the Germans built up their forces along the Soviet frontiers and continually violated Soviet air space. His argument was that Germany could not successfully fight a two-front war;[16] thus, she had a disincentive for attacking the Soviet Union.

Zhdanov enjoyed a brief period of rewards for his role in bringing about the pact of Germany; he was placed in charge, for instance, of the absorption of Estonia into the USSR.[17] At first, Zhdanov displayed relative moderation in carrying out his duties as the Soviet "proconsul" in charge of the "consolidation" of Estonia. When his "recommendations" concerning the composition of the Estonian cabinet were resisted by President Päts, however, Zhdanov arranged a Communist "uprising," forcing Päts to accept the Leningrad leader's choice of personnel.[18]

As relations with the Nazis deteriorated in mid-1940, several notables among the Soviet leadership with unmistakably pro-German records were demoted ostentatiously. In addition to sinister manifestations of Berlin's intentions vis-à-vis Moscow, such as German military movements in Romania[19] (not to mention the second thoughts concerning the pact with Hitler that Stalin must have had as soon as Paris fell), the Kremlin may have become aware, during the late summer of 1940, of initial plans concerning what subsequently became Operation Barbarossa. This development was to have adverse effects on Zhdanov's (as on Molotov's) influence.

It is now known that the German decision, in principle, to attack the Soviet Union eventually was made on July 31, 1940.[20] According to subsequent Soviet and Western accounts, in August 1940 Richard Sorge, the star Soviet agent in Japan, became aware that a German-Japanese alliance was being discussed, initially between German ambassador Eugen Ott and Tokyo officials; early in September, Heinrich Georg Stahmer was dispatched to Tokyo to continue these negotiations. Sorge was briefed concurrently both by Ott and Stahmer.[21] Such discussions must have concerned Moscow.[22]

According to the memoirs of Marshal A. M. Vasilevskii, in

---

*Zhdanov stated: "I permit myself to express a personal opinion. . . although my friends do not share it. They still think that in beginning negotiations on a pact of mutual assistance with the USSR, the English and French Governments had serious intentions of creating a powerful barrier against aggression in Europe. I believe. . . that the English and French Governments have no wish for a treaty on terms of equality with the USSR, but only [for] *talks* about a treaty in order to play upon public opinion in their countries about the supposedly unyielding attitude of the USSR and thus to make it easier for themselves to make a deal with the aggressors."[15] One wonders whether the "friends" who disagreed with Zhdanov and preferred a deal with the West included Malenkov.

September 1940 Marshal Shaposhnikov was assigned to give a briefing regarding likely German invasion routes into the USSR. While Stalin was reported to have disagreed with Shaposhnikov's choice of likely routes, it appears that Stalin was indeed becoming concerned about the possibility of a German invasion.[23] This concern was manifested by a series of moves.

On August 12, 1940, Stalin made public major structural and personnel changes in the military establishment, bearing witness to his growing anxiety regarding the course of Soviet-German relations. In a key move, *yedinonachaliye* ("unitary command") was introduced, thereby eliminating the role of military commissars at the tactical level.* In the following month, Lev Z. Mekhlis (whose culpability in the massive purge of the Red Army, which contributed to the poor Soviet showing in the Winter War with Finland, has been well documented) was removed from his post as chief of the Main Political Administration of the Red Army and transferred to the Commission for State Control.[26] (However, as will be seen, this did not mean that he was downgraded in his civilian capacity.) Soon after, referring to the replacement of Marshal B. M. Shaposhnikov by Marshal K. A. Meretskov as chief of the General Staff, Stalin stated specifically that he was trying to "show the world that there had been a complete change in the military leadership since the Finnish War." (No such reference could bode well for Zhdanov, who, as indicated earlier, was implicated in the disaster.) Stalin added that he hoped to "lessen international [that is, Soviet-German] tension" by means of this move.[27]

Thus, it appears that Stalin was reasserting professional control of the army, thereby attempting to upgrade its competence. Perhaps, at the same time, he intended to send a signal to Berlin that the USSR was not unconcerned about German moves, nor would it be unwilling or unable to defend itself should the situation so demand. These military changes in Moscow were accompanied by alterations in the political establishment.

Specifically, the September 7, 1940, edition of *Pravda* contained two items announcing a series of very significant personnel changes. The top of the first page displayed three decrees promulgated the day

---

*In place of the commissar, Stalin created an assistant commander for Political Affairs (referred to generally by the abbreviation "Zampolit"), subordinated to the unit commander, who now bore responsibility both for the military and political affairs of the unit. Political commissars were reintroduced, however, on July 16, 1941, following the utter collapse of Soviet defenses during the early stages of Operation Barbarossa, presumably in an attempt to "stem the rot." On October 9, 1942 (with military competence the supreme requirement during the initial stage of the battle for Stalingrad, prior to the successful Soviet counterattack of November 19, 1942),[24] Moscow again replaced the Commissar with the Zampolit.[25]

before. The first two, signed formally by M. Kalinin and A. Gorkin, in the name of the Presidium of the Supreme Soviet, served to undermine Molotov, in his capacity as chairman of the Council of People's Commissars of the USSR. The first "ukaz" provided for a People's Commissariat for State Control, under the direction of Lev Z. Mekhlis.[28] This body was given broad supervisory authority over Molotov's Council of People's Commissars. Moreover, in the second of the three decrees, Mekhlis himself was appointed also deputy chairman of the Council of People's Commissars.[29] Thus, not only was he placed in charge of a body with oversight capacity over Molotov's Sovnarkom, but he was also given a position immediately below Molotov within the latter organ; thus, Molotov was being enveloped both from above and below. The third "ukaz" (signed formally by Molotov himself, along with K. Khlomov, both representing the Council of People's Commissars), saddled Molotov, in his capacity as People's Commissar for Foreign Affairs, with Andreii Ya. Vyshinsky, as deputy people's commissar for Foreign Affairs.[30]

On page 3 of the same edition of *Pravda*, there appeared an announcement that Zhdanov was being released from his post as chief (*nachal'nik*) of the Department of Propaganda of the Central Committee of the CPSU (b) and would be replaced by the young man who, at the time, was his deputy, G. F. Aleksandrov.* Although the decree specified that Zhdanov would be left with supervisory power over that department, the loss of direct control most probably spelled a demotion, which may have been due to the perceived linkage between his approach and a pro-German line.[31]

Molotov's downgrading during this period, like Zhdanov's, probably was a function, in great part, of the same linkage. In this context, it may be significant that in November 1940, upon their return to Moscow from an abortive mission to Berlin, Molotov jokingly remarked to his companion, General A. S. Iakovlev, "Ah, here is the German! Well, now we both will be held responsible." (Perhaps Molotov was implying that he himself already was being held responsible for the failures of

---

*G. F. Aleksandrov had started his career under the aegis of Zhdanov, but maintained also an association with Malenkov (see Chapter 5). His promotion at Zhdanov's expense in 1940 may have contributed to a subsequent, postwar rift with his former patron. (There is no indication that Aleksandrov had opposed Zhdanov in any way prior to the younger man's sudden elevation in September 1940). In the post–World War II period, in 1947, when Zhdanov overshadowed all his colleagues and rivals, Aleksandrov was to become the object of a furious tirade published by the Zhdanovites. At that time, and subsequently, during Malenkov's brief period of glory following Stalin's death, Aleksandrov appears to have been linked closely to Malenkov. With Khrushchev's rise to power, Aleksandrov descended into obscurity, following his alleged involvement in a sex scandal. (See Appendix B).

the pro-German line.) Molotov went on to explain, "Well did we dine with Hitler? We did. Did we shake hands with Goebbels? We did. We shall have to repent."[32]

In addition to being burdened with a part of the onus for having led the USSR into an increasingly damaging relationship with Nazi Germany, Zhdanov (together with his protégé, N. A. Voznesenskii, then chairman of the defense industry's Economic Council and supervisor of the People's Commissariat of Armaments) was seriously culpable with regard to Soviet military unpreparedness for Operation Barbarossa; early in 1941, while dealing with production of artillery and armor, Zhdanov was accused openly by Colonel-General B. L. Vannikov of "tolerating disarmament in the face of an approaching war."[33] Moreover, it is known that Zhdanov insisted, during the period from late 1940 at least until February 1941, that "Germany is incapable of fighting on two fronts" and was too "bogged down" in the war with Britain to open such a front against the USSR.[34]

Almost certainly in response to the visibly growing threat to the Soviet western flank, an announcement by the Presidium of the Supreme Soviet, on May 7, 1941, informed the world that Stalin had assumed the position of chairman of the Council of People's Commissars, replacing Molotov who, it was explained, had pointed out repeatedly that he was too busy with his tasks as People's Commissar for Foreign Affairs to meet his additional obligations as Sovnarkom chairman. Consequently, Molotov was relegated to the post of deputy chairman.[35] Nevertheless, only a week before Operation Barbarossa was unleashed, Molotov was to tell Admiral Kuznetsov that "only a fool would attack us."[36] It would appear that Molotov, like Zhdanov, had a major stake in the continuing viability of the pro-German line.

In the meanwhile, Malenkov had been promoted to the rank of candidate member of the Politburo early in 1941.[37] With the German attack on the Soviet Union, Zhdanov's stock was to decline still further. During the period immediately after July 22, 1941, Malenkov and Beria, two candidate members of the Politburo, were virtually running the newly created State Defense Committee, which also included Molotov and—nominally—Voroshilov, Stalin apparently being in a state of shock and withdrawal at the time. Yet, Zhdanov, a full Politburo member, was given the far more limited role of controlling the Leningrad Military District.[38] The dissident Soviet historian, Anton Antonov-Ovseyenko, who for a brief period during the "thaw" had access to classified material, testifies that the "German invasion struck fear in Stalin's heart."

> . . . He shut himself up in his Kremlin apartment. . . . While the leader hid himself from the people like a coward, Beria

and Malenkov zealously sawed away at the chair holding Andreii Zhdanov, the first in line to succeed Stalin. They laid the groundwork for his transfer to the doomed city of Leningrad. No place was found for Andreii Zhdanov, Stalin's favorite, even when the structure of the State Committee of Defense was revamped. . . . Malenkov gained special favor in the eyes of the Master. It was no longer Zhdanov, but Malenkov who seemed destined to become the aging Leader's successor. . . . For Zhdanov the fall of Leningrad would have meant the end of everything. If the city surrendered, the triumvirate of Molotov, Malenkov, and Beria would totally supplant him in the Master's favor. For days on end Zhdanov didn't sleep.[39]

Later, Stalin returned to full-time activity in the State Defense Committee and added Mikoyan, Kaganovich, Bulganin, and even Zhdanov's ally Voznesenskii to its membership. Zhdanov, whose predilections for a pro-German policy apparently continued to be remembered, never was permitted to join that august body, despite the fact that it was being enlarged.

Throughout the war, Malenkov and his associate Beria* provided indications of the intense nature of their conflict with Zhdanov, reportedly by hampering their adversary's efforts as political commissar in overall charge of the Leningrad front and by attempting to undermine his reputation with Stalin. According to allegations by Terenti Shtykov (one of the few Zhdanov allies not purged during the 1949 "Leningrad Affair"), during the initial six months of the war Beria, who had enjoyed vast discretionary power as N.K.V.D. chief and had been placed in charge of partisan operations, in effect undermined paramilitary and partisan activities in the Leningrad area.[41] Reportedly at Beria's instigation, Stalin reprimanded Zhdanov at a key moment during the initial German assault (in August 1941) for forming a council of defense to plan civilian and paramilitary activities without obtaining Moscow's permission.[42] According to Antonov-Ovseyenko, "Stalin fell upon Zhdanov and Voroshilov [who had been dispatched to Leningrad in the meantime]: 'Why wasn't the Gensek [General Secretary, that is, Stalin himself] informed?' "[43] Of course, Zhdanov's move had detracted from Beria's control over the civilian population. It seems that Beria incited Stalin by drawing his attention to the implications of Leningrad's alleged in-

---

*The long-term Malenkov-Beria tie is fairly well established. Stalin's daughter, in but one example, stated that: "until March, 1953, one could always see Malenkov and Beria walking arm in arm. They always moved as a couple and as such used to come to my father at his dacha, in appearance the closest of pals. This friendship, so obvious to everyone, must have been based on their joint dealings in some debatable matters."[40]

subordination.[44] Moreover, while Zhdanov was attempting a very difficult retreat and consolidation operation, in the face of overwhelmingly superior German forces, the Leningrad party was accused by Stalin of being "specialists in the art of retreat," and the Soviet dictator insisted that Zhdanov "concerns himself with only one thing—how to retreat."[45]

Stalin's attitude may have been engendered by N.K.V.D. rumors that the Leningrad population was disloyal. Jealousy of Moscow's sudden rise in stature was evident among Leningraders, who had traditionally viewed Moscow as "a big provincial city."[46] After all, Leningrad had been not only the imperial capital, but also a major revolutionary center, during the 1825 Decembrist uprising, the 1905 revolution, and the two 1917 revolutions. Stalin, on his part, had felt personally threatened by Leningrad party bosses Grigorii Zinoviev, in 1927, and Sergeii Kirov, in 1934. These are indications that this historical rivalry engendered suspicion of the great cultural center on the Neva in Stalin's parochial mind (the Kirov affair and the post–World War II Leningrad affair bore some resemblance to one another).*

Zhdanov's nadir politically came during the late summer of 1941, when the military situation dictated that abandonment of Leningrad be considered. Malenkov and Molotov were sent to the front to evaluate the situation. (According to Antonov-Ovseyenko, Molotov, at this stage, had joined the anti-Zhdanov front: "Molotov barely concealed his hostility toward Zhdanov. . . . Molotov [in addition to Malenkov and Beria] suggested to Stalin the idea of sending Zhdanov to Leningrad." The same source also reports that the delegation sent to review Zhdanov's performance in the north included two marshals and an admiral.[48] When the delegates returned, the State Defense Committee demoted Zhdanov, as well as Marshal K. Ye. Voroshilov, the military commander of the Northern Front. Whereas the two

---

*It is interesting that during the postwar Zhdanovshchina, a cultural purge of major proportions, Zhdanov himself felt compelled to attack Leningrad chauvinism, perhaps in order to assuage Stalin's anxieties concerning the Zhdanovite power base. Voznesenskii's evidence (his last outburst prior to the announcement of his death sentence, as related to us by Khrushchev, who claimed to be Voznesenskii's supporter) is most interesting in this respect:

> I was with Stalin when he was told what Voznesenskii said just before it was announced that he had been sentenced to be shot. Voznesenskii stood up and spewed hatred against Leningrad. He cursed the day he had set foot in the city, when he came to study from the Donbass. He said that Leningrad had already had its share of conspiracies; it had been subjected to all varieties of revolutionary influence, from Biron to Zinoviev.[47]

Perhaps the Zhdanov group actually had assumed conspiratorial dimensions in its final period of ascendancy. (Of course, Voznesenskii conceivably may have thought that Stalin wanted to hear that there had been a conspiracy and was trying to save himself by admitting that, indeed, there had been a plot.)

leaders had been in charge of the entire complex of armies in the region, now Karelia was split off from their command. Moreover, the Leningrad group was reprimanded by Stalin for its tactics in defending its lines.[49] The upshot of these criticisms was the replacement of Voroshilov by Marshal Georgii K. Zhukov in September 1941. Zhukov's relations with Zhdanov quickly revealed signs of uncongeniality.[50] Some of Zhdanov's military and political associates later were to intensify hostility toward Zhukov, contributing first to the termination of his command over the Soviet Occupation Zone of Germany and, afterward, to his transfer from his Odessa command to a more remote post (see pp. 31–32).

As the war continued and a murderous, prolonged siege of the northern city ensued, Beria and Malenkov reportedly continued to hamper Zhdanov. At one point, in an astonishing display of arrogance, Beria allegedly responded to Stalin's order to send nine hundred tanks to Leningrad by telling Marshal N. N. Voronov, "I'll give you four hundred machines and this conversation is finished." Only upon threat of appeal to Stalin is Beria supposed to have relented.[51]

However, Beria and Malenkov were unable to stay on top indefinitely. One major chink in Malenkov's armor seems to have been his affiliation with Lt. Gen. Andreii A. Vlasov, who went over to the Germans and eventually commanded ex-Soviet troops on their side.[52] According to Antonov-Ovseyenko, Malenkov bore a share of the responsibility "for the disaster in Leningrad, when the Second Shock Army under General Vlasov was trapped. . . .Vlasov, who went over to the Germans, had been a protégé of Malenkov. . ."[53] The impact of the debacle on Malenkov's influence may not have been immediate, but led to longer term results. Thus, the 1943 decree to abolish the Comintern was signed for the CPSU by Manuilskii, the secretary-general of the organization, and by Zhdanov, still supervising partly blockaded Leningrad. Borkenau claimed that Malenkov at the time was apparently in charge of the conduct of foreign relations on behalf of the Central Committee, so that he, rather than Zhdanov, should have been one of the signatories.[54]

According to the eyewitness account by Enrique Castro Delgado, a former member of the Politburo of the Spanish Communist Party, however, Zhdanov, in fact, soon played a major role in the "Ghost Comintern" (after the pro forma dissolution of the Comintern), and regularly received one of only two top-secret reports,[55] the other going to the nominal leader of "Institute Number 205," G. M. Dimitrov.[56] According to Castro Delgado, nothing changed after the "dissolution" of the organization, not even the building in which it met.[57] Moreover, this account stresses also that, on matters of any significance, Dimitrov never took a stand without glancing first at D. Z. Manuilskii,[58] who apparently asserted direct authority during meetings (even if only through stern glances), although Dimitrov formally presided over them. Manuilskii very probably was Zhdanov's alter ego at the meetings. (For Manuilskii's affiliations, see note on p. 101, Chapter 10—The Founding Meeting of the Cominform.)

Nevertheless, the close of the war found Zhdanov in a somewhat secondary area, on the Allied Control Commission in Finland, while Malenkov and Beria still remained relatively powerful figures. In 1944, Malenkov was appointed to chair a key committee to deal with the dismantling of German industry (in payment of reparations to the USSR), having been nominated in the previous year, together with Beria,* to the Committee for the Rehabilitation of the Economy of the Liberated Areas.[60] Yet, Zhdanov, in addition to leading Leningrad in its desperate resistance against German encirclement, had coordinated a vast evacuation effort of Leningrad industries during the heat of the siege.[61] By comparison, the dismantling and transfer to Russia of German industrial plants, adminstered by Malenkov's committee during the chaos of immediate postwar conditions, were less than successful; much complex machinery was taken apart, and there is no evidence that it was reassembled to any meaningful extent. Not only was a considerable amount of material lost in the shuffle, but much was destroyed deliberately, lest Germany receive it when the Soviet Union withdrew, along with the other occupying powers, leaving a unified, neutralized, disarmed Germany. (Malenkov's and Beria's advocacy of continued dismantling apparently reflected their expectation of an eventual Soviet evacuation of Germany—see pp. 88–89) Still more material was disassembled and shipped to storage facilities in the USSR where, if the elements did not corrode it first, the *tolkach* (the "pusher"—a middleman employed in illegal economic activities) availed himself of vital parts.[62]

Zhdanov and Voznesenskii led a campaign to investigate Malenkov's committee. The resulting inquiry, headed by Mikoyan (who, as minister of foreign trade, had an interest in German production), recommended that the dismantling process cease and that Soviet corporations be set up instead, in the Russian occupation zone of Germany, to manufacture goods for the USSR.[63] This indictment led to a brief demotion of Malenkov from his position in the Secretariat

---

*Beria had a major interest in these committees because much of the dismantled industrial material to be transferred from Germany was to be incorporated in the economic enterprises of the N.K.V.D., under the heading of "rehabilitation."[59]

of the Central Committee.* It is known now that Malenkov was replaced as party secretary in May 1946 by N. S. Patolichev, at a meeting
with Stalin, attended, significantly, only by A. A. Zhdanov, and
Zhdanov's protégé A. A. Kuznetsov.[64] (Further details of this important
episode are presented on p. 30)

According to the "memoirs" of Dmitri Shostakovich "as related to"
Solomon Volkov, there was an additional dimension to the conflict:

> . . . Malenkov wanted to become Stalin's main ideological
> adviser, a rather important position, right below Stalin's top
> executioner, Beria. He would be the executioner on the
> cultural front. Malenkov and Zhdanov fought to prove them-
> selves worthy of that honored position. The war with Hitler
> was won and Malenkov decided to stress public relations and
> to glorify the homeland. . . . Malenkov worked out grandiose
> plans, one of which was a series of deluxe editions of Russian
> literature from antiquity to the present. . . . The series began
> with *The Lay of Prince Igor* and ended. . . with Akhmatova
> and Zoshchenko. . . . With the aim of getting rid of Malenkov,
> Zhdanov attacked Malenkov's ideas and proved to Stalin,
> like two plus two, that it was vigilance that Malenkov had
> lost. Zhdanov, unfortunately, knew what and how Akhmatova
> and Zoshchenko wrote, since Leningrad was Zhdanov's own
> turf.[65] (The details of this significant aspect of the "Zhdanov-
> schina" appear on pp. 56–57.)

While it is difficult to establish whether the "economic," the "aviation," or the "cultural" aspects proved decisive in causing Malenkov's
temporary relegation and Zhdanov's ascent to hegemony, there is little
doubt concerning the fact that, as Antonov-Ovseyenko testifies, "after

---

*There exists an alternative (or perhaps supplementary) explanation of Malenkov's poli-
tical decline during this period. During the war, Malenkov, who in the State Defense
Committee exercised supervisory authority over Soviet aviation, dressed down in public
Stalin's undisciplined son Vasilii, saying "Major Stalin, the combat performance of your
fliers is revolting. . . . What is it? Did you forget how to fight?" We are told that "the short
major's face flushed," and he seems to have managed to get his revenge in the period
immediately after the war, when Malenkov was implicated in the indictment of A. I.
Shakurin, the former people's commissar of the Aviation Industry, who allegedly had
allowed production of defective airplanes during the war. According to the Khrushchev
memoirs, not only was Malenkov dropped from the Central Committee Secretariat in
connection with this affair, but he was briefly shipped off to Tashkent, until Beria
interceded on his behalf. See Major-General S. D. Luganskii, "Na glubokikh virazakh,"
pp. 83–85, in Bialer, *Stalin and His General*, pp. 454–55; Talbott, *Khrushchev Remembers*, pp. 252–53; Soviet *Encyclopedic Dictionary*, vol. II, April 1954, as quoted in
Conquest, *Power*, p. 470, stating "As a member of the State Defense Committee G. M.
Malenkov directed work for equipping. . . . Soviet aviation with aircraft and engines."

the war a struggle broke out around the Gensek's throne. The
Malenkov-Beria group decided to put an end to Zhdanov's claim to the
succession. He was a dangerous rival, who missed no chance to stir up
Stalin's suspicion against Malenkov himself and who had succeeded
once in having Malenkov sent out of Moscow."[66]

3 THE ZHDANOV GROUP
Attitudes and Personalities

Zhdanov, by contrast, began to make a well-nigh meteoric come-back after the war ended. Soon, he was responsible for Party policy over a vast array of ideological and cultural matters, including art, philosophy, literature, and music. At the same time, Zhdanov began to reassert himself in the realm of foreign affairs.

A noted expert on the topic of Soviet international policy during the 1940s, Dr. Alexander M. Nekrich, a former senior scholar of the Institute of World History of the USSR Academy of Sciences, points out that, in his role as head of the Foreign (International) Department of the Central Committee of the CPSU, Zhdanov at this time was again in direct charge of Soviet relations with foreign Communist parties.[1] Moreover, Zhdanov was also chairman of the Committee on Foreign Affairs of the Supreme Soviet,[2] a "legislative" position, which, although presumably of little substantive importance given his party functions, was symbolic of Zhdanov's standing in the realm of foreign policy. By its very nature, Zhdanov's Foreign (International) Department was in competition with some of the activities of the Committee on Liberated Areas. Moreover, since the Main Political Administration of the Red Army was taken over in 1945 by I. V. Shikin, another Zhdanov follower, after the death of Zhdanov's close associate, A. S. Shcherbakov,* Zhdanov also maintained leverage over the military commanders of occupied areas through their *Politruks*. According to Nekrich, the overlapping of areas of responsibility and influence was Stalin's deliberate policy, whereby he attempted to ensure that, rather than conspiring against him, his underlings would be too busy competing with one another. Nekrich stresses that Stalin was a master at inciting one group against another. If it was Stalin's intention to bring about friction between his subordinates in the context of Soviet occupation policy in Germany, he was to prove highly successful in that endeavor.

Having long maintained a position particularly hostile to the West (as shown, for example, in his July 1939 *Pravda* article), Zhdanov con-

*Shcherbakov's name was linked to Zhdanov's in death (*TASS* announcement on "Arrest of Group of Saboteur-Doctors," *Pravda*, January 13, 1953) as it was in life (Conquest, *Power*, p. 100).

tinued to thrust in that direction.* Indeed, he seems to have become the unofficial leader in the communist world of the proponents of a "forward," or militant, anti-Western foreign policy. He appears even to have been establishing an international power base in the new Soviet East European empire, well beyond his original Leningrad and Finnish fiefdoms. (While Zhdanov and his followers, in their struggle with a rival faction, "raised their banners high over the battlefield" i.e. espoused a particular approach toward international affairs, in order to "score points", that does not prove at all that the competing groups were motivated by issues rather than by "feudal" chieftain-retainer relationships and the need to prevail in the contest for power.)

The essential elements of Zhdanov's line were to be propounded by Zhdanov himself at the November 1946 anniversary commemoration of the 1917 Revolution and again at the September 1947 founding conference of the Cominform, as well as implicitly, by Zhdanov's close ally, N. A. Voznesenskii, in his highly publicized book, *The Wartime Economy of the U.S.S.R. during the Great Patriotic War* (published in 1948).

The doctrinal pronouncements emanating from the Zhdanov-Voznesenskii group to some extent drew upon Stalin's reports to the seventeenth and eighteenth party congresses and his February 9, 1946, preelection address,[3] which, in turn, traced their line of descent loosely from Lenin's *Imperialism, the Highest Stage of Capitalism*. The line promulgated soon after the victorious conclusion of the global conflict was based upon the theory that the "first stage in the general crisis of world capitalism," brought about by the "uneven development" of capitalism which led to World War I, had culminated in the subtraction of the "socialist sixth" from the world market for which the imperial powers competed. This loss of a significant portion of the outlets for excess capital and production helped to trigger the Depression and, ultimately, World War II. That global conflagration had resulted in the further subtraction from the imperialist global market of the "new democracies" established in Eastern Europe, thus inaugurating the "second stage in the general crisis." Consequently, still more intense conflict would be triggered among the imperial powers, particularly the United States and Britain, for redivision of a constantly diminishing world market, resulting, ultimately, in a third (and devastating) stage in the general crisis (in which the "correlation of forces" would shift irreversibly in favor of the Soviet camp).

---

*The main difference, of course, between Zhdanov's prewar and postwar postures was that, in 1939, he displayed antagonism to Britain and France, whereas, from 1945 onward, he expressed hostility toward the United States and Britain, with increasing emphasis on the former.

Thus, the West was declining as a result of objective factors, and a "leftist," militant, "forward" Soviet line would be not only appropriate but, indeed, incumbent upon the Kremlin. Since the British had emerged from the war as the weaker party in the Anglo-American duumvirate, a policy calculated to pry Britain away from its erstwhile ally would be in order. In a period expected to be marked by unbridled competition for markets among the imperial powers, British (not to speak of French, German, or Japanese) antipathy to Washington was probable. Perhaps some of these "secondary adversaries" would even take a neutral stand in the rivalry that would develop inevitably between the USSR and its new "principal antagonist," the United States.

Moreover, the Zhdanov group's line was both to assume that the East European "new democracies" were embarked irreversibly on the path leading to "socialism" and to ensure that this, indeed, was the case, through measures imposing maximal Communist Party control in those countries. This was an integral part of a strategy based implicitly on the proposition that the "second stage in the general crisis" had been reached, offering opportunities to the Soviet camp that must be seized boldly. (See Chapter 6—The Varga-Voznesenskii "Debate".)

Zhdanov's postwar comeback may have been aided by Stalin's bouts of illness and periods of recuperation during 1945 and 1946 (and reportedly even in 1947). Apparently, the Soviet dictator suffered cardiovascular incidents during 1945, one of them two months prior to the Potsdam Conference and another during that meeting.[4] (See Appendix D: Stalin—Possible Limitations on his Activities; his Appearances, Statements, and Publications, 1945–52.) As a result, serious measures were taken to safeguard his health. A medical commission recommended that he take five to six months' rest each year and that his work schedule in general be much less strenuous. A commission to supervise Stalin's health was established and charged with making "Comrade Stalin a centenarian." The members of the commission were Beria, Malenkov, and Molotov.[5] Thus, in mid-1945, when Stalin was still present in Moscow on a full-time basis, Malenkov and Beria evidently remained important figures while Zhdanov and his associates had not yet moved back from the sidelines toward the center. In the fall of 1945, however, Stalin departed for the mild climate of his vacation home in Sochi, on the Black Sea.[6] Clearly he had decided to take doctors' orders very seriously, since, in a break with peacetime tradition, he was absent from the rostrum during the huge annual parades commemorating the October Revolution both in 1945 and in 1946. During the winter of 1945/46, Zhdanov and his supporters apparently began to stage a comeback.

Western attention to the personalities on the rostrum of the November 1946 parade commemorating the Bolshevik Revolution was confined, at the time, primarily to the absence from the proceedings, for the second straight year, of Stalin.* In fact, more careful analysis would have revealed very significant developments. Missing from the podium were Beria and Malenkov, two leaders recently promoted to full membership of the Politburo. Moreover, also absent were such long-time members as Mikoyan, Molotov, Voroshilov, Andreyev, Kaganovich, and Khrushchev. Instead, the reviewing stand was dominated by A. A. Zhdanov and filled with other public figures, the great majority of whom were known then or identified by subsequent events as Zhdanovites, while few of them could be compared in standing, reputation, or seniority to the leaders who were absent. Zhdanov himself was ensconced squarely in the center of the rostrum and clearly was meant to be viewed as the man presiding over the proceedings. Also on the dais (not necessarily listed in order of their location) were:[8]

N. A. Voznesenskii. He had been reappointed that year (in place of Malenkov's associate, Saburov) as chairman of the Soviet State Planning Commission (Gosplan) and promoted a few weeks earlier to membership in the unpublicized but most important Politburo Commission for Foreign Affairs (although his elevation to full membership of the Politburo itself was not to be announced until the following year). He had reached prominence first as Zhdanov's appointee to the post of chairman of the Leningrad City Planning Commission in the mid-1930s, when Zhdanov was first secretary of the Party there, being promoted subsequently to deputy chairman of the Leningrad City Soviet, and his brother, A. A. Voznesenskii, had been made rector of Leningrad University under Zhdanov's aegis toward the end of the war. Eventually, both brothers were to become victims of the notorious Leningrad Affair of 1949–50, in which almost all Zhdanovites were purged.[9]

A. N. Kosygin. He had just been promoted to candidate membership of the Politburo in March of that year, only weeks before Malenkov was demoted from the post of party secretary and replaced by N. S. Patolichev. During Zhdanov's "Leningrad purges" of Kirov supporters, Kosygin "served on the Committee of the city's Vyborg Borough. He caught. . . Zhdanov's eye and was taken into the hierarchy. In June, 1939, . . . Kosygin was appointed head of the Industrial Transport Department of the Leningrad Region's Party Committee.

---

*"During the winter of 1946–47 Stalin was seriously ill for some weeks with recurrent heart trouble, aggravated by high blood pressure."[7]

Four months later, he was designated [chairman of the Leningrad Executive Committee], making him a partner of. . .Zhdanov." At the Eighteenth CPSU Congress, thanks to Zhdanov's pervasive influence, Kosygin became a member of the CPSU Central Committee.[10] He was associated intimately with Zhdanov in the defense of Leningrad, being in charge of the evacuation of industry and of a part of the population from the beleaguered city. Later, during the war, Kosygin (together with the quartermaster, General A. V. Khrulev) was deputy to N. A. Voznesenskii, at the head of the Traffic-Transit Committee, which, from 1942 onward, handled the gigantic task of evacuating Soviet industry across the Urals. In the "memoirs" (*Khrushchev Remembers*) imputed to him, Khrushchev mentioned Kosygin as one of the bright young men who, together with N. A. Voznesenskii and A. A. Kuznetsov, rose to prominence in this period, pointing out snidely, however, that only Kosygin managed somehow to survive the Leningrad Affair.[11]

A. A. Kuznetsov. He had been elevated to the post of secretary of the Central Committee in the previous year and, subsequently, to membership in the Orgburo. He had been Zhdanov's deputy during the defense of Leningrad and succeeded him as first secretary of the Leningrad party toward the end of the war, when Zhdanov began to move back to the national scene. Khrushchev later revealed that upon his promotion to the Secretariat, Kuznetsov had been entrusted "with the supervision of the State-security organs" and that this fact had "alarmed Beria."* Thus, Kuznetsov's rise indicated a setback for Zhdanov's rivals, Beria and Malenkov. Kuznetsov, like Voznesenskii, perished in the aftermath of the Leningrad Affair; as reported in Khrushchev's "memoirs," the entire group was condemned for excessive "Russian nationalism."[12]

Admiral N. G. Kuznetsov. According to his own voluminous memoirs, he had been on terms of intimacy with Zhdanov who, in his capacity as "Central Committee secretary in charge of naval affairs," had personally pushed through Kuznetsov's appointment, in March 1939, to replace P. A. Smirnov-Svetlovskii as first deputy people's commissar of the Navy. No people's commissar was appointed at the time, and Zhdanov told Admiral Kuznetsov, "You decide and call me on the more important or doubtful questions. . . .We'll get it done." Thereafter, they worked in close personal proximity and traveled together

---

*Beria had reason to be concerned; declassified C.I.A. material (CIACR 76-12971, July 1976, "Who's Who in Soviet Government, January 1948," collected DSOS 1948–66, Uncl. 1, 2 of 39) shows that, in the period March 19, 1946–October 19, 1946–February 24, 1947, the senior positions in MVD and MGB were filled by appointees none of whom were to be included among the "treacherous group of conspirators" shot together with Beria in 1953 (*Pravda*, December 24, 1953; Conquest, pp. 440–47).

frequently and over long distances. Kuznetsov subsequently became commander-in-chief of the Soviet Navy and was linked personally, on many occasions, with Zhdanov's defense of Leningrad.[13]

G. M. Popov. His position represented an attempt by the Leningrad group to establish a foothold in Moscow. A protégé of A. S. Shcherbakov (Zhdanov's brother-in-law,[14] "close associate," and "ally"), Popov eventually "inherited" Shcherbakov's posts of Moscow city and provincial first secretary of the party and secretary of the CPSU Central Committee. In the wake of the Leningrad Affair, Popov was removed from all these positions, and all four Moscow provincial secretaries who had served under him disappeared. Popov, however, unlike most of the Leningraders, was not shot.[15]

General A. V. Khrulev. A deputy minister of defense, he had been an intimate associate of N. A. Voznesenskii and A. N. Kosygin on the Traffic-Transit Committee, securing Soviet defense industry from seizure by the enemy during the war, when Khrulev was quartermaster and chief of Red Army Rear Services. In this capacity, he went to Leningrad briefly in 1942 to aid Zhdanov. Reportedly, Malenkov and Beria blamed him for grave errors during the war, his wife was arrested, and Stalin finally demoted him. His official position in 1946 did not necessarily warrant appearance on the podium. In an article of wartime reminiscences fifteen years later, he refers, out of context, to "such outstanding leaders as...A. A. Zhdanov."[16]

N. S. Patolichev. He had just become a party secretary, replacing the demoted Malenkov. In his memoirs, Patolichev leaves no doubt as to the persons to whom he owed his advancement. In May 1946, he was summoned by Stalin's personal secretary, A. N. Poskrebyshev, to the Kremlin, where the only persons present, apart from Stalin, were A. A. Zhdanov and A. A. Kuznetsov (himself newly promoted to party secretary). Originally alarmed by the summons, "from the expression of Zhdanov's and Kuznetsov's faces I could see that the situation was calm." Stalin suddenly offered him advancement to party secretary, and Patolichev glanced at Zhdanov and Kuznetsov for guidance: "Zhdanov, smiling, threw his arms wide, as if to say, 'you do the deciding yourself.'" Thus encouraged, Patolichev intimated that he had no hesitation, whereupon Stalin dictated over the phone" "Write down a second point in that Central Committee decision—to approve Comrade Patolichev as Secretary of the Central Committee.' What the first point was I did not know. It became known only later. It stated that G. M. Malenkov was relieved of responsibilities as Secretary of the Central Committee." Obviously, Zhdanov and Kuznetsov had maneuvered to have Malenkov replaced by Patolichev. Moreover, when in need of patronage a few years earlier, Patolichev had recourse to another Zhdanovite, General A. V. Khrulev, "who had been a comrade-in-arms of Patolichev's father during the Civil War, and who had had an emotional meeting with Patolichev junior at a Central Committee gathering." However, Patolichev took care also to maintain long-term ties to other "patrons," particularly A. A. Andreyev, and may have collaborated for a brief period with L. M. Kaganovich.[17] Such "flexibility" may have helped him to survive (politically and physically—to this very day) the subsequent annihilation of nearly all other leading adherents of the Zhdanovite faction. This is particularly surprising since, with his promotion to secretary of the Central Committee, Patolichev was placed in charge of the Administration for Inspection of [Leading] Party Organs, which was set up in 1946 as part of the tightening up of party control that was a hallmark of the Zhdanovshchina. Thus, he must have been linked intimately with other Zhdanovites, particularly A. A. Kuznetsov, in implementing what amounted to a major purge.[18] (See pp. 55–56 of this study.)

Marshal L. A. Govorov. The commander of Leningrad during the siege, he had worked intimately with the Leningrad Defense Council under A. A. Zhdanov* and A. A. Kuznetsov. He took Zhdanov's side in disputes with the State Defense Committee in Moscow and with commanders of other fronts. He played a prominent role in the 1943 May Day proceedings in Leningrad, in which the city was full of "portraits of Stalin and Zhdanov—more of Zhdanov than of Stalin."[19] His name was linked, subsequently, with Zhdanov's and Shcherbakov's, as one of the "victims" or "intended victims" of the "Doctors' Plot". In 1941, he had been threatened with liquidation by Beria because of a youthful association with the "white" Admiral Kolchak, and he was to be prominent among the military personalities who denounced Beria in 1953.[21]

Marshal I. S. Konev. He shared some of Govorov's attitudes and was another alleged intended "victim" of the "Doctors' Plot." Later, in 1953, he presided over the special session of the USSR Supreme Court that "sentenced" Beria, who had denounced the "Doctors' Plot" as a fraud.[22]

It seems also that a further factor linking Govorov, Konev, and the Zhdanov group was their shared dislike of Marshal G. K. Zhukov.†

---

*Despite Harrison Salisbury's account, in *900 Days*, Zhdanov must have come to know Govorov prior to the siege of Leningrad, since the latter had been chief of staff of one of the Soviet armies in the Finnish Winter War of 1939–40.[20]

†In April of 1946, Zhukov was dismissed as commander-in-chief of the Soviet Occupation Forces in Germany. Zhukov's German policy had differed considerably from the line advocated by Colonel S. I. Tiul'panov, Zhdanov's man in Germany; in fact,

As these brief descriptions indicate, there is little serious doubt concerning the linkage of the personalities mentioned with the Zhdanov-Voznesenskii group.

The others present on the dais are factionally identifiable with less

several months prior to its announcement, Tiul'panov was confidently predicting Zhukov's ouster from his post in Germany.[23] After departing the Soviet occupation zone, Zhukov was demoted again, this time losing his posts as commander-in-chief of the Ground Forces of the Red Army and deputy minister of the Armed Forces, and was relegated to the command of the Odessa Military District.[24] What is more, he was ousted from the CPSU Central Committee. This rapid sequence of events followed immediately upon the concentration of power in the Main Political Directorate (Administration) of the Red Army, during February of 1946, within the hands of Colonel-General I. V. Shikin, one of Zhdanov's Leningrad cronies and A. S. Shcherbakov's political heir, as well as a future victim of the Leningrad Affair.[25] According to one source, Zhukov had strongly opposed the appointment of Shikin because the Marshal feared a Zhdanovite purge of the Red Army.[26] Zhukov was succeeded as commander-in-chief of Soviet Ground Forces by Konev, who had developed a personal rivalry with Zhukov during World War II.[27] Zhukov's post in Germany was assumed by Marshal V. D. Sokolovskii, at one time Konev's chief-of-staff in charge of the Western Front,[28] who was to cooperate closely with the Zhdanovite faction in the Soviet occupation zone. During the following year, 1947, Govorov was appointed chief inspector of the Soviet Army. In this capacity, according to a Soviet emigré account, he was rumored to have given Zhukov's Odessa district a very poor rating, which led to Zhukov's transfer to an even more obscure post, this time in the Urals.[29] Govorov and Zhukov, apparently, fell out while the former was serving under Zhdanov on the Leningrad front because of what Govorov felt to be Zhukov's excessive interference in his command.[30] Zhdanov certainly had cause himself for resenting Zhukov, who had been sent in to rescue the military situation in Leningrad—an implicit rebuke to the leadership there. At a Berlin press conference (June 1945), Zhukov proudly referred to his role in Leningrad, at which point Andreii Vishinsky added, "Yes it was Zhukov who saved Leningrad."[31] This was a serious matter for Zhdanov, since the heroic defense of Leningrad had provided him with the means of atoning for his egregious political errors in promoting the ill-fated Ribbentrop-Molotov Pact and the highly embarrassing Winter War with Finland. Since Zhukov had so many other victories to his credit, it must have been infuriating to hear him impinge on Zhdanov's personal glory by dwelling on the Leningrad episode. Clearly Zhdanov had every incentive to move Zhukov away from the spotlight.

Moreover, according to American intelligence sources in 1946, Zhukov opposed provocative measures against the West because of what he considered the unpreparedness of the Red Army to fight.[32] This posed evident problems for Zhdanov's militant approach. Only when Malenkov achieved power was Zhukov to be brought back, initially as first deputy minister of defense in 1953.[33]

Thus, the inclusion of Konev and Govorov on the dais with the Zhdanov group may have symbolized mutual interests vis-à-vis Zhukov, rather than being necessarily a manifestation of their unqualified backing of the Leningraders in the conflict with Malenkov and Beria. Western observers saw indications, moreover, that, despite his seniority, Konev's place in the limelight, at this stage, was being taken by Govorov—if true, this was unlikely to enhance harmony between the marshals.[34]

This is not to minimize, of course, Stalin's possible role in Zhukov's demotion. Wolfgang Leonhard recalls rumors circulating at the time in the Soviet occupation zone of Germany to the effect that the marshal's removal was related to Stalin's growing concern about Zhukov's popularity, both within the Soviet Union and in the "new democracies."[35] Boris Meissner asserts that, in order to avert Bonapartism, Stalin played off Zhukov and Konev against one another.[36]

assurance, although, in several cases, the data also are highly suggestive:

M. F. Shkiriatov. Long a prominent member of the Party Control Commission, he was placed on the Special Secret Political Department of State Security in the 1930s. Together with Yezhov, he and two other members of the department were in charge of "arrangements" for Kirov's removal (whose fiefdom, Leningrad, thus fell into Zhdanov's hands). During the "Yezhovshchina," the same group, together with Zhdanov himself, purged Kirov associates and appointees, particularly in Leningrad. (Of 154 Leningrad delegates to the 1934 Seventeenth CPSU Congress, only two reappeared at the 1939 Eighteenth Congress, one of them being—Shkiriatov.)

This may not constitute definitive evidence of Shkiriatov's factional allegiance, since he had not actually served with or under Zhdanov; he managed also to survive the years 1948–50, the period marked by the political (and, in most cases, the physical) annihilation of the Zhdanovites.* It is clear, at any rate, that there could have been no love lost between him and the faction that opposed Zhdanov. His most important party appointment was to be a brief appearance in the enlarged Party Presidium of October 1952–March 1953. That he was removed from that body after Malenkov's ascent to power implies that he was not a Malenkov supporter. Moreover, there are indications that he may have been connected with the plans for the implementation of a major purge in connection with the "Doctors' Plot"; this means that he hardly could have been a Beria supporter. (Beria had been accused implicitly of insufficient "vigilance" in connection with the "crimes" of the "murderous doctors" and obviously felt himself threatened, since one of his first actions after Stalin's death was to denounce the "plot" as a blatant fabrication.) Shkiriatov, therefore, may be counted among the adversaries of Zhdanov's opponents—presumably "my enemy's enemy is my friend."[37]

Army General (subsequently Marshal) *N. A. Bulganin.* He had been sent to exercise political supervision during the first three years of the war on the western sectors of the front, as Zhdanov had on the northwestern and Khrushchev on the southwestern sectors. Bulganin worked under the general direction from Moscow of Zhdanov's brother-in-law, A. S. Shcherbakov (in the latter's capacity as chief of the Main Political Administration† of the Red Army, from 1942 until his death in 1945).

---

*For possible links with Zhdanov, during and after the Yezhovshchina, see Appendix A.

†The terms "Main Political Administration" and "Chief Political Directorate" are used synonymously.

Bulganin formally signed the order of the day for the October Revolution anniversary, an honor Stalin normally reserved for himself. Bulganin had just become a candidate member of the Politburo, as well as being a deputy defense minister. In the following year Stalin was to relinquish to him the position of minister of defense. However, the fact that he was raised to full membership of the Politburo only in 1948 (when the Zhdanovshchina already had terminated), as well as other factors, leave his factional affiliation at this time a question mark.[38]

The Chief of Staff, *Marshal A. M. Vasilevskii*. He was to be included subsequently among the alleged intended "victims" of the "Doctors' Plot," together with Marshals Govorov and Konev, his name being listed immediately after those of the main "victims" themselves: A. A. Zhdanov and A. S. Shcherbakov. (The fact that the TASS announcement of the "Doctors' Plot" in January 1953 was followed within three days by the "rehabilitation" of A. A. Zhdanov's son Yurii, who was permitted to publish a major polemical article to which *Pravda* devoted considerable space—and who, four and a half years earlier, just before his father's death, had been the object of political humiliation in *Pravda*—strengthens the supposition that the fabricated "Doctors' Plot" was meant to rehabilitate Zhdanovites in general.) Thus, the appearance of Vasilevskii's name on the January 13, 1953, list cannot be dismissed as insignificant.[39]

V. V. Kuznetsov. The head of the trade unions and a member of the Orgburo, his greatest talent appears to have been the ability to survive, irrespective of changes in the power structure. He passed through the 1949–50 Leningrad Affair period unscathed, even politically. However, during the period 1940–43, he had served as N. A. Voznesenskii's deputy at Gosplan.[40] Thus, his presence on the dais may well have resulted from his recent association with Zhdanov's close ally. Moreover, in view of his demotion from the Party Presidium after its reduction in size in March 1953, when Malenkov briefly stood at the apex of power, there is cause for believing that the Malenkovites regarded him as hostile.[41]

Colonel-General K. A. Vershinin. He had achieved renown as aviation commander during the war. Documentation concerning him is insufficient to indicate whether he can be identified with particular factions.[42]

Marshal S. M. Budenny. A deputy defense minister, he was Stalin's old crony, but had no real political standing, and his presence at these parades had become traditional as an "Old Bolshevik" symbol.[43]

N. N. Shvernik. The chairman of the Presidium of the Supreme

Soviet, he was a rather shadowy figure whose presence, as "Head of State," would have to be considered a matter of protocol.[44]

Thus, of the seventeen personalities on the rostrum, counting Zhdanov himself, no less than ten appear to have been part of, or at least to have maintained close connections with, the Leningrad group: A. A. Zhdanov, A. A. Voznesenskii, A. N. Kosygin, A. A. Kuznetsov, N. G. Kuznetsov, G. M. Popov, General A. V. Khrulev, N. S. Patoli-chev, and Marshals L. A. Govorov and I. S. Konev. Moreover, M. F. Shkiriatov's memoirs reveal distinct Zhdanovite links. Marshal A. M. Vasilevskii, judging by the "Doctors' Plot," well may have had similar affiliations, and this would seem to apply also to N. A. Bulganin (at least prior to 1948). S. M. Budenny and N. N. Shvernik probably were present for reasons of protocol, while evidence concerning V. V. Kuz-netsov's and General K. A. Vershinin's affiliations remains insufficient to reach definite conclusions. It is evident, therefore, that the dais was "packed" with Zhdanovites and persons hostile to Beria and Malen-kov, and that, in any case, no one of stature was present with apparent links to Zhdanov's adversaries. Moreover, the accompanying article in *Pravda* summing up the anniversary (of the October Revolution) proceedings was indicative of Zhdanov's control. In listing the persons taking the salute at the parade, the following order was given: A. A. Zhdanov, N. E. Shvernik, N. A. Voznesenskii, N. A. Bulganin, A. N. Kosygin, and A. A. Kuznetsov. Of these first six persons named, four were hardcore Zhdanovites and the other two (Shvernik and Bulganin) virtually had to be listed prominently as a matter of protocol.

It should be emphasized, once more, that issues are not the critical factor entitling analysts to regard some one dozen Zhdanovites on the dais as a faction; indeed, only Zhdanov and Voznesenskii prominently articulated views on policy and, once they fell, the rival faction showed no inhibition about adopting portions of their "platform". Rather, the men on the rostrum were linked by biography, that is, by personal bonds of "feudal" protection, assistance, obligation, and service, which led to promotion, power, and prestige during the ascendency of their patrons and to humiliation, expulsion, and execution once their adversaries triumphed. Appearance on a purge list depended less on the prospective victim's views than on the question to whom he owed his appointment. However, while a power struggle was in full tilt, the policy "platform" of their faction certainly constituted a "battleflag" around which the members were expected to rally. Not surprisingly, therefore, the unprecedented massing of Zhdanovites on the review stand was accompanied by attempts to promulgate an ideological and political line which, were it to prevail over other concepts, would herald the imminent victory of the Leningrad clique and demonstrate to fence sitters that it was high time to line up with the winners.

For Stalin, such emblems of domination by one group were likely to have been alarming. Never before (or again) in the dictator's lifetime was one faction permitted to dominate a May or November parade to such an extent.

This "Parade of the (temporary) Victors," in the fall of 1946, constituted the first in a series of highly symbolic triumphs for the Zhdanovites, following more than eight months of the draconian decrees covering the greater part of the Soviet artistic and intellectual scene that have become known as the Zhdanovshchina (see Chapter 5).

In fact, traces of the militant lurch "leftward," so typical of the Zhdanov ascendancy, had become visible already in the previous year. One might note an assertion published by Earl Browder, the former general secretary of the American Communist Party, several years after Zhdanov's death. In mid-1945 Browder was denounced for his moderate and conciliatory line, above all toward the West and, particularly, the U.S., ostensibly by Jacques Duclos, the French Communist Party leader (who, ironically, was to be attacked for similar "rightist" deviations two years later by Zhdanov and the Yugoslavs). Soon after coming under fire, Browder was deposed at Moscow's behest. In retrospect, Browder remarked that:

> When from 1945 on I found myself in deep and growing disagreement with the international line of the Communist movement, so much so that I no longer call myself a Communist, I believed and still believe that the 1945 collapse of the American Communist Party was one of the by-products of Stalin's retirement from active operational leadership.[45]

Clearly, he felt that more militant, leftist, and adventuristic elements (which, in this context, presumably meant Zhdanov and Voznesenskii) were assuming responsibility for day-to-day conduct of international affairs in place of the ailing Stalin. (Of course, it is naive to assume that, even while convalescing near the Black Sea coast, Stalin somehow could be "overruled.") Phillip Jaffe, one of Browder's closest associates in the American Communist Party and his biographer, even suggests that Zhdanov probably wrote the "Duclos" article denouncing Browder.[46]

Certainly Stalin himself, a by-word for caution, had shown no indication of preferring an "adventuristic" line during this or earlier periods. He had made prudent (albeit empty) gestures toward the West following Hitler's attack upon the USSR, eliminating (at least official-ly) the revolutionary Comintern and changing the Soviet anthem from the "Internationale" to a national hymn less objectionable to the West (and to many Russians tired of ideological exhortations). Moreover, he preferred "salami tactics" to more overt means of seizing power after the war. As will be seen, he repeatedly lectured the Yugoslav Commu-nists during the wartime and immediate postwar periods on the dangers of overt provocations of the West. (For more on Stalin's apparent policy predilections, see pp. 116–29.) This is not to say for one moment, of course, that Stalin, whatever the state of his health, was actually being "supplanted" from 1945 onward. However, other hands also were beginning to leave an imprint on the day-to-day conduct of policy.

That imprint increasingly reflected the line propagated by A. A. Zhdanov, who had given a more elaborate exposition of his particular view of the world on the eve of the November 1946 parade, having been chosen to deliver this symbolic annual message on behalf of the party leadership. (Foreign observers noted the absence of Stalin's "vaca-tioning in the south," and the fact that the traditional order of the day to the Soviet Armed Forces, issued in Stalin's name, did not bear his signature.)[47] Zhdanov's speech, initially in somewhat muted tones, de-veloped the theme of opposing blocs and the antagonism between them:

> One could have expected that [the] clear-cut program for the establishment of general peace and security would be achieved without much difficulty and arguments, but this was not so. On the contrary, this peace program met with the organized resistance of reactionary elements in a number of states, especially in Britain and the United States, which have been using as camouflage a number of small countries who have expressed their willingness to follow in the wake of Anglo-American policy. . . .Two tendencies were particularly evident in connection with the question of the direction in which international cooperation must develop at present.
>
> One policy, that pursued by the Soviet Union, consists of fully realizing. . .the consolidation of peace and prevention of aggression. . . .
>
> The other [policy] is the direction of those reactionary forces and circles who are not loath to renounce declarations made only yesterday, . . .to clear the way for the forces of expansion and aggression. . . .

Imperialist circles...are interested in a free hand to conquer world supremacy and expand aggression. But our people did not shed streams of their precious blood to clear the way for new pretenders to world supremacy....[The] anti-Soviet campaign is directed by the reactionary imperialist circles for whom war is a profitable business....

The slander campaign being waged against the USSR...is calculated to undermine the increased confidence in, and the authority of, the Soviet Union among the peoples of the democratic countries.... [This] is not new, and...already more than once this course has come to a sad end as far as its initiators are concerned....

For every inch of criticism of the United States published in *Pravda*, at least a thousand inches of anti-Soviet criticism is published in the American press.

The forces of democracy have grown and multiplied, while the forces of reaction, no matter how they strive to retain their positions...have grown weaker.

Zhdanov emphasized the consequent "responsibility" of "the Soviet intelligentsia":

You know that the Party Central Committee recently exposed intolerable instances of lack of ideology in our literature and art. ...These are precisely those remnants of capitalism in the people's consciousness which we still have to overcome and extirpate. ...[We must intensify] the uncompromising Bolshevik attitude to all sorts of ideological perversions... The Soviet regime cannot tolerate youth being educated in a lack of ideology and indifference to politics. It is vital that our youth should be protected from harmful alien influence.

Significantly, Zhdanov also called for mobilization of scientific resources, but without placing ideological constraints upon that field of activity, with its obvious military implications:

The Soviet state attaches particular importance to the development of science....It is well known what energetic measures the Soviet government is taking to provide our scientists with all necessary conditions for the development of scientific activities,...not only to catch up but also to outstrip within the immediate future scientific achievements outside our country.[48]

Less than three years later, the USSR was to announce its first successful nuclear test.

In the context of the increasingly advantageous international situation for Soviet and communist forward moves, with "the forces of democracy [having] grown and multiplied, while the forces of reaction. . .have grown weaker," Zhdanov paid particular homage to

> the brilliant victories of democracy in the *fraternal Slav countries* [emphasis added] of Yugoslavia, Czechoslovakia, and Poland. In those countries a new, true democracy is flourishing. . . .The peoples of these countries have taken the fate of their countries into their own hands. . .and are waging an active struggle against the forces of reaction. . . .
>
> An unprecedented upsurge of democracy and activity of the popular masses is in progress also in the countries which only yesterday were Germany's satellites—Italy, Bulgaria, Rumania, Hungary, and Finland. Only a few days ago we were witnesses of a major victory for the Fatherland Front in Bulgaria which represented fresh proof of the strengthening of democratic forces in post-war Europe.[49]

The Panslav theme is unmistakable, as is the peculiar pecking order, with Yugoslavia awarded first place. Tito's pet irredenta, Trieste, was emphasized in Zhdanov's address as the first of two major topics of dispute between the blocs at the Paris Conference, while Albania, the object of Yugoslav annexationist aspirations, significantly was omitted altogether from Zhdanov's list of independent East European and Balkan countries experiencing a major "democratic" upsurge. Moreover, among former Axis satellites, Zhdanov picked out for special praise another Slav country, Bulgaria, under G. M. Dimitrov (Zhdanov's former collaborator in the "Ghost Comintern" and Tito's ally, as this study hopes to demonstrate). Noteworthy also is Zhdanov's statement: "striving for freedom and democratic development has. . .spread to the peoples of colonial and dependent countries which are trying to achieve free national development. Millions. . . organized themselves. . . .I am thinking of the importance. . .of the World Federation of Democratic Youth." (This communist "front organization" with paramilitary aspects was to have a role in sponsoring the February 1948 Calcutta Conference of Youth and Students of Southeast Asia Fighting for Freedom and Independence, at which Yugoslav delegates encouraged the ill-fated 1948 uprisings in that region. See pp. 111–14.)

The Panslav theme in Zhdanov's speech paralleled a distinctly Great Russian nationalist, indeed chauvinist, note in the same address:

> The kind of "information" about *Russia* which fills the columns of many newspapers in the United States and Great Britain is beginning to choke even many bourgeois leading personalities. . .to write something about *Russia* it is sufficient to mix a little slander, a little ignorance. . . . Many "investigations" have also appeared recently as regards the character of the Soviet people in general and *the national character of Russians in particular*. . . .We read and wonder how quickly *the Russian people* must have changed. When *our blood* was flowing on the battlefield, *our courage, gallantry, high moral qualities, and unbounded patriotism* evoked universal admiration. [emphases added][50]

As far as the identification of the "principal adversary" is concerned, it should be noted that, while Zhdanov still excoriated "Anglo-American imperialism," particular venom was reserved for anti-Soviet attacks in the *United States* and on the part of "such warmongers as Churchill," who had been *out of office* in Britain for well over a year. As against these comments, Zhdanov devoted relatively friendly comments to the British and French governments:

> The defeat of the conservatives and the victory of the Labour Party in Britain, as well as. . .the victory of the left-wing party bloc in France, constitute an important shift of those countries toward the left.

Zhdanov extolled the importance of the new Five-Year Plan—a form of tribute to its author, his close ally, N. A. Voznesenskii.* He developed the line which soon was to become the official posture of the followers of Zhdanov and Voznesenskii in their polemics against E. S. Varga (see Chapter 6),† claiming that, unlike the Soviet Union, the Western countries would emerge from the war only to be beset by imminent economic crises because of an inherent inability to plan their

---

*Voznesenskii presented the Fourth Five-Year Plan to the Supreme Soviet on March 15, 1946. See N. A. Voznesenskii, *Piatiletnii plan vosstanovleniia i razvitiia narodnogo khoziaistva SSSR na 1946–1950 gg.* English text: *Five Year Plan for the Restoration and Development of the National Economy of the U.S.S.R. for 1946–50.*

†Although the Voznesenskii book, which figured prominently in the anti-Varga polemics, *Voennaia ekonomika SSSR v period Otechestvennoi voiny* [*The wartime economy of the U.S.S.R. during the great patriotic war*], was not published formally until the following year, there can be very little doubt that the manuscript was already available to Zhdanov, particularly given the tendency in the Soviet Union for major works to be circulated within high circles well in advance of formal publication.

economies:

> The Soviet Union has emerged from World War II firm and
> strong. As distinct from capitalist states, our country has
> resumed its peacetime production without any crises or up-
> heavals. . . .The postwar period in [Great Britain and the
> United States] is marked by grave economic and political
> crisis. The reconversion from war to peace in capitalist
> countries has caused an acute narrowing of markets, a drop
> in the production standard, the closing down of factories and
> a growth of unemployment. . . .We have none of the anarchy
> in production characteristic of capitalism, which leads to a
> cycle of boom and crisis, shaking to its very foundations the
> whole economic system and creating among the workers a
> constant insecurity regarding the future. Our economic life is
> being directed by a single plan of popular economy.[51]

This statement flatly contradicted, in effect, an article the
Hungarian-born Soviet economist Varga had published earlier in the
year.[52] Varga (director of the Institute of World Economics and World
Politics) had prognosticated an *increase* in American exports during
the postwar period. Moreover, while Zhdanov stressed the advantages
accruing to the Soviet Union from its ability to plan—an option lacking in the West, so he asserted—Varga was to be attacked, in the following year, for having claimed in his book *Changes in the Economy of
Capitalism as a Result of the Second World War* (Moscow: September,
1946, i.e., published also prior to Zhdanov's speech) that during the
global conflagration the West had achieved the ability to impose a
certain degree of state regulation in times of war, which would carry
over into peacetime. (See pp. 62–64, 67–69.) Judging by an extended
interview with Harold Stassen published only five months after
Zhdanov's address, Stalin himself appears to have accepted many
of Varga's notions regarding Western postwar economic policies—
particularly with regard to planning. (See pp. 124–30.) The differences
between Varga's position and those of Zhdanov and Voznesenskii were
soon to provide the catalyst that precipitated a major "ideological"
confrontation, with evident factional roots and clear policy
implications. (See Chapter 6.)

Significantly, the *Pravda* edition of November 6, 1946 (the day of
Zhdanov's address), in publicizing Soviet industrial progress, singled
out the Zhdanovite Leningrad fiefdom for special achievements, with
Zhdanov's former bailiwick of Gorkii receiving second billing.[53]

4 THE BELGRADE CONNECTION
Balkan Jacobinism

The details of the "leftist" Zhdanov-Voznesenskii line in international affairs, as in ideological-cultural questions, will be discussed later in this study. At this stage, however, it should be pointed out that perhaps the only major Communist leaders during this period who projected an image as stridently militant in word and deed as Zhdanov's and Voznesenskii's belonged to the Communist Party of Yugoslavia (C.P.Y.). In fact, it had been Tito who, as early as 1945, first suggested to Stalin the establishment of the Cominform,[1] although, of course, after Belgrade's expulsion in 1948 from that organization, Vladimir Dedijer was to claim that the Yugoslav concept had been far different from the Stalinist monolith that actually developed.[2] Yet, as will be shown later, Yugoslav behavior at the founding meeting of the Cominform does not support the argument that Tito had intended merely that a consultative framework be set up.

In any case, Zhdanovite-Titoist linkages, the focus of a sizable segment of this study, like the bonds between the individual members of Zhdanov's faction, derived from personal ties and obligations that antedated ideological convergence.

Tito's own career in the movement was launched, it should be recalled, by serving in the Comintern—first in its Moscow central offices, where he worked after his release in 1933 from a Yugoslav prison, and then in Paris, from which he coordinated the movement of Communists and other antifascists being smuggled into Spain to fight in the civil war.[3] Tito's period of service in the Comintern coincided with the purge by Stalin of virtually the entire Central Committee of the C.P.Y. Certainly, at that time, Tito must have been a "good Stalinist." His ability to survive the purge, alone among his party's Central Committee members in Moscow, might cause cynics to question whether, just possibly, he might have "fingered" his comrades. Afterwards, he recruited several of his immediate subordinates in the newly established Central Committee from among the Yugoslav "Spaniards," who had been hand-picked by him.[4]

The Spanish Civil War was the scene of mass purges by Comintern agents among the Communist volunteers in the International Brigades.

Thus, Tito was well acquainted with the real character of international Communist organizations (Comintern or Cominform) and their operations. As a Comintern agent, Tito had worked closely with the Bulgarian Georgi Dimitrov, who reached Moscow practically at the same time as Tito and had become secretary-general of the organization. Tito was assigned for some time to the Balkan Secretariat, where he collaborated both with Dimitrov and with Otto Kuusinen (who, as noted previously, was one of Zhdanov's colleagues).[5] Almost a decade and a half later, Stalin was to treat Dimitrov and Tito as co-conspirators in the "Balkan Federation Affair." A few months prior to that, in 1947, Tito's and Dimitrov's delegations to the founding meeting of the Cominform were to act as Zhdanov's closest collaborators in lecturing the Communist parties of Western and Eastern Europe, respectively, how to seize and consolidate power.[6]

It should be noted that the Yezhovshchina from which Zhdanov benefitted significantly (see Appendix A) was also instrumental in enabling Tito to ascend to the leadership of the Yugoslav Communist Party, following the liquidation of Milan Gorkić, the general secretary of the party until 1937. Along with Gorkić, over a hundred other leading Yugoslav Communists were killed. It was Dimitrov who informed Tito officially that he had been chosen to succeed Gorkić.[7].

Significantly, while much of the leadership of the Bulgarian Communist Party was also eliminated, Dimitrov not only was able to survive (perhaps it would have been awkward to purge, so soon, the "Hero of the Reichstag Fire Trial"), but was also in a position to protect his brother-in-law, V. Chervenkov, until he could be "interceded for."[8] It would seem, therefore, that Dimitrov wielded some clout among the perpetrators of the Yezhovshchina.* Thus, it may not be unreasonable to speculate that, given his role in the Balkan Secretariat, Dimitrov could have been influential in picking out Tito to survive and "inherit" the Yugoslav party. According to Dedijer, Tito "often met" Dimitrov during his first years in the Balkan Secretariat, and he implies that Dimitrov may have saved Tito.[9] One of the two Soviet representatives in the same Secretariat was Manuilskii, who seems to have served subsequently as Zhdanov's alter ego in the "Ghost Comintern." After Tito returned to Yugoslavia, he sent his son Žarko (born in 1924) to the Comintern School (which, like the rest of that organization, was evacuated to Ufa, in the Bashkir ASSR, until the post-Stalingrad period, when the whole apparatus was moved back to

---

*Another personality to survive this purge unscathed, who emerged, subsequently, as a member of Zhdanov's entourage, was Otto Kuusinen. (See Conquest, *Great Terror*, p. 587.)

Moscow). This institution was packed with children of the elite cadres from the various Communist parties. Not only was Tito's son there but so was the daughter of Dolores Ibarruri ("La Passionaria"). The young men and women in this school were privy to secret Comintern documents. Clearly, the Comintern trusted Tito and his family, and Tito, in turn, entrusted his son to it.[10]

Yugoslav proclivities toward an international policy of a "forward" type revealed themselves soon after the Nazi invasion of April 1941. Repeatedly, during the war, the Yugoslav Partisans were chided by Stalin for behaving far too overtly like militant international Communists, rather than adopting the pose of being good Yugoslav nationalists. For example, as early as 1942, Stalin questioned why Tito saw fit to irritate the British government (which was providing the USSR with vital military assistance) by calling his units "Proletarian Brigades."[11] During Djilas's 1944 trip to Moscow, Stalin again asked the Yugoslav Partisans to be less provocative toward the British, exclaiming, "What do you want with Red Stars on your caps? The form is not important, but what is to be gained, and you—Red Stars! By God, stars aren't necessary!"[12]

The Soviet leader may have had another consideration in mind as well, of course. His "spheres-of-influence" agreement with Winston Churchill in October 1944 had provided for "90 percent" British control of Greece (traditionally an object of British concern and affection, as symbolized by the locale of Lord Byron's untimely death). This was the only Southeast European state in which Britain was accorded majority control (insofar as the ambiguous agreement had any concrete meaning at all). Stalin may have wished to avoid developments that might jeopardize Soviet control over Romania, Bulgaria, and Hungary, which London appeared willing to accept. The October 1944 agreement left Tito's Yugoslavia apportioned "50-50" between the Soviet Union and Great Britain.[13] Stalin, however, could hardly instruct Tito to constrain himself at home in Yugoslavia, as well as in Greek Macedonia, in fulfillment of a "gentlemen's agreement" with the leader of Great Britain's Conservative Party! The rambunctious Titoist leadership, moreover, could not be expected to accept with equanimity the parceling out of Yugoslav sovereignty.

In fact, according to Vladimir Dedijer, the Yugoslav Communists, through Randolph Churchill, discovered the existence of this agreement in 1944.[14] Tito left little doubt about his views on the subject in late May of 1945, in a speech delivered in Ljubljana:

> We believe that by virtue of our struggle, our sacrifices, and our exertions for the allied cause, we have given proof enough

that we are loyal to the general cause of the allies. . . . After the last war. . . some politicians had no qualms about giving away slices of our country. . . .Today the situation is different. There is a new Yugoslavia today. . . .This Yugoslavia is not an object for *barter* or *bargaining* [emphasis added].[15]

Yugoslav discovery of the Churchill-Stalin "deal" may well have contributed further to Yugoslav militancy; since the last thing Tito would have wanted then was an amicable Anglo-Soviet arrangement for partitioning the Balkans, he may have hoped that his policies would have a catalytic effect, triggering tension between the USSR and the West. The Yugoslav leaders consistently demonstrated more incontinently anti-American and intermittently anti-British attitudes than did Moscow, prior to Zhdanov's 1946 ascendancy in the foreign policy realm.[16] As the war came to a close, the Yugoslavs agitated furiously for extension of their borders to include Austrian Carinthia, the Trieste–Venezia Giulia area of Italy, and Greece's Aegean Macedonia. In pursuit of these irredentist goals, Belgrade even precipitated military confrontations with Western forces.

Early in 1946, Tito's military forces shot down two American planes which allegedly had strayed too close to Yugoslavia. Obviously fearing an escalation of the conflict, Stalin, via his foreign minister, Molotov, warned Belgrade against shooting down any more planes.[17] Tito was particularly unrestrained on the Trieste issue, evoking comments by Moscow that the Yugoslavs apparently were willing to provoke a war between the USSR and the Anglo-American allies.[18] Tito seems to have conceived of an expanded Yugoslavia, federated eventually with Bulgaria, Romania, and Greece, should the rebels win there. It was intended that, subsequently, the new unit would link up with a northern federation of "people's democracies," including Hungary, Czechoslovakia, and Poland[19] (although this was contingent upon an overt and total Communist takeover in each of these countries, a process which, in fact, had not yet been completed at the time). Beyond that, the Yugoslavs had spoken even of becoming eventually "a constituent part of the USSR."[20]*

As this study indicates, and as was suggested earlier in this chapter, the links between Tito and Zhdanov's entourage were forged, apparently, during the murkiest period of the "twilight of the Comintern" and bore, therefore, an essentially personal, factional

---

*In viewing Tito's relations with Britain (pp. 43–45), one should note that, on March 13, 1943, Djilas, Velebit, and Popović apparently offered the German General Dippold to cease fire and to "fight the British should [they] land in Yugoslavia." (Walter R. Roberts, *Tito, Mihailović and the Allies, 1941/1945*, pp. 106–12.)

character. However, the fact that "objective realities" had impelled Tito's Partisans, during and after World War II, to adopt a "leftist" and expansionistic posture provided the Zhdanov group in the USSR with a particularly tempting incentive to turn Yugoslavia into a "favored instrument of policy." The militant Zhdanovite "platform" on international affairs, which seemed to provide a particularly useful tactical weapon for undermining factional rivals who (as will be shown) were vulnerable to the charge of "lack of vigilance" and "capitulationism," coincided conveniently with the slogans and actions that characterized Tito and most of his followers.

This offensive and irredentist aspect of (pre-1948/49) Titoism found especially significant expression in Yugoslav behavior vis-à-vis Albania and Greece, issues that were to assume major symbolic importance when Stalin decided finally to put an end to the Zhdanov group and its Balkan allies in the winter of 1947/48. Consequently, the Albanian and Greek "episodes" in Tito's international operations require exposition in some detail, particularly since they illustrate the role played by the establishment of factional linkages across international frontiers.

Albania

In addition to its other territorial aspirations, Belgrade apparently desired to annex Albania. An opportunity for achieving this objective, the Yugoslavs were to claim later, was offered to Tito by Stalin, in unsolicited fashion: "We agreed to Yugoslavia swallowing Albania!"[21] Milovan Djilas subsequently asserted that he was shocked by the crude offer, and explained to Stalin, "It is not a matter of swallowing, but of unification."[22] However, events would prove that — at the time of and even prior to Stalin's "offer" — control of Albania really was of major concern to the Yugoslav government. Belgrade fully backed a faction, under Koci Xoxe, that favored incorporation of Albania into Yugoslavia, against a group led by Enver Hoxha and Mehmet Shehu,* in a bloody Albanian feud.[23] The conflict in Albania ended only after the Kremlin broke with Tito, when Stalin intervened openly in favor of Hoxha, apparently having secretly backed him earlier. So intense was the Hoxha-Xoxe struggle over the question of Yugoslav control that

---

*In an analysis (April 18, 1947) of the implications of the lessons of World War II for the composition and strategy of the Albanian army, Mehmet Shehu ignored the recent precedent of the campaigns waged by the Yugoslav Partisans, while emphasizing Soviet doctrine, even when dealing with Partisan warfare. One would have thought that Soviet victories resulting from large-scale armored battles, such as Kursk, would be less relevant to Albania than warfare waged in the mountains of Montenegro or Bosnia.[24]

the key factor in the Albanian-Soviet rift, a decade later, was to be Tirana's opposition to Khrushchev's policy of rapprochement with Belgrade from 1954–55 onward.[25]

Between 1945 and May Day of 1948, before Zhdanov's downfall had become evident outside the USSR and prior to Tito's expulsion from the Cominform, Enver Hoxha, apparently unlike Shehu, labored under the impression that Moscow was not yet prepared to wrest Albania from Yugoslavia's tender mercies. Consequently, as late as his May Day address of 1948, Hoxha believed that he had to pay homage to Tito:

> Our people are determined to strengthen more and more their relations with the peoples of New Yugoslavia and to strike mercilessly at the head of all those who may dare to destroy these relations. Our people are closely linked with the peoples of Marshal Tito's Yugoslavia. They are closely marching the same path, and there is no power in the world which can hinder them from doing so.[26]

Thus, a mere month prior to the Cominform's expulsion of the C.P.Y., Hoxha still felt unable to resist de facto control of Albania by its northern neighbor. Of course, it is unclear to what extent Hoxha was cognizant of relations between Tito and various Soviet personalities. Hoxha may have been particularly fearful of potential Yugoslav moves against Albania during this period of uncertainty — perhaps as a manifestation of Tito's resolve to defy pressure from a (suddenly) unfriendly Soviet leadership. While a year earlier Shehu had been prepared to risk making implicitly anti-Yugoslav statements, Hoxha may have felt insufficiently secure to do so in the spring of 1948, particularly since Albania had common borders only with Yugoslavia and Greece, neither of which was under Soviet control by that time.

In October 1946, in contravention of international law, the Albanians (then under Yugoslav domination) had mined the Corfu Channel, sinking two British ships and exacting a high toll in British lives.[27] Ironically, by the time this case was considered at the International Court of Justice in 1949, the Albanian Communist Party had been taken over completely by Hoxha, who refused to pay compensation for the (mis)deeds of his predecessors, who had been operating under the direction of the now-discredited Marshal Tito.[28]

Greece

Even more militant and expansionistic was Tito's policy toward

Greece, where, without question, he was a prime factor in fueling the Civil War—which was to provide "hot proving grounds" for the emerging Zhdanovite-Titoist strategy. As an East-West confrontation, of course, this was a far graver issue than control of Albania. In 1948, Stalin left little doubt as to his more cautious approach to the Greek situation (although, of course, this may have been an ex post facto revision of view). He queried Tito's intimate friend Kardelj regarding the chances for a successful outcome: "Do you believe in the success of the uprising in Greece?" The Slovene leader replied affirmatively, "If foreign intervention does not grow and if serious political and military errors are not made."[29] Stalin's response was quite harsh:

> If, if! No, they have no prospect of success at all. What do you think, that Great Britain and the United States—the United States, the most powerful state in the world—will permit you to break their line of communications in the Mediterranean Sea! Nonsense. And we have no Navy. The uprising in Greece must be stopped, and as quickly as possible.[30]*

Characteristically, Stalin tended to be "serious"—that is, careful—in the face of adversaries. His position contradicted not only Yugoslav policy, but also the line regarding the allegedly declining strength of the West (permitting a more militantly offensive Communist policy) which Voznesenskii and Zhdanov had been propounding over the previous two years, as will be demonstrated. Stalin, after all, unlike his various lieutenants, was not compelled to engage in factional games, not being a contender for the succession or having to demonstrate his supremacy, so that he alone could afford to deal realistically with "concrete factors."

The Yugoslav role in Greece certainly was to be an element exacerbating relations with Stalin. Quite apart from the question whether the Yugoslavs were adopting a more provocative posture than Stalin considered appropriate, perhaps more significantly, they were cultivating a pro-Tito faction within the K.K.E., the Greek Communist Party. (Unlike the results of the internecine struggle ensuing in Albania during this period, Tito's expulsion from the Cominform was to be followed not by the liquidation of the pro-Belgrade group in Greece, although its leader, Markos Vaphiadis, disappeared for decades, but "only" by the expulsion of its members from the party.)

Stalin had authorized Tito to "swallow" Albania, not Greece, and he was hardly likely to appreciate Tito's sponsorship of a group rivaling the Muscovite section of the K.K.E., led by Nicholas Zakhariadis.

---

*Stalin, in all probability, was impressed by the promulgation of the Truman Doctrine.

The Zakhariadis faction (reflecting the view that we know to have been endorsed by Stalin subsequently) maneuvered cautiously during the early part of the civil-war period, preferring, in the short run, to pursue a legal, constitutional road to power, while recruiting and training an armed force for subsequent use.[31] As late as May 13, 1947, with hostilities in Greece well in progress, Zakhariadis apparently informed the Yugoslav leadership that the aims of the K.K.E. were free elections, a general amnesty, equal friendship with all great powers, and Greek neutrality, to be protected by the United Nations.[32] Zakhariadis, presumably reflecting Stalin's concern to maintain, at least temporarily and in appearance, the "percentage" arrangement with Churchill,[33] stated in 1945 that the British and the USSR constituted "two poles" around which Greek policy would have to revolve.[34] During the same period, he stressed that "the K.K.E. never did stand for social revolution. The K.K.E. has always striven, as it does today, to gain the support of a majority of the nation."[35]

In contrast, the faction which became affiliated increasingly with Tito was led by Markos Vaphiadis, who had developed ties to the Yugoslavs while in Macedonia.[36]* This group, influenced no doubt by the success of the Yugoslav Partisans during World War II, was oriented toward guerrilla warfare, which it wished to unleash immediately.[38] The Tito regime's role in arming its Greek clients during the civil war is well documented. On December 15, 1945, a group of Yugoslav officials, including Ranković, reportedly promised aid to the K.K.E. and coordinated plans for the struggle.[39] Later, Zakhariadis specified that the decision "to proceed into the organization of the new armed struggle" was made on February 12, 1946, with Tito's support.[40] (The previous phase of fighting had occurred more than a year earlier, when British forces had to combat EAM/ELAS insurgents in Athens, despite Stalin's recognition of the pro-British Greek government.)

Zakhariadis later claimed that:

> Tito and his clique promised us the most substantial aid. This played a decisive role in our decision [to initiate renewed armed struggle], because in Yugoslavia, the main factor in the Balkans at that time, our new revolutionary move did not have an opponent who could pose insurmountable obstacles.[41]

In fact, Yugoslav sources allege that Zakhariadis resisted this decision to renew hostilities, reportedly despite pressures from various

---

*The Yugoslav leader who appears to have been dealing directly with the Greeks was Svetozar Vukmanović(-Tempo), the chief of the Political Department of the Yugoslav Army General Staff.[37]

Greek Communists, including Markos, who later repeated the Yugoslav allegations.[42]

On December 24, 1947, after the dominance of the Yugoslav and Zhdanovite line was established at the founding meeting of the Cominform, Markos set up a "free democratic provisional government," dedicated to the "liberation" of Greece. Zakhariadis, the secretary-general of the K.K.E., was not included as a member of the "government," at least in part by his own choice.[43] Slightly more than a year later, at the January 30–31, 1949, Fifth Plenary Session of the Central Committee of the K.K.E.[44*] (after the June 1948 expulsion of Yugoslavia from the Cominform, but before the July 10, 1949, announcement of the "progressive closing" of the Yugoslav border to the Greek rebels),[46] Markos was dismissed from his posts as head of the "government" and of the "democratic army," together with his Yugoslav adviser, General Popović. Subsequently, Markos and some of his comrades were to be dismissed from the Central Committee of the K.K.E.[47]

The Fifth Plenum also marked a major change in K.K.E. policy regarding the Stalin-Tito rift. Suddenly, the K.K.E. committed itself to an independent, unified Macedonia within a federation of Balkan peoples, conforming to the Bulgarian (and Soviet) view on this issue;[48] that approach conflicted with Belgrade's concept of a Yugoslav Greater Macedonia including the Pirin (Bulgarian) and Aegean (Greek) sections, as well as the Vardar (Yugoslav-controlled) region.[†]

An authoritative Yugoslav account of this period was published in 1950 by Svetozar Vukmanović(-Tempo), who had been directly in contact with the Greek Communists during World War II, when he played a key role in Macedonian affairs,[50] and during the Greek civil war, when he was the chief of the Political Department of the Yugoslav Army General Staff.[51] In his book, Vukmanović blames Zakhariadis for not taking the offensive, for not waging partisan warfare, thereby failing to utilize the lessons that should have been learned from the campaigns of Tito's troops during World War II, and for supporting Greek national claims against Albania with respect to Northern Epirus (in the June 7, 1945, Resolution of the Politburo of the Communist Party of Greece).[52] Of course, Greek control of Northern Epirus would have been of little practical consequence in 1950 from the Yugoslav point of view, since Hoxha's welfare was hardly still a matter of

---

*Late in the fall of 1948, despite the events of the preceding June, the Yugoslav representatives at the United Nations still were fervently espousing Markos's cause. On September 29, 1948, Kardelj addressed the General Assembly, supporting the Greek revolutionaries in general and Markos in particular.[45]

†*Borba*, August 27 and 27, 1946, featured maps of this proposed Yugoslav Greater Macedonia.[49]

Belgrade's concern. However, in 1945, Greek claims to Albanian soil
constituted overt defiance of Yugoslavia, which at that time made little
secret of its desire to incorporate Albania into Tito's realm; thus,
implicitly, Vukmanović was reasserting Greater-Yugoslav aspirations as
late as 1950.

Vukmanović clearly intended to place blame squarely on Zakhari-
adis's shoulders, pointing to the decline in the fortunes of the "Libera-
tion Movement in Greece, particularly after the mysterious removal of
Markos."[53] He repeatedly cited a letter from Markos to the Greek
Communist Party of August 4, 1947, noting that, in contrast to
Zakhariadis, "the Markos leadership did try to utilize the rich
experience of the Yugoslav Army during the Second World War."[54]
Vukmanović stresses that:

> With Markos' removal there was an end to Markos' tactics
> of keeping on the offensive, by which the Democratic Army
> had achieved great victories, and which had shown vital value
> in all the campaigns up to that point. Instead of Markos' tac-
> tics of the offensive, Zakhariadis' tactics of "fortified
> mountains" were introduced. . . .These were tactics of dig-
> ging in and frittering away the revolutionary army.[55]

Significantly (in continuation of the Yugoslav line at the founding
meeting of the Cominform, September 1947 [see pp. 103–4]).
Vukmanović, as late as 1950, was still maintaining the offensive
against the previous, "rightist" approach of the French and Italian
parties, stressing that they had been "defeated" at the end of the war
because of "internal weaknesses," and that the failure of the K.K.E.
was due to its emulation of the P.C.I., the Italian Party, which had
committed the serious error of entering a "bourgeois-democratic
government, in which the bourgeoisie would hold the reins." Thus, even
in 1950, when the Yugoslav leadership, ousted from the Cominform,
could have been expected to embark upon a much more moderate "path
to socialism," it was still attacking other European Communist parties
from the "left."[56]*

It is unclear to what extent the Yugoslav leaders felt they had a
go-ahead on Greece (implicit or explicit) from the Zhdanovite group
(particularly after the Cominform was founded and its headquarters
established in Belgrade). According to some views, it would not have
been inconceivable for the Yugoslav "leftist" zealots to have operated

---

*Since Cominform excommunication of the Yugoslav "heretics" challenged Tito's
legitimacy as a Communist leader, he continued attempting to demonstrate his leftist
ideological "purity," by showing that Moscow—not Belgrade—had succumbed to
"rightist deviation" (or "degeneration").

independently in what they regarded as their backyard. However, Titoist contacts with the Zhdanovites were resumed quite early after the Partisans seized power in Yugoslavia, and it would be most surprising if such questions were not discussed and coordinated, at the latest during the Panslav Congress, early in 1946. This is highly probable, all the more so since the two groups were linked by personal ties, as well as being in accord, conveniently, on basic ideological postures and their tactical applications to the realm of international relations.

Zhdanovite-Titoist Ties

Given their similar ideological predilections, in addition to the personal links discussed, it is hardly astonishing that the Zhdanov camp and Belgrade would join forces overtly during 1947. The first major public intimation that Tito's group might be cooperating with Zhdanov preceded the September 1947 inaugural meeting of the Cominform. Zhdanov's aforementioned November 6, 1946, October Revolution anniversary address, in which he asserted the complete dichotomy between the Western and Communist blocs, and the hostility of the West toward the "democratic" states, as well as the declining strength of the adversary in Europe, was an important indicator of this trend. At a time when U.S.-Yugoslav relations were very tense over the Trieste issue, Zhdanov, in effect, publicly backed Tito and cited Trieste as a prime example of the "antidemocratic" nature of American and British policies.[57] Thus, Yugoslavia was presented by Zhdanov as an outstanding case of a threatened ally to be supported by Moscow, whereas Stalin, as we now know, had been attempting for some time to constrain the exuberant Belgrade leaders.

It is difficult to pinpoint the first contacts between the Zhdanov and Tito groups after the end of the war, when Zhdanov resumed his position in the central *Apparat*. From an account by Ilya Ehrenburg we know that, in April 1945, the Panslav Committee gave a dinner in honor of Tito at which G. F. Aleksandrov was in attendance.[58] At that juncture, it appears that Aleksandrov was still essentially a representative of Zhdanov's sector of the bureaucracy (see Appendix B).

Zhdanov himself was to travel to Belgrade late in October of that year, presumably in his capacity as chief of the CPSU Central Committee department in charge of relations with foreign Communist parties.[59] At the time at which Zhdanov visited Yugoslavia, Georgi Dimitrov, the venerable leader of the Bulgarian Communist Party (and Zhdanov's close collaborator in the "Ghost Comintern," as well as Tito's patron) was allowed to return to Bulgaria,[60] where his policies were to be coordinated closely with Tito's during the following three years. At the same time, during the founding meeting of the United Nations in San Francisco, another of Zhdanov's and Dimitrov's associates, D. Z. Manuilskii, in front of Czech and Polish officials, went out of his way to outflank the Soviet foreign minister, V. M. Molotov, in praising the Yugoslav leadership and in lauding Tito's role during the war as exemplary.[61] Thus, there are signs that, in the fall of 1945, Zhdanov, Tito, and apparently Dimitrov were initiating the "Leningrad"-Belgrade-Sofia ties which were to become more evident in 1947.

These contacts between the Tito and Zhdanov groups seem to have been consolidated further during the Belgrade Panslav Conference early in 1946. There, as Djilas revealed much later, he had "some very interesting discussions" with A. A. Voznesenskii,[62] (N. A. Voznesenskii's older brother), then rector of Leningrad University, who was to be promoted subsequently to the post of Minister of Education of the R.S.F.S.R., prior to being liquidated, like so many other Zhdanovites, in the aftermath of the Leningrad Affair.[63] (Panslavism, like Great-Russian nationalism, experienced a marked revival during the Zhdanovshchina.)[64]

Remaining true to form, Belgrade in 1947 refused even to consider accepting Marshall Plan aid, in contrast, initially, to Czechoslovakia and Poland (which, as enemies of Germany freed by the Red Army, presumably had been within the competence and under the influence of Malenkov's Committee for the Rehabilitation of the Economy of the Liberated Areas). As late as the Fifth Congress of the CPY, on July 21, 1948, Kardelj followed the Zhdanovite line precisely in rejecting such assistance, claiming that the plan was intended simply to reduce Europe to an American colony and that the U.S. headed a camp antagonistic to the socialist bloc to which Yugoslavia belonged by virtue of Belgrade's policy of "close collaboration with, and all-round support of, the peace-loving, democratic, antiimperialist policy of the Soviet Union and the People's Democracies."[65]

5 THE ZHDANOVSHCHINA

If, thus, significant personal and organizational linkages can be traced between the Zhdanov and Tito groups, and their approaches to foreign policy were substantially compatible, so too were both leaders oriented (perhaps temperamentally) toward a tough, militant, dogmatic line domestically, aimed at total consolidation of power and elimination of outside influence—"clearing the decks," in effect, for the expected international conflict. Of course, this policy took somewhat different forms within the Soviet Union and Yugoslavia, respectively, given the difference between the two states in socioeconomic development, culture, history, and location.

Zhdanov's very name came to be linked to this line. In 1946, he initiated the "Zhdanovshchina" (as it came to be called), a massive, crude, cultural purge, aimed at extirpating "pernicious" bourgeois traits and, above all, foreign (that is, non–Great Russian) influences (subsumed indiscriminately under the pejorative "cosmopolitan," which came to have blatantly antisemitic overtones). This campaign went hand in hand with chauvinistic, ecstatic praise for all matters Great Russian and with a rehabilitation of Panslavism, particularly as pertaining to the intimate links between Russia and the Balkan Slav "new democracies,"* Yugoslavia and Bulgaria.[1]

As was pointed out earlier, "international" and "domestic" aspects of policy do not exist in watertight compartments, particularly for an elite habituated to view developments in terms derived from an all-embracing, "scientific" ideology. During the period covered by this study, "foreign affairs" were intertwined with such "internal" matters as the direction of the Soviet economy, of Russian culture and science, and of Communist Party management, which have to be addressed, therefore. Moreover, the "resolution" of Soviet factional struggles, by their very nature, demanded control of "cadres," or purges, which must be the object of attention in any analysis of this kind.

---

*The term "new democracy" was borrowed by the Kremlin, without attribution to the real author, from the work of that title by Mao Tse-tung, published in 1940, which addressed the issue of transitional rule before attaining the path to socialism (precisely the stage Eastern Europe was assumed to be entering at the end of World War II).

The launching of the Zhdanovshchina was authorized in a series of Central Committee resolutions that were portrayed as essential for the fulfillment of the Fourth Five-Year Plan, which, of course, was the task of Zhdanov's firm ally, N. A. Voznesenskii.[2] On March 27, 1946, the Central Committee announced that it was instructing

Party organizations to develop broadly their mass political work in acquainting all working people with the law on the Five-Year Plan for the restoration and development of the national economy of the USSR during the period 1946–50. . . . [and] in mobilizing the Soviet people to struggle to fulfill and overfulfill the new Five-Year Plan. The Central Committee of the VKP(b) proceeds from the assumption that this task is not one [that can be achieved in a] short term campaign, but will comprise a most integral part of the Party's agitation and propaganda work in the forthcoming period.[3]

This was followed by another Central Committee resolution on July 26, 1946,[4] which concerned itself with "qualitative" improvements in the party following the mass admissions of candidates (in part to replace comrades killed in battle) during the previous few years. The result of the new line was that criteria for admission became considerably tougher. On August 2, 1946, yet another resolution was promulgated,[5] addressing itself to the training and retraining of party members. (Shortly thereafter, Zhdanov's protégé, A. A. Kuznetsov, appeared to be taking credit for this development.)[6] Consequently, several levels of higher party schools were established, and the Academy of Social Sciences was inaugurated. The upshot of the campaign was a flood of meetings of "criticism and self-criticism" (so typical of purge periods), massive retraining programs, centralized inspection,[7] and highly selective positioning and repositioning of cadres (that is, an even more centralized *nomenklatura* system).[8] Thus, the door was opened to still tighter central party control over appointments and education, and large-scale personnel changes clearly were underway.

In October 1946, the CPSU Central Committee sponsored a conference of heads of personnel departments of local and regional party committees, at which new policy was outlined with regard to assignment of cadres. By October 1947, some forty thousand members had been trained as new "reserves" to be used mainly in replacing officials who were designated for dismissal, demotion, or reassignment. Included in these categories were officials as high as first secretaries of Obkoms, Kraikoms, and Central Committees of Union Republics; chairmen of

Councils of Ministers of Union and Autonomous Republics; and chairmen of Krai and Oblast Executive Committees (*Ispolnitelii Komitet*). Other "reserves" were available as replacements at lower local levels. Thus, officials purged for alleged inadequacies could be replaced instantly. In fact, by the fall of 1947, more than one hundred five thousand officials had been investigated by the Cadres Administration of the Central Committee, in conjunction with such state organs as Voznesenskii's Gosplan, to see if they were operating in accordance with the economic and political tasks of the Five-Year Plan.[9] Thus, under the watchful eyes of A. A. Kuznetsov and Voznesenskii, Zhdanov's adversaries and their appointees were likely objects of the purge being prepared. Moreover, in the meantime, the wave of "criticism and self-criticism" had inundated the realm of literature.

The opening salvos were fired at two Leningrad-based literary magazines, *Zvezda* and *Leningrad*. Zhdanov was particularly harsh on Mikhail Zoshchenko and Anna Akhmatova, two leading Leningrad literary figures who were "unanimously" expelled from the Writers' Union.[10] Scholars have wondered why Zhdanov initiated the purges by an attack on Leningrad literature. Some have suggested that he wished to consolidate power in his own backyard prior to embarking on expeditions into more perilous regions.

However, material that has become available recently throws new light upon this episode and demonstrates its significance in the context of the power struggle between the Zhdanov and Malenkov factions. The memoirs attributed to Dmitri Shostakovich state:

> Akhmatova and Zoshchenko were the victims of a struggle . . .
> between Malenkov and Zhdanov. Allegedly Malenkov wanted to become Stalin's main ideological adviser, a rather important position, right below Stalin's top executioner, Beria. He would be the executioner on the cultural front. Malenkov and Zhdanov fought to prove themselves worthy of that honored position. The war with Hitler was won and Malenkov decided to stress public relations and to glorify the homeland. . . .
> Malenkov worked out grandiose plans, one of which was a series of deluxe editions of Russian literature from antiquity to the present. . . .The series began with *The Lay of Prince Igor* and ended believe it or not, with Akhmatova and Zoshchenko. But Malenkov's idea didn't work and Zhdanov outguessed him. He knew Stalin better and considered that laudatory editions were fine, but steadfast struggle with the

enemy—vigilance, so to speak—was more important.

With the aim of getting rid of Malenkov, Zhdanov attacked Malenkov's ideas and proved to Stalin, like two plus two, that it was vigilance that Malenkov had lost. Zhdanov, unfortunately, knew what and how Akhmatova and Zoshchenko wrote, since Leningrad was Zhdanov's own turf.

This was Zhdanov's argument: The Soviet Army is victorious, we are advancing on Europe, and Soviet literature must be an aid in this, it must attack bourgeois culture, which is in a state of confusion and decay. And do Akhmatova and Zoshchenko attack? Akhmatova writes lyric poetry and Zoshchenko writes derogatory prose. Zhdanov won, Stalin took his side, and Malenkov was removed from leading the cultural front. Zhdanov was empowered to strike a blow at harmful influences, at "the spirit of negative criticism, despair, and nonbelief."

Zhdanov later announced, "What would have happened if we had brought up our young people in the spirit of despair and nonbelief in our work? What would have happened was that we would not have won the Great Patriotic War." Now, that scared them. Just think, one short story by Zoshchenko, and the Soviet regime might have toppled.[11]

In his speech at the time, Zhdanov did indeed stress ominously "how weak must be the *vigilance* [emphasis added] of those citizens of Leningrad in the leadership of *Zvezda* for it to place in this journal works that are poisoned with the venom of zoological hostility to the Soviet leadership."[12] The term "vigilance" in the USSR, of course, almost invariably marks the onset of a purge; August 1946 proved to be no exception to this rule. (As has been shown, Zhdanov's protégés, A. A. Kuznetsov and N. S. Patolichev, were initiating such a purge at that very time.)

Zhdanov's barrage led to a resolution of the Central Committee (August 14, 1946) to close down the magazine *Leningrad* and replace V. Sayonov, the editor-in-chief of *Zvezda*, with A. Yegolin, deputy chief of the Propaganda Bureau of the Communist Party in Leningrad.[13]

One of the publications to which Zhdanov took particular exception in his attack was a parody of *Evgenii Onegin*, written by an author named Khazin, which drew invidious comparisons between the vibrant Saint Petersburg of the Pushkin era and the gray Leningrad of the mid–twentieth century. Zhdanov clearly viewed this as a personal slur upon his administration of his fiefdom; in effect, he was taking revenge upon the editorial board of *Leningrad* for publishing this piece.[14] He hastened to add that "in the city magnificent work is going on, the city is healing the wounds inflicted by the blockade, the people of Leningrad are full of enthusiasm. . .of postwar restoration."[15] Clearly, Zhdanov would allow nothing and no one to tarnish the reputation of his Leningrad bailiwick and to undermine his control of the region.

No one was safe from Zhdanov's verbal thrusts (and from the ensuing political and personal dangers). Such great artists as the composers Dmitri Shostakovich, Sergeii Prokofiev, and A. I. Khachaturian were attacked during the Zhdanovshchina.[16] Similarly, Zhdanov assailed the brilliant Soviet film-maker Sergeii Eisenstein.[17] While some of the criticism levied by A. A. Zhdanov, the "expert" in the realms of art, music, literature, cinematography, and philosophy, was fatuous and seemed to be capricious, much probably was carefully calculated. For instance, a signal for "leading cadres" that Malenkov was still slipping (and should be shunned) was Zhdanov's move, on June 24, 1947, in attacking the philosopher and apparatchik G. F. Aleksandrov, a former Zhdanov protégé who, apparently, had gone over to Malenkov some time earlier (see Appendix B). Zhdanov called Aleksandrov "toothless vegetarian" and accused him of "pseudo-objectivism" and of failing to criticize Western bourgeois philosophers.[18]* Similarly, one of the major assaults against musicians was launched upon an obscure Caucasian composer, Vano Muradelli, whose only distinction to date had been the composition of a "Song of Beria."[19] It is hardly probable that Zhdanov picked on Muradelli by accident.

One of the by-products of the Great-Russian chauvinism which characterized the Zhdanovshchina was antisemitism. This prejudice had been associated particularly with Zhdanov's brother-in-law, A. S. Shcherbakov.[20] Djilas recalls that, during a trip to Leningrad early in 1948, the Yugoslav delegation (which had just encountered trouble in Moscow, ostensibly over the proposed Balkan Federation) was told proudly by its cordial escort, a local representative of Zhdanov's "machine" named Lesakov, that "Comrade Zhdanov purged all the Jews from the apparatus of the Central Committee."[21] By contrast, Beria seems to have adopted a posture considerably more moderate on the "nationalities question"; to some degree, he even had a reputation of understanding for Jews. He appears to have played a key role in

---

*Less than a year earlier, Aleksandrov's book, *The History of Western Philosophy* (now the object of Zhdanov's attack), had been awarded a "Stalin Prize." See Corbett, "Aleksandrov Story," p. 163.

giving the Czechoslovak Communists Slansky and Geminder to understand that weapons should be provided for the nascent state of Israel in its war of independence. (See p. 81.) Moreover, the important publications in Beria's fiefdoms of Georgia and Azerbaidzhan, *Zaria Vostoka* and *Bakinskii Rabochii*,[22] never adopted the antisemitic tone propagated by *Pravda* during the period of February–March 1949 (when this and certain other aspects of the Zhdanovshchina continued, and were even intensified in some respects, despite Zhdanov's death during the previous year). (See p. 155.)

Israel Emiot, an emigré once linked with the Jewish Anti-Fascist Committee, presents an eyewitness account of the cooperation extended in the immediate postwar period by one General Nikishov,* Beria's official in charge of the administration of the notorious Kolyma prison camp, to the Jewish settlers of Birobidjan.[23] Moreover, as Dr. Mark Kuchment has pointed out, given the wartime contacts of the Jewish Anti-Fascist Committee with the West, including trips there by individual members and the receipt of funds from the American Joint Distribution Committee, it would be inconceivable that Beria's security service was not involved intimately in the surveillance of Jewish affairs, lest a very narrow opening to the outside become a two-way street.[24]

Apparently, conflict between Zhdanov and his adversaries extended into the realm of science. There is reason for believing that Zhdanov opposed T. D. Lysenko, the "Marxist" agrobiologist, whose contention it was that acquired traits could be inherited and that environment, rather than genetics, was the key, despite the traditional theories of Gregor Mendel and Thomas Hunt Morgan. In effect, he rejected genetics. In 1939, Lysenko was brought in to undermine his one-time patron, S. I. Vavilov (until then one of the most prestigious Soviet biologists), as head of Leningrad's Soviet Plant Production Institute.[25] Vavilov had come to oppose Lysenko's increasingly eccentric pseudoscience; consequently, he was arrested (reportedly on Beria's instructions) and eventually died in a prison camp.[26] It is not unlikely that Zhdanov resented the insertion of an outsider into his domain to replace Vavilov, who, as a prestigious Leningrader, could not but have had frequent dealings with the party boss of the region. This intrusion and Vavilov's misfortune occurred, appropriately enough, at the very time when Zhdanov's influence was declining because of Soviet humiliation at the hands of the heroic Finns, during the Winter War of 1939–40. There is evidence that Zhdanov became embroiled in the "Lysenko Affair," at least by proxy, and that it played a symbolic role in his downfall.

Zhdanov's son, Yurii A. Zhdanov, a biochemist, who was also an

---

*Nikishov was also a candidate member of the CPSU Central Committee.

important figure in the Science Division of the CPSU Central Committee, was a consistent critic of Lysenko, voicing his opinions in print from time to time. As will be discussed later, several weeks before his father's death in the summer of 1948, and around the time when Malenkov suddenly replaced the older Zhdanov as the secretary who signed Central Committee decrees and messages, Yurii A. Zhdanov was compelled to publish an abject recantation in *Pravda* addressed to Stalin himself,* apologizing for having criticized Lysenko.[27] For the cognescenti in the USSR, this publication signalled the death knell of Zhdanovism (and of the older Zhdanov himself—indeed, Roy Medvedev asserts that this issue was used by Stalin as the reason for purging A. A. Zhdanov).[28]

The journal *Voprosy Filosofii*, which the Zhdanovites controlled completely after the publication of the onslaught on G. F. Aleksandrov, was careful to avoid defending ideological intrusions into the hard sciences and even published an implicitly anti-Lysenko article prior to Zhdanov's death. However, shortly after Zhdanov's demise in 1948, this journal suddenly began to glorify Lysenko and his "Michurinist" biology.[29] Although it is true that the now triumphant Lysenko was among the many who delivered public eulogies after Zhdanov's death (for that matter, Malenkov and Beria were among his pall-bearers), it is noteworthy that the eulogy made no pretense whatever that Zhdanov ever supported Lysenkoism.[30]

It may seem strange that Zhdanov, who so adamantly opposed Western influences in the arts, was willing to defend the Morgan-Mendel contribution in the sciences.† However, if Zhdanov anticipated a confrontation with the West, as is implicit in his whole posture, it would be reasonable to expect him to attempt elimination of the influence of Western thought in the USSR, and thus to consolidate the domestic base of the leadership; it would be equally logical for him to exploit Western science and technology to strengthen the industrial and agricultural infrastructure, should war come. In any case, the decisive question was probably whose factional ox was being gored, and the Lysenko Affair demonstrates once again that obscure issues may be manipulated by rival factions in order to score points against their opponents.

---

*Ironically, a year after his humiliating apology to Stalin and his father's death, Yurii would become Stalin's son-in-law, marrying the dictator's daughter Svetlana.

†The Lysenko case was by no means an aberration. *Voprosy Filosofii*, while under Zhdanov's control, published work by the physicist M. A. Markov, who was attacked by A. A. Maksimov, another physicist, for ignoring the dialectic. After Zhdanov's death, the editorial board of the magazine was purged and the subsequent number reversed its previous position of support for Markov and opposition to Lysenko. By and large, the campaign to restrict the sciences along ideological lines was a post-Zhdanov phenomenon.[31]

Tito, like Zhdanov (albeit in a fashion reflecting Yugoslav circumstances), had embarked upon domestic policies that had to be viewed as radical, both in comparison with those of the other "new democracies" and even compared with Bolshevik policies at a similar stage — that is, at the end of the civil war and intervention, when Russia adopted the "rightist" N.E.P., not a militantly "leftist" approach. The Yugoslav leaders already had nationalized 82 percent of all industry by the end of World War II and continued to expropriate private enterprises, culminating in a very strict nationalization law of April 1948.[32] In April 1947, two years earlier than the other "new democracies," Belgrade promulgated its First Five-Year Plan, a very ambitious project, based upon studies of the Soviet system.[33] Similarly, the 1946 Yugoslav Constitution was based almost entirely upon the 1936 "Stalin Constitution," and the Belgrade leadership spoke of the "dictatorship of the proletariat" as appropriate for Yugoslavia and other East European states.[34] If agrarian measures lagged somewhat behind the nationalization of industry, it could hardly be asserted that the Law on Agrarian Reform of August 23, 1945, did not constitute a major step toward collectivization. It provided for confiscation of all major holdings (churches and monasteries were dealt with separately) and limited considerably the size of peasant plots.[35]

Thus, if anything, the Yugoslavs were too "Communist" in their domestic policies. While they were pushing a rapid (almost "Maoist") drive toward socialism, Stalin (and the anti-Zhdanovites) apparently were skeptical about the future of Yugoslavia and the rest of the "new democracies," doubting whether they could be unlinked from the West and welded to the Soviet Union. (This was to emerge clearly from the Varga "debate.") Consequently, the Moscow anti-Zhdanovites backed the quick exploitation of East European resources by the notorious Soviet "joint-stock companies" while the going was good.[36]

6 THE VARGA-VOZNESENSKII "DEBATE"

Two major developments occurred in 1947, providing arenas, so to speak, for what were intended to be elimination bouts between the various opposing forces, both the rival Soviet factions and their respective allies and surrogates among the other Communist parties. In chronological order, these events were the Varga "debate" and the founding meeting of the Cominform. With respect to each of these developments, the analyst is the beneficiary of ample documentation, the authenticity of which is not seriously in question. In each instance, the original meetings were held in secret but, for various reasons, their contents were publicized some months later: in the case of the Varga "debate," an apparently complete transcript of the closed sessions of May 7, 14, and 21, 1947, appeared in print; the contents of the key speeches to the founding meeting of the Cominform also were published subsequently, in the first two issues of the journal of the new organization (supplemented by the invaluable eyewitness account of Eugenio Reale, who verified the general authenticity of the printed texts).

The attack upon Eugene S. Varga, sustained almost certainly by Zhdanov's ally N. A. Voznesenskii and implemented at least in part by persons clearly linked to the Zhdanovites, may be viewed as a proxy for the conflict between Zhdanov and his adversaries. In this context, it is of great significance that Varga was unwilling to accept the contention of his critics that a qualitative change was occurring, which was weakening the West, probably irreversibly, in other words, that conditions were "ripe" for an assault upon the enemy. No less noteworthy, however, was the denigration by Varga of the "democracies of a new type," particularly Yugoslavia and Bulgaria, and the anger this aroused among his critics.

Varga's major work—the object of the controversy—was his book *Changes in the Economy of Capitalism as a Result of the Second World War*,[1] published in September 1946 (although portions had appeared earlier in article form). Voznesenskii's final riposte took the shape of his magnum opus, *The Wartime Economy of the U.S.S.R. during the Great Patriotic War*, which was prepared for publication in 1947 and later awarded the Stalin Prize plus a substantial emolument of 200 thousand rubles.[2] Varga had been people's commissar of finance in Hungary under Bela Kun, fleeing to Russia in 1920.[3] At the time of the "debate," Varga was the prestigious director of the Institute of World Economics and World Politics,[4] and was known to have maintained friendly personal relations with Stalin. However, Varga could hardly be counted among the leaders of the USSR. Voznesenskii, by contrast, ranked among the top dozen political figures in the Soviet Union. By the time his book appeared, he was a full member of the Politburo, chairman of the State Planning Commission (Gosplan), and deputy chairman of the Council of Ministers of the USSR.[5] Yet Varga was to survive the confrontation unscathed and to be rehabilitated in the Soviet Union as a favored political economist, reaching a ripe old age,[*] while Voznesenskii fell from power barely two years after the "debate" started and was liquidated in the aftermath of the Leningrad Affair. These facts alone — not to speak of the almost unique phenomenon that a man like Varga, under almost constant public attack for over a year, while retreating a little, refused to recant fully, yet escaped arrest in Stalin's Russia — lead to the unavoidable conclusion that Varga enjoyed the protection of patrons in the very highest positions.

Varga analyzed the international situation in a way that implicitly demanded a cautious or "rightist" Soviet policy. In brief, he contended that, contrary to the view that a new qualitative stage was being reached in the "general crisis of world capitalism," the development of state regulation during World War II would delay this process, at least by some years. Control of the economy had evolved, to a certain extent, in all bourgeois countries, both belligerent and neutral, during the war, when at least some degree of economic regulation (although not quite "planning" in a socialist mode) had been introduced in these states.[6] Labor productivity and the technological base were said to have increased substantially, especially in the U.S., Canada, and the neutral states. On the other hand, regulation could delay cyclical crises of overproduction.[7] Clearly, this thesis implied that the West was not substantially weakened by the war and, thus, the time for an activist or forward Soviet foreign policy had not yet come.

Varga took some pains not to portray international communism as having been strengthened significantly by developments in the client states of Eastern Europe (dubbed the "countries of a democracy of a new type"). Varga's opponents, on the other hand, proclaimed that a

---

[*]Rather unkindly, Trotsky once ascribed Varga's invulnerability to his willingness to parrot Stalin's line (Ypsilon, Pseud., *Pattern of World Revolution* [New York: Ziff-Davis, 1947], p. 159).

qualitative international change—the arrival of the "second stage in the general crisis of world capitalism"—was attributable precisely to the fact that periodic crises of overproduction would encounter a shrunken capitalist world market, from which not only the USSR but also the newly socialized countries had been subtracted. Eventually, these states would create a new "world socialist system," in place of the "world's only socialist state," to confront the "capitalist system." Varga's denial that this was a correct interpretation of the situation constituted yet another factor requiring caution on the part of an essentially weak Soviet Union, as well as presenting an implicit affront to the Communist leaders of Eastern Europe.

Varga asserted that, in the "countries of a democracy of a new type," state capitalism predominated. He did not include these states in the socialist bloc, but continued to regard them as part of the capitalist camp: "The relative weight of these countries in *capitalist* world economy as a whole is comparatively small."[8] In contrast to Varga, N. A. Voznesenskii's book, which was to be published some months later (although final drafts must have been circulating for some time among the Soviet leadership), stressed the importance of these states, including, of course, Yugoslavia (described already as "people's democracies"—i.e. well on the path of transition toward the attainment of socialism), in tipping the balance against the West:

> As a result of the Second World War and the democratic trans-
> formations in eastern and central European countries, new
> people's republics, countries of people's democracy, have arisen.
> World capitalism has lost its power in yet another series of
> democratic countries. The forces of democracy and socialism
> have grown, and the general crisis of capitalism has become
> more acute.[9]

Varga, on the other hand, in addition to downplaying the role of the East European states as a whole, refused to give prominence to Yugoslavia and Bulgaria in his discussions. His listing of "the countries of democracy of a new type" is significant: "Czechoslovakia, Poland, Romania, Yugoslavia, etc."[10] Considering that Czechoslovakia had to be freed from the Nazis by the Red Army and General Patton (not to mention General Vlasov, changing sides once more), and, at this stage, was still ruled by a genuine multiparty coalition, including pro-Western democrats; that Poland was occupied by the Red Army which had imposed a puppet regime upon the country; and that Romania was a former Axis state with a leadership imported from Moscow and sitting on Soviet bayonets, placing Yugoslavia at the end of this list (and omitting Dimitrov's Bulgaria altogether) was hardly less than a resounding slap.

Such treatment of these "new democracies" contrasted starkly with the respectful attitude toward them displayed by most participants at the closed meetings held on May 7, 14, and 21, 1947, in Moscow, of members of the Institute of Economics of the Soviet Academy of Sciences and of the Faculty of Economics of Moscow University (plus a guest, who will be discussed later). K. V. Ostrovitianov, in the chair, spoke of "Yugoslavia, Bulgaria, and other countries of the new democracy,"[11] in that order, and his approach was echoed by other speakers, such as V. E. Motylyov, who stressed that "such countries as Yugoslavia, Bulgaria and Poland *have already* ceased to be part of the capitalist world. And the remaining countries of the new democracy *will* cease to be such." [emphases added].[12] Varga's critics were merely echoing, of course, the paeans to these East European states and the Panslav "pecking order" that emanated from A. A. Zhdanov's October Revolution speech, six months earlier.

At these May 1947 gatherings, the details of which will be analyzed further, Varga was attacked for his writings by most, but not all, of the participants. He was allowed to defend himself and ended up by delivering a highly qualified *mea culpa*, by no means surrendering his dignity.

While the Yugoslavs and other foreigners, of course, were not invited to the closed meetings, their views were represented forcibly at the gathering. K. V. Ostrovitianov stated at the conclusion of the proceedings (after Varga had retracted a part of his earlier assertions regarding the "new democracies") that "Yugoslavia, Bulgaria, and other countries of the new democracy, who were at first disoriented by Comrade Varga's wrong assertions regarding state capitalism, will welcome this presentation of the question."[13] Clearly, Tito's and Dimitrov's representatives must have complained to someone about Varga's writings — how, otherwise, could Ostrovitianov have known and stated (so delicately) that they "were" (not "they may have been") disoriented?

Moreover, Ostrovitianov's remarks, in effect, amounted to an admission that Yugoslavia and Bulgaria were being represented at these closed meetings by someone in contact with their leaders. How, otherwise, could he be so confident of their reactions to what was being said in these hallowed premises ("[They] will welcome this presentation...")? It must be borne in mind that, in fact, the transcripts were not to see the light of day for many months — an indication, together with the whole character of the gathering, that, originally, no publication seems to have been intended. At this point, an educated guess may be in order as to just who Tito's informant might have been. One cannot overlook the likely significance of the presence of one outsider, in this context, V. V. Reikhardt from Leningrad University. (It is to be presumed that he was the only outsider, since he was the only participant to be introduced specially to the members, with particular reference to his institutional affiliation.)[14] His attendance would hardly have been possible without the permission, indeed the request, of the rector of his university, who just happened to be. . .A. A. Voznesenskii, older brother of the same N. A. Voznesenskii whose book, in effect, constituted a polemic against Varga's writings; the older Voznesenskii, as was pointed out earlier, had established personal contact with the Yugoslav leaders at the 1946 Belgrade Panslav Conference (the Panslavism that was so typical a feature of the whole Zhdanovshchina). Djilas has provided valuable evidence concerning this contact, although even he continues to be discreet and elusive about the details of their "very interesting discussions."[15]

Reikhardt made it abundantly clear that he was attending the gathering as an emissary of the Leningrad group. He announced that Varga's work was the object of great interest in Leningrad, not only at the university, but also in the economics section of the lecturers' group of the party's City Committee.[16] It should be recalled that, while Zhdanov himself had moved to the Kremlin, he had bequeathed the Leningrad city and regional party apparatus to his protégé, P. S. Popkov (Zhdanov's immediate "heir," A. A. Kuznetsov, having followed his patron to Moscow). This was the official who was to receive the Yugoslavs so warmly, early in 1948, when in Moscow the "frost" in Soviet-Yugoslav relations was already becoming apparent.[17] Needless to say, P. S. Popkov was purged in the Leningrad Affair.[18] Professor Reikhardt, of course, had come to criticize Varga, although he was careful, at this stage, to be reasonably polite.

Reikhardt, for instance, espoused a resoundingly revolutionary slogan for the colonies, stating that, "I think the colonies can attain independence, but only in one way—the revolutionary way." (As will be demonstrated, this was precisely the advice given by Kardelj to Asian, and particularly Indian, Communists in 1947, and the line advocated by members of the Yugoslav delegations to the ill-fated Calcutta Conferences early in 1948.) Reikhardt's statement constituted a blunt rejoinder to Varga's assertion that some colonies (especially India) already *had* achieved independence in nonviolent fashion. Varga explained that this had been possible because, during World War II, European imperial powers had needed colonial raw material imports which, in many cases, they were unable to repay. Consequently, they had declined from creditor to debtor status vis-à-vis their own colonies, some of which had exploited the situation to extort political independence from their former overlords. Thus, revolutionary struggle was unnecessary in such instances.[20] At the same time, Varga prognosticated that the United States would replace Britain as the main exporter to the colonial market. Thus, the increasingly powerful United States, and not just the weaker European imperial states, would have an interest in combatting colonial social insurrections. Therefore, on the one hand, revolutionary struggle for political independence would be unnecessary, and, on the other, social revolution would confront a more formidable adversary. On both counts, it would behoove the USSR and the communist movement to pursue a moderate, "rightist," cautious line, appropriate to nonrevolutionary situations. Challenged by his adversaries during the meeting to demonstrate that India was genuinely independent, Varga responded in uncharacteristically naive fashion that, since India now had an ambassador in Moscow, this proved her independence![21]

On the central topic, that is, the question whether a qualitative change — a new stage — was imminent in the "general crisis of world capitalism," Varga remained cautiously skeptical. He contrasted the economic situation in the United States with that in war-devastated Western Europe. For the U.S., the war had resulted in general and broadly spread enrichment and the construction of a large number of new factories. In the belligerent states of Europe there had been impoverishment and massive destruction of means of production. As a result, in the U.S., the neutral bourgeois states, and Canada, there would be overproduction; however, in the formerly belligerent, bourgeois countries of Europe, there would be a corresponding degree of underproduction. Thus, the states experiencing overproduction would find it in their interest to bolster the economies of those suffering from underproduction, so as to utilize them as markets for their own goods. Wartime regulation of their economies had provided capitalist states with a control mechanism for delaying crises.[22] As mentioned earlier, Varga's thesis had already been contradicted flatly, if implicitly, in A. A. Zhdanov's 1946 October Revolution anniversary address.

The Hungarian-born economist, of course, did not reject the theory of *eventual* collapse of world capitalism. He thought, however, that after a minor crisis of overproduction, two or three years after the war, aid from the overproducers would stabilize the economies of the underproducers. Eventually, production in the capitalist states of Europe would rise sufficiently to bring about a major crisis of overproduction, but this might begin only some ten years after the first, minor, crisis. Thus, Varga was implicitly advocating a "rightist" Soviet policy of caution, appropriate for a period of relative "capitalist consolidation," to last more than another decade.[23]

Voznesenskii's book, although shunning explicit mention of Varga's name, clearly attacked his propositions. There could be little doubt to whom it was referring;* for example:

> The talk of naive people, and more frequently of malicious liars, about the "popular" capitalism in the U.S.A. is a fairy tale for fools. Suffice it to say that in 1944 in the U.S.A. one hundred of the largest capitalist monopolies obtained 75 percent of all war orders and thirty giant monopolies obtained 49 percent of all war orders.[24]

Furthermore:

> The discussions of certain theoreticians who consider themselves Marxists about "the decisive role of the state in the war economies of the capitalist countries" are nonsense, not worthy of attention.[25]

> The fundamental distinction between the planning of the national economy of the USSR and economic "planning" in the capitalist countries abroad lies in the fact that the Soviet Union's planning rests on the social method of production. [In the West] . . . the tendency towards state capitalism, resting on monopoly capitalism, was strengthened during the war.[26]

Thus, rather insultingly, Voznesenskii dismissed Varga's assertions regarding the flexibility offered by capitalist economies' state regulation, contending that this was not "planning" in the socialist sense, but mere "state capitalism." In fact, Voznesenskii foresaw an *impending* full-scale crisis of capitalism:

> The high levels of productivity and of technology which were reached in the U.S.A. during the war make the contradiction peculiar to capitalism more acute, and created the basis for a new devastating economic crisis and chronic unemployment.[27]†

---

*There was little room for uncertainty among "leading cadres" that Varga indeed was the target of Voznesenskii's attack, since, as will be discussed subsequently, accounts of the high level conference at which the book was condemned and Varga was induced to deliver a qualified retraction, had already been published.

†It is worth noting that in January 1947, a considerable period prior to the release of Voznesenskii's book, Edvard Kardelj, then vice premier of Yugoslavia and a leading member of the Politburo, published an extensive article in which he asserted that:

> Not only did the Second World War fail to bring stabilization to the capitalist

Voznesenskii disagreed with Varga concerning the feasibility of the United States temporarily bolstering the failing (presumably European) economies: "The unevenness of the development of capitalist countries, which was intensified during the Second World War, creates new contradictions and conflicts and makes the general crisis of capitalism more acute."[30]

Unlike Varga, Voznesenskii claimed that immediate dangers to the USSR were posed by imperialism, clearly identifying the United States as the "primary antagonist":

Having waxed fat on the people's blood during the Second World War, monopoly capitalism of the United States of America stands now at the head of the antiimperialist and antidemocratic camp and has become the instigator of imperialist expansion everywhere in the world. Imperialist expansion of the U.S.A. is moving toward a new war as a means of seizing world domination, and as a means of crushing democracy, preventing an economic crisis, and opposing the working class within the country.[31]*

---

world but, on the contrary, it still further deepened and sharpened the general crisis of the system. . . .[28]

The Second World War has not only failed to extricate capitalism from its general crisis, but has rendered this crisis even deeper. . . . It is unlikely that the capitalist world is moving toward some sort of relative stabilization in the coming years. It is, on the contrary, far more likely that the economic crisis, and the sharpening of all contradictions, will in the coming years result, not merely in a serious economic crisis, but also in extremely violent political upheavals for the capitalist world.[29]

The similarity between the line propagated by Zhdanov late in 1946, Kardelj early in 1947, and Voznesenskii subsequently, in sharp contradiction to the views of Varga and *his* patrons, is unlikely to have been coincidental.

*A similar sentiment already had been voiced by Kardelj in January of 1947 (see p. 104), and was supported emphatically by Tito (almost simultaneously with Zhdanov's enunciation of the same doctrine at the founding meeting of the Cominform—see p. 105):

Unable to satisfy fully the imperialist appetite, international reaction, headed by American imperialists, is undertaking the most virulent campaign of slander against the democratic countries, especially against the Soviet Union and Yugoslavia.[32]

Dimitrov, who soon was to be assailed by Stalin (as were Tito's emissaries) for the ill-fated Bled Agreement (concerning the proposed East European federation), also expressed the view, early in 1948, that the United States now was the primary antagonist, particularly in Europe, being run by a few trusts

in France, Blum and Ramadier, who are in the service of American imperialism, will secede and then the true Socialists, those who remain, will join the Communist Party. We must make people understand what the Truman Doctrine is and tell them the truth about that dark Marshall Plan. . . . We do not want either the honey or the sting of the American bee—and by the American bee I do not mean the American people but the American trusts.[33]

Again in contrast to Varga, Voznesenskii (as mentioned earlier) stressed the importance of the "people's democracies" (including, of course, Yugoslavia), in tipping the global balance against the West:

> As a result of the Second World War and the democratic trans-formations in central and eastern European countries, new people's republics, countries of people's democracy, have arisen. World capitalism has lost its power in yet another series of democratic countries. The forces of democracy and socialism have grown, and the general crisis of capitalism has become more acute.[34]*

In sum, therefore, Voznesenskii refuted Varga's advocacy of a "right-ist" policy by stressing that: (1) the alleged favorable swing in the global balance—due to the arrival of the "second stage in the general crisis of world capitalism"—made a "leftist," forward, militant Soviet policy *feasible*, and (2) the violent hostility of the "main antagonist," the U.S. (born of desperation), made such a policy *essential*.

In all of these propositions, Voznesenskii merely summarized the points made already by Varga's critics during the May 1947 sessions, that almost certainly were reported immediately to the Zhdanovite leadership (which must have provided the catalyst for the attack on Varga—if, indeed, Voznesenskii and company did not write the script for this drama).

While Varga emphasized the West's newly developed regulatory capabilities during World War II, Voznesenskii used the example of the war to praise Soviet accomplishments in this realm, particularly the evacuation of industries eastward during the initial German attack.[36] Thus, Voznesenskii utilized the opportunity for some nasty infighting against the rival Malenkov-Beria faction by evoking the memory of the Zhdanov group's most noteworthy success, which, of course, served as a foil to the apparent shambles of the Malenkov-Beria operation in dis-mantling and relocating German industrial plants after the war. Voznesenskii then proceeded to milk this episode for all it was worth

---

*Kardelj, of course, was no less emphatic concerning the strategic advantages accruing to the USSR as a consequence of the establishment of "people's democracies," as well as (implicitly) of the changing status of some colonial and ex-colonial countries:

> The emergence of people's democracies in the countries of Eastern and Southeastern Europe, as well as the beginnings of such democracies in certain other countries, are significant, not merely in that they constitute a qualitative change in the relation of forces in the sphere of international politics, but also in that they introduce a new element into the latter, breaking the system of capitalist encirclement of the first country where the construction of socialism has been achieved, and opening up new vistas for the struggle of the democratic, progressive, antiimperialist forces in the world.[35]

by lavishing special praise upon the Leningrad group by name, for its performance *after* the evacuation, stating that

> truly superhuman instances of industrial work were exhibited in Leningrad, which was for a long time under artillery fire. In spite of the evacuation of ninety-two of the largest enterprises, in spite of a prolonged blockade, bombings, and artillery blows, the workers of Leningrad gave to the front a large amount of war production.[37]

The May 1947 meetings concerning Varga's book had some aspects that, perhaps, were unique for this period in Soviet history. While Varga certainly was placed on the defensive by his critics, he was not forced to make anything like a wholesale retraction. He was treated with relative deference by other participants; in fact, he was even defended by some colleagues, such as M. A. Arzhanov, who analogized the Hungarian-born economist to a messenger who is punished for bringing bad news—a rather biting comment, implying that the Zhdanovites refused to face up to a situation unpropitious for adventures, preferring to have the facts suit their predilections.[38] Arzhanov pointed out that Varga was only analyzing the facts, not making normative judgments. In other words, if the situation in the West was not as bad as certain persons might have hoped, this was their problem, not Varga's. Another of Varga's colleagues, V. A. Maslennikov, defended him to the point of drawing unfavorable attention to himself.[39]

These exceptions notwithstanding, the majority of the participants was critical of Varga's positions, although K. V. Ostrovitianov, presiding, concluded the meetings on a rather moderate note, accepting Varga's partial modifications of his earlier views as satisfactory, apparently because Varga consented to amend some of his implicitly contemptuous references to the "new democracies," led by Yugoslavia.[40] The transcript leaves the impression that this was really the crucial point, and the presence of Leningrad's V. V. Reikhardt "observing" the proceedings no doubt ensured a "satisfactory" outcome on this issue.

Eventually, the ideological battle between the two "economists" was to culminate in an apparently more clear-cut victory for Voznesenskii, although, of course, his triumph was to be of very brief duration. On September 15, 1947, *Bol'shevik*, the official publication of the Central Committee of the CPSU (at that time still under Zhdanov's control), carried an article by I. Gladkov, reporting the three May meetings at the Institute of Economics of the Academy of Sciences but condemning Varga's work in far less qualified terms than those of the actual participants. The piece drew attention to Varga's admission concerning the significance of the "new democracies"[41] and failed to report the favorable views of his work that had been expressed at the meetings.

Early in October 1947, the Presidium of the Academy of Sciences announced a decision:

> To fuse the Institute of Economics with [Varga's] Institute of World Economics and World Politics into an Institute of Economics and to appoint K. V. Ostrovitianov [the presiding official at the May meeting criticizing Varga's works] as Director of the Institute.[42]*

The new institute was placed under the sway of the State Planning Commission, Gosplan, headed at the time, of course, by N. A. Voznesenskii.[44]

Thus, Varga was deprived of his power base; he lost control of an important institute with access to sensitive information and influence on policy makers and was demoted to deputy editor of the journal *Problems of Economics*.[45] Nevertheless, he survived this period of danger, later to be promoted again to positions of prominence.

In a *Pravda* article on December 24, 1947, Varga, without apology for previous "heresies," moved slightly toward the Zhdanov position. He agreed that, in contrast to West European states, the "new democracies" (ranked in the Zhdanovite order, beginning with Yugoslavia and Bulgaria) had been able to control inflation during the postwar period:

> In spite of the fact that these countries suffered more from the war, the campaign against inflation is being waged with marked success in Yugoslavia, Bulgaria, Czechoslovakia, and Romania.

---

*Ostrovitianov (along with M. Galaktianov) was soon to review the Voznesenskii opus in highly complimentary terms. Although, for the most part, they merely quoted or summarized the assertions of the Gosplan chief, the reviewers praised both the book's theoretical contribution and its practical utility, particularly in training cadres:

> The book is of great theoretical interest and contains a searching analysis of the motive forces and regular laws of the socialist wartime economy. . . .Comrade Voznesenskii's book [constitutes] an important step forward in the creative treatment of the problems of the war time economy of the U.S.S.R., and a valuable contribution to the political economy of socialism,. . . [it] will prove to be an important aid to our cadres in the task of studying the established laws of Socialist economy, and will contribute to their application in the practice of socialist construction.[43]

However, Varga made no reference to any role of the new regimes of these states in strengthening the "progressive" forces.

In somewhat of a departure from his previous approach, he did concede that:

> In the U.S.A., the money continues to decrease in value, as demonstrated by the fact that prices there continue to rise month after month. Prices of foodstuffs, on the average, have doubled in comparison with prewar. All this testifies that American capitalism is being weakened rather than stabilized, that an economic crisis is imminent.[46]

However, Varga refrained from agreeing that imperialist war would be the logical American response to such an economic crisis, and he ignored the issue of British relations with the colonies, one of the key points of contention during the conference at his former institute, some months earlier. The *Pravda* article signaled some concessions, but was far from reflecting full adherence to the Voznesenskii line.

That Varga was allowed to defend himself with impunity at the May conference, that he retracted only some statements (and several of those only partially), that Voznesenskii, an important member of the Politburo, refrained from attacking him by name, and that he was demoted, but not liquidated, in a period when most comparable "heretics" among academicians (e.g., Vavilov) simply disappeared, would seem to indicate that someone more powerful even than Zhdanov (who proved unable to protect Vavilov) or Malenkov was devoting attention to such fallout of the factional struggle and was interceding to prevent the elimination of the underdogs (at this time, undoubtedly the "rightists," among them Malenkov, Beria, and Varga). Such intervention would ensure that the faction in ascendancy should not become so powerful as to endanger potentially someone at the very top.

That "someone" had to be Stalin himself, particularly an ailing Stalin with a severely reduced work schedule and prolonged absences from the center,* who would be all the more sensitive concerning the implications for himself of any really major shift in the delicate balance of power that had enabled him to play off his would-be heirs against one another. The Kirov Affair (as it may be reconstructed now on the

---

*Stalin undoubtedly remembered only too well how one leader's ailments (Lenin's strokes and prolonged recuperation periods) and another's absence (Trotsky's rest cure near the Black Sea) had enabled an ambitious junior competitor (Stalin himself) to seize power and eliminate all his rivals. Moreover, the controversy over the text of Stalin's interview with Stassen (see pp. 124–29) would seem to indicate that, in fact, Stalin was not prepared to permit the anti-Varga line to triumph totally; in turn, this attitude appears to have irked whoever "edited" that interview for broadcast abroad.

basis of N. S. Khrushchev's revelations) showed very plainly Stalin's suspicions of any Soviet "crown prince" and his willingness to take ruthless action to cut down such a pretender to the throne.[47] Undoubtedly, the Zhdanov-Malenkov struggle played a major role in Stalin's calculations; in all probability, he welcomed and encouraged it, now lending support to one faction and then to another. Varga may have owed his survival to this factor.

Not only did the Voznesenskii line prescribe militant Soviet international thrusts in the face of presumed Western weakness, while Varga intimated that Soviet caution was required in the light of continued Western strength, but the two contending approaches also identified different "main antagonists" as leaders of the "enemy camp." The Zhdanov-Voznesenskii faction viewed the United States and Great Britain as having incompatible interests, with the former having become the stronger and far more dangerous adversary of the USSR; logically, therefore, the correct tactic would be to woo the weaker power away from the stronger with a Soviet foreign policy that was militantly anti-American and more open-ended toward Britain, at least in Europe. Varga regarded the United States as being too powerful at the moment to be confronted actively. Moreover, America was relying upon Britain as a market for the glut of goods likely to be manufactured during the forthcoming period of United States overproduction. Thus, a confrontation with Washington well might result if the Soviet Union wooed the British too assiduously or successfully. Consequently, gestures toward Britain would be counter-productive.* On the contrary, the only safe Soviet policy would be accommodation of the United States itself, at least for the interim period of a decade or more until qualitative intensification became apparent in the crisis of capitalism. These points, although not explicit, could be deduced from Varga's and Voznesenskii's theses by any reader with elementary education in historical and dialectical materialism.

---

*Varga, together with all politically sensitive Soviet personalities, no doubt recalled that, with brief exceptions, such as 1941–45, the British Empire had been regarded as Moscow's "main adversary," particularly by Stalin himself.

7 THE YUGOSLAV FACTOR
Further Considerations

It is significant that Andrija Hebrang, one of the dissident Yugoslav leaders (together with Sretan Žujović) purged by Tito in May 1948, had proposed acting in conformity with Varga's original line as far as the socioeconomic position of the "new democracies" was concerned: "For the moment, we still will not set up a long term plan, nor integrate the different sectors of the economy into the parameters of an overall plan."[1]

This paralleled Varga's contention that "new democracies" had developed no further than "state capitalism":

> The case is such that, at this time, in these states, they cannot have a planned economy in the same sense that we have. That is impossible due to the continuation of private ownership of the means of production. They could not know how to plan, such as in a socialist system, where all the means of production are nationalized.[2]

In a major speech delivered at the Fifth Congress of the Communist Party of Yugoslavia, in July 1948, Boris Kidrič, the chairman of the State Planning Commission,[3] addressed himself to the topic of "The Construction of Socialist Economy in the F.P.R.Y." He repeatedly attacked Žujović and Hebrang for resisting the Yugoslav "socialist offensive":

> When, in 1946, the C.C. of our party decided to introduce clear and definitive socialist forms of organization and methods of work into the state sector of our economy, Hebrang and Žujović offered fierce resistance to the concrete elaboration and enactment.[4]

> They did not believe in the economic strength of our country or in the creative strength of our working class and working people, or in the possibilities of the construction of socialism in our country.[5]

> It is a fact that Žujović offered fierce resistance to the introduction of the turnover tax on goods as a typically socialist form of socialist money accumulation, tried out in practice in the Soviet Union, and that he gave preference to the *Capitalist*

(not our present!) form of profit in state economic enterprises.[6]

Not altogether surprisingly, Yugoslav sources have alleged that Hebrang maintained close ties to Beria (one of the adversaries of the Zhdanov-Voznesenskii faction).[7]

Thus, it appears that the Yugoslavs had their own version of the Varga affair, with the rightist, minimalistic group—corresponding to Varga—being linked to Beria's security apparatus.

Although Kidrič did not specifically tie Hebrang and Žujović to Varga, the Yugoslavs demonstrably were well aware of the Varga episode and sided completely with Varga's opponents. As late as the July 1949 issue of the Belgrade *Kommunist*, Edvard Kardelj repeatedly attacked Varga by name, specifically invoking the May 1947 conference, which had criticized Varga, and quoting K. V. Ostrovitianov's patronizing endorsement of Varga's subsequent recantation of his earlier skeptical position regarding the "new democracies." Kardelj, however, also quibbled with Ostrovitianov for not having adopted a posture that was sufficiently antagonistic to Varga. In any case, there is little doubt that the Yugoslav leadership sympathized with Varga's enemies.[8] Thus, it is hardly surprising that (according to Wolfgang Leonhard) Voznesenskii remained very popular in Belgrade in 1949, and that his works were still widely available there.[9]

On the issue of the "principal antagonist," also, the Yugoslavs sided with the Zhdanov faction; Tito had some incentive for pursuing an anti-American rather than an anti-British policy after the announcement of the Truman Doctrine early in 1947. As a regime that was enthusiastically supporting the Communists in the Greek civil war, the Belgrade leadership subsequently was to be lectured by Stalin on the dangers of confronting United States interests in Greece. As will be seen, both Zhdanov himself (in full accord with Voznesenskii's propositions) and the Titoists were to continue until 1948 to emphasize the anti-American approach, in theory and practice alike. The functionaries of the Soviet Foreign Ministry under V. M. Molotov, on the other hand, apparently danced to someone else's tune and on at least one important occasion in 1947 seemed very clearly to be pursuing a primarily anti-British policy. It is noteworthy that, as the Soviet-Yugoslav dispute began to intensify, the Kremlin, in a letter to the Belgrade leadership dated May 4, 1948,[10] accused the Yugoslav Foreign Ministry of being infested by *British* spies, such as Vlatko Velebit, the first assistant minister, and Ljubo Leontić, the Yugoslav ambassador to London.

Eighteen months later, however—with Zhdanov safely in his grave and his supporters routed in the Leningrad Affair—the international affairs issue no longer provided battleflags, behind which the competing factions could rally. Consequently, the victors were free now to raise the fallen banners of the defeated, as has happened so often in Soviet history. Thus, when in November 1949 the Cominform charged the Communist Party of Yugoslavia with being "in the power of murderers and spies,"[11] its resolution added: "The Tito clique transformed Belgrade into an *American* center for espionage and anti-Communist propaganda."[12]* Thus, when contrasting the Soviet charges against Yugoslavia in May 1948 and November 1949, it becomes evident to what extent the (by then ascendant) anti-Zhdanovite faction in 1948 focused on Britain rather than the U.S. as an adversary, a view that had been implicit, to some extent, in Varga's thesis.

To be sure, the close relationship between Tito and his associates, on the one hand, and Sir Fitzroy Maclean, Major Randolph Churchill, and Colonel William F. Deakin, key members of the British military intelligence community, on the other (who continued their personal contact with the Yugoslav leadership after the war), might have raised questions even in minds less suspicious than that of Stalin[13] (However, see p. 45, fn., on Tito's ambivalence.)

Indeed, Stalin was not the only person to comment on the high degree of British Yugoslav cooperation during this period. In November 1947, the American ambassador to Yugoslavia, Cavendish W. Cannon, sent a secret dispatch to Washington in which he pointed to his concerns regarding a separate British entente with Belgrade:

> For some time I have observed a shift in British policy here clearly showing reversion to "soft phase" toward Tito regime such as has recurred at intervals since 1943. It is probably grounded in persistence of the idea that there is possibility of an independent British Yugoslav policy separate from British Soviet or other British policies. This misapprehension that Tito is free agent may now be supplemented by doctrine setting up Britain as leader of democratic socialist countries with noble task of bridging widening East-West gap.

Cannon in fact was suggesting that the Yugoslavs and British were in the process of implementing the Zhdanovite policy of cooperation between the newly strengthened "progressive" bloc and its secondary adversary, the declining British Empire, to the detriment of the primary

---

*Antonov-Ovseyenko, however, asserts that even in 1949, during the Leningrad Affair, Stalin linked the (Zhdanovite) accused "to the British imperialists" (p. 298), and that, as late as 1952/53, at the time of the "Doctors' Plot," he suggested that one of the physicians be charged with "British espionage" (p. 302).

adversary, the United States:

> Recent phase may date from [Philip] Noel-Baker visits and [Fitzroy] Maclean talks and shows consistent line thru the interrupted negotiations for an air agreement, the *gratuitous* [emphasis added] offering of shipping and claims agreement to the major British-Yugoslav economic negotiations still underway, the press exploitation of Yugoslav delegates to the Youth Railway and compromises of General Steele and Churchill in Carinthia which incidentally were commended in the Foreign Office. . . . If this theory is sound it may in part explain new attitude on Trieste.
>
> I wonder whether this long series is only local manifestation of deeper problem indicating general fatigue and frustration in carrying on in this part of Europe in view of serious economic situation at home and Bevin's trouble with elements in his own party. . . .
>
> Yugoslav Government ever watchful for signs like this will draw every advantage from circumstances such as Britain's urgent need of trade. . . . British Ambassador told me "we simply must have food from Yugoslavia." Local reaction is already evident and there is marked falling off in anti-British propaganda in Yugoslavia.
>
> This means that we must henceforth take into account the possibility that Yugoslav Government may now consider that British are no longer an important element as regards either Greece or Trieste and probable Yugoslav Government's confidence that it can work out something as far as British are concerned as regards Carinthia when time comes. . . .
>
> That would mean that it is today only US which stands in Yugoslav Government's way in achievement its program.

Cannon went on to state that the U.S. still could count on the British for "general" support, and "perhaps full cooperation at moments of crisis." However, he finished on an ominous note: "but I do feel that our basic policy must in the future be shaped on assumption we must carry the burden and at times we may have to go it alone."[14]

Jacques Duclos, probably delighted at the chance of revenge for the rough treatment meted out to the P.C.F. at the founding meeting of the Cominform by Zhdanov personally and by Tito's representatives (see pp. 103–10) was to level the same accusation at Tito:

> We know, for example, how Churchill refused to send arms

to the French Francs-Tireurs and partisans.

But on the other hand, we know that Churchill's attitude to Tito was quite different. And since the old British reactionary never lost sight of the interests of reaction for one moment, the question arises: What guarantee was Tito able to give him at the time? We have the right to assume that during the war the [British] Intelligence Service had its agents among those who were closest to Tito.[15]

8 The Principal Adversary
Focus on the Middle East

There is significant evidence that the analysis submitted here rests on more than pure fancy. At a time in 1947 when no ominous cloud yet appeared to darken the Moscow-Belgrade relationship, Yugoslavia and the rest of the bloc split over an issue related directly to the adoption, respectively, of a primarily anti-British or anti-American posture. To the astonishment of those acquainted with the violently anti-Zionist course pursued by the Bolsheviks ever since Lenin, the Soviet diplomat A. A. Gromyko, on May 14, 1947, endorsed the creation of a Jewish state in Palestine,[1] declaring:

> If this plan [a unitary Arab-Jewish state] proves impossible to implement, in view of the deterioration in the relations between the Jews and Arabs. . . then it would be necessary to consider the second plan. . .which provides for the partition of Palestine into two independent autonomous states, one Jewish and one Arab.[2]

British policy, guided by Ernest Bevin, at that time followed a blatantly pro-Arab and anti-Zionist policy, while the United States, or at least the White House, tended to sympathize with the Jewish national cause. A U.N. Special Commission on Palestine (UNSCOP) sent to investigate the situation, on August 31, 1947, published a Majority Report that was endorsed by its Czechoslovak member and, like Gromyko three months earlier, supported the creation of a Jewish State.[3] The Yugoslav member signed a sharply dissenting Minority Report, calling essentially for the establishment of an Arab state that would contain a Jewish canton with limited autonomy, as envisaged by Bevin and the British authorities in Palestine.[4] When the issue was put to the vote in the U.N. General Assembly on November 29, 1947, the Soviet Union and the other countries of the bloc lined up behind the Majority Report, *together with the United States*, while the Yugoslavs, *together with Britain*, abstained.[5] In the parliamentary situation then prevailing at the U.N., abstention was tantamount to support of the Arab states, almost as much as a negative vote. Interestingly enough, at the very time of the international debate on the topic, between the publication of the UNSCOP report and the final vote, Zhdanov (as was to be discovered later) delivered his policy address to the secret founding meeting of the Cominform, in which, like the Yugoslavs and the British, he expressed pro-Arab sentiments, particularly regarding Egypt and Syria.[6] To put it mildly, this did not square with the views presented or the votes cast by the Soviet delegation to the U.N. in 1947. On the other hand, late in 1944, Malenkov had been reported (by a Soviet representative in Iran) to have expressed his support for Jewish territorial claims in Palestine.[7]

A fascinating, detailed, firsthand account of East European and Soviet military aid to the Palestinian Jewish defense forces during 1947–48 has been provided by Meir ("Munya") Mardor, who, together with several colleagues, was charged with obtaining arms for the *Yishuv**[*] during this period.[8] (Until May of 1948, it must be recalled, Palestine remained under the control of the British Mandatory Government, which tried to disarm the Jews.) It seems that, as early as December 1947,[9] Israeli emissaries had received permission from Prague to buy weapons manufactured in Czechoslovakia. Although a secret agreement on this topic with the Beneš government was reached before the February 1948 Communist "coup," the Jewish representatives were unable actually to obtain the arms, partly because the political upheaval in Czechoslovakia interrupted the process, and partly because of the logistical problems posed by the need to transport hardware (secretly) across the Mediterranean from a land-locked European state. While Romanian (Communist) leaders expressed sympathy for the Jewish cause (although they claimed that they were unable to help, because of a munitions shortfall in Romania), the Yugoslavs declined simply to help the *Yishuv* at all.

Subsequently, after the Communist takeover in Czechoslovakia, the promised secret shipment of weapons crystallized in the form of "German" hardware manufactured at the famous Skoda armaments plant. Even during the period of uncertainty in Prague in January 1948, however, Palestinian Jewish emissaries were allowed to visit freely Czech arms factories.[10] This would seem to imply that Beria's[†] security services at this stage viewed the Jewish cause favorably, since it is inconceivable that the sophisticated Czechoslovak weapons industry, which had been developed further under the German occupation, was not carefully guarded by the appropriate Soviet agency.[11] Once the situation in Czechoslovakia had stabilized, the representatives of the *Yishuv* were still faced by serious logistical problems. Clandestine arms transport by

---

[*]The Yishuv was the collective name of the Jewish sector of Palestine.

[†]By 1948, Beria appears to have reestablished the hegemony in the security services that was challenged earlier by A. A. Kuznetsov.

sea required Hungarian and Yugoslav collusion. In March 1948, the Yugoslavs refused to cooperate in this respect, and finally did so only after considerable pressure was applied, "from above," perhaps by Stalin himself,[12] possibly at the initiative of Beria and Malenkov.

It seems unlikely that Tito would have attempted to deviate on a matter so marginal to Belgrade's own interests, particularly at such a critical juncture in Soviet-Yugoslav relations, unless he had cause to believe that he had powerful friends in the USSR who also disagreed with the line given expression in Gromyko's U.N. speech and with the de facto cooperation extended by the USSR in supplying arms to the *Yishuv*.[13]

Although, in fact, Tito subsequently continued to be associated closely with the Arab position in the Middle East, it is unlikely that his position at this particular time was based on primarily personal predilections (such as the friendship he was to develop with Nasser during the 1950s), rather than the essentially "pro-British,"* anti-American line that the Yugoslavs (particularly in the UNSCOP vote) and the Leningrad group (during the Varga controversy) had come to adopt.†

Under duress, Belgrade eventually was to allow arms shipments to the *Yishuv* to pass through Yugoslavia intermittently. Once the Jewish leadership obtained some DC-3s, its dependence on Yugoslav ports was alleviated somewhat.[14] However, Yugoslavia's docks continued to be used as "funnels" from time to time until late in the summer of 1948,‡ when, with the sudden decline of the Zhdanov group and the subsequent demise of its leader (shortly after the June 1948 Cominform expulsion of Tito), Belgrade no longer had any incentive to appease Moscow. (The rift had deepened to the point of no return, and Zhdanov, Tito's patron in the USSR, had been undermined to the point of being compelled, by June, to add his name to the condemnation of his Yugoslav friends and allies only a few months after they had demonstrated their intimate

---

*That is, supportive of Bevin's line on Palestine.

†As it turned out, the Egyptians were to fight the 1948 war with British Spitfires, a symbol of Britain's fundamentally pro-Arab position, identified correctly by the Yugoslavs. Ironically, the Israelis depended upon Czech-built Messerschmitts (it was typical of the Soviet approach during this period that the USSR sold "German" weapons, which, of course, were not readily identifiable as Soviet-bloc armaments); thus, the Battle of Britain, in a way, was refought in the Middle East, with the Israelis, in a strange reversal of roles, flying the Messerschmitts. (See Gavriel D. Ra'anan, "The Evolution of the Soviet Use of Surrogates in Military Relations with the Third World, with Particular Emphasis on Cuban Participation in Africa," Santa Monica, Cal.: The Rand Corporation, 1980, P-6420.)

‡Col. Benjamin Kagan, *The Secret Battle for Israel*, pp. 133–40, 145–48, refers to isolated instances where Yugoslavia granted overflight and other facilities as late as the turn of 1948–49.

association at the 1947 Szklarska Poreba founding meeting of the Cominform. Zhdanov clearly was doomed, as indicated by the ominous publication on August 7, 1948, of his son, Yurii Zhdanov's, "letter of apology" to Stalin.)* Thus, Tito no longer felt compelled to take into account Moscow's policy considerations and began to follow his own inclinations in the Middle East, which the next three decades would reveal to be essentially pro-Arab.[15]

Paradoxically, despite the victory of the anti-Zhdanov group, Soviet relations with Israel themselves were to cool off soon afterward, apparently because of primarily domestic considerations in Moscow. The arrival on September 6, 1948, of Golda Meir, Israel's first ambassador to the USSR, precipitated manifestations of local Jewish solidarity with the fledgling state, apparently in excess of any developments anticipated by the Soviet regime. On September 11, the Israeli representatives were mobbed by Jewish enthusiasts at the Moscow synagogue, and five days later their visit to the Jewish theater evoked similar reactions. Even more significantly, applications for immigration to Israel began to arrive in large numbers at the Israeli legation in Moscow.[16] On September 21, 1948, Ilya Ehrenburg published an article in *Pravda* denying that "Zionist nationalists" were a significant force in the USSR and denying also the existence of the Jewish people as a nation (as opposed to being merely a religious and cultural group).[17]

It is now known that, at the time, negotiations were proceeding in Moscow regarding the possibility of *Soviet* arms supplies to Israel. This topic led to a meeting, on October 5, 1948, between the Israeli Major-General Yochanan Rattner and General Antonov, representing the Soviet chief of staff, Marshal Vasilevskii. Later in October, Mrs. Meir spoke to Mr. Bakulin of the Middle East Division of the Soviet Foreign Ministry and submitted a detailed list of requests (including T-34 tanks, fighter planes, artillery, and anti-aircraft guns), stressing the urgency of an answer. However, she never received a reply, and the request was never fulfilled.[18]

The period of friendly Israeli-Soviet relations ended at this point. Moreover, late in 1948, a major crackdown on Jewish activities was carried out in the USSR, including an intensification of the antisemitic ("anticosmopolitan") campaign which led to the arrest and eventual execution of most of the leadership of the Jewish Anti-Fascist Committee.[19]

By 1950, the Soviet Union was to come out publicly against Israel, citing the young state's ties to the United States. Already on November 2, 1949, *Vechernaia Moskva* published a TASS cable from Tel Aviv,

---

*These developments are discussed in subsequent chapters.

quoting the Israeli Communist Party journal *Kol Ha'am*, which attacked Ben-Gurion for allegedly "openly joining the *American* camp of warmongers and the policy of cold war against the USSR."[20]

The shift in Soviet policy, while undoubtedly influenced by the national fervor suddenly demonstrated by Soviet Jews during this period, also may have resulted from the clear identification, *after* Zhdanov's death, of the *United States* as the primary adversary (see Chapter 15); the result was a different Soviet Middle-Eastern policy, reflecting the change in "objective circumstances."

In this connection it is significant that Varga, having finally conceded his past errors (the "Varga approach" and the "general line" having converged, presumably, by this time, with Stalin's recovery and return to full-time work followed by the destruction of the "Leningrad Group"—see Appendix D), now asserted that American imperialism "virtually forced England out of the Ruhr, Palestine, Greece...."[21] This presentation of the United States as the primary antagonist constituted a clear shift from Varga's previous statements and from earlier official Soviet foreign policy statements, which had condemned the Arab League and Trans-Jordan as being controlled by the British.[22] Thus, after their downfall, the Zhdanovites (and their Yugoslav allies) ironically received ex post facto vindication, at least as far as their views of the "principal adversary" were concerned.

This approach, and its application to the Middle East, of course was not the only, or even the major, topic linking the Titoists and the Zhdanovites. The most obvious attraction that the Voznesenskii position offered the Yugoslavs was its insistence that the "new democracies,"[23] of which Yugoslavia was the preeminent example, should be regarded as very important components in the antiimperialist struggle. Moreover, in general, Voznesenskii's implicit advocacy of a militantly anti-Western line was likely to enhance the willingness of Soviet leaders to aid Belgrade in its efforts to gain control of Trieste, Carinthia, and Aegean Macedonia, if necessary by force.

9 THE SOVIET OCCUPATION ZONE OF GERMANY
Factional Rivalry

Given the focal role of Germany in Soviet policy at all times, it is not surprising that the Soviet occupation zone became a factional battleground.

In this context, it is necessary to reiterate certain essential considerations: it is perfectly true that, from the late 1930s to Zhdanov's demise, the rival factions propagated their respective "platforms" on the vital German question in a particularly coherent, lucid, and consistent manner. This was, of course, precisely the period during which the Zhdanovite-Malenkovite struggle was waged, and this study has repeatedly advanced the proposition that, as long as such a contest for power continues, the adversaries tend to adhere to their competing doctrines, if only because the latter serve as "battleflags", indicating who is winning and whose star is waning. Policy reversals become possible, indeed probable, only when one side has suffered irreversible defeat, at which point issues cease to serve as convenient weapons for scoring tactical points against opponents. Consequently, one should not assume that, because factional advocacy of particular approaches to important questions of international affairs has been prolonged and expressed in a logical, plausible, and elegant manner, it follows that one is dealing with primarily issue-oriented groups rather than with "feudal" chieftain-retainer associations that exploit policy questions in a power struggle. If that assumption were left unchallenged, it would be difficult to comprehend why victorious factions show so little compunction about picking up the fallen banners of their rivals from the battlefield, or why biographical data seem to play such a central role in determining the composition of the various political "clans."

Thus, as will be seen, the chief spokesman for the Zhdanovite approach to Germany, Colonel S. I. Tiul'panov, was not linked to that faction primarily because he agreed with its views on this issue, but because he had risen in Zhdanov's Leningrad machine, had been rescued from Siberia by Zhdanov and transferred to Germany, and was responsible to Colonel-General I. V. Shikin, another Zhdanovite. These personal links long antedated Tiul'panov's role in Germany; clearly, therefore, he was not a Zhdanovite necessarily because he shared the German policy propagated by that group — rather, he articulated its views because he was a Zhdanovite.

As for the great utility of "issues" as potent tactical weapons in the power struggle — particularly in the German context — suffice it to recall that the dismantling of East German industry (during the "reparations versus sovietization" debate) at the end of World War II provided the Zhdanovites with ammunition to bring about Malenkov's (temporary) demotion, without which Zhdanov's hegemony of 1946–47 hardly would have been feasible.

The essentially pro-German aspects of Zhdanov's policy preferences were to be indicated once more toward the end of World War II. On February 9, 1945, an editorial appeared in *Krasnaia Zvezda*, attempting to create a less Germanophobe mood among the ranks of the Red Army occupying German territory:

> "An eye for an eye, a tooth for a tooth" is an old saying. But it must not be taken literally. If the Germans marauded, and publicly raped our women, it does not mean that we must do the same. This has never been and never shall be. Our soldiers will not allow anything like that to happen — not because of pity for the enemy, but out of a sense of their own personal dignity. . . .They understand that every breach of military discipline only weakens the victorious Red Army. . . . Our revenge is not blind. Our anger is not irrational. In an access of blind rage one is apt to destroy a factory in conquered enemy territory — a factory that would be of value to us. Such an attitude can only play into the enemy's hands.[1]

Since Zhdanov's brother-in-law, A. S. Shcherbakov, was in charge of the Main Political Directorate of the Red Army (which, it is safe to assume, supervised unsigned editorials in the army's organ, *Krasnaia Zvezda*), one may deduce that this approach was consistent with Zhdanovite views.

Two months later, G. F. Aleksandrov (in charge of Agitprop, a Central Committee department that, it will be recalled, had been left under Zhdanov's general supervision by the September 1940 decree, elevating Aleksandrov to be its chief) criticized an article by Ilya Ehrenburg called "That's Enough!", which had appeared on April 11 in *Krasnaia Zvezda*. Ehrenburg, a member of the Jewish Anti-Fascist Committee, was criticized on two counts: he was said to have been unable to distinguish between the Germans responsible for the war and other, nonculpable Germans. Moreover, Aleksandrov attacked Ehrenburg's assertion that the German decision to transfer some divisions from the Western to the Eastern Front was based upon the Germans' greater fear of Russian than of Western retribution:

> At the present stage the Nazis are following their own mischievous policy of sowing distrust among the Allies. . . . They are trying, by means of this political military trick, to achieve what they could not achieve by purely military means. If the Germans, as Ehrenburg says, were only scared of the Russians, they would not, to this day, go on sinking Allied ships, murdering British prisoners, or sending flying bombs over London. "We did not capture Königsberg by telephone," Ehrenburg said. That is quite true; but the explanation he offers for the simple way in which the Allies occupy towns in Western Germany is not the correct one.[2]

Aleksandrov was minimizing the degree of alleged German hatred of the Russians. Apparently, the Zhdanov group was attempting to clear the way for eventual Soviet rapprochement with Germany or with a portion thereof (there is no evidence that Aleksandrov and Zhdanov had come to a parting of the ways prior to Aleksandrov's rapid rise to political prominence during 1946 [see Appendix B])

This approach was consistent not only with Zhdanov's pro-German bent in the years preceding Operation Barbarossa, but also with his postwar policy preferences in general. If even part of Germany could be subtracted from the "capitalist camp" (in Voznesenskii's terms, thereby reducing still further the markets available for alleviating periodic crises of overproduction in the West), not to speak of actually establishing Soviet control there, this would bolster Zhdanov's case for a "forward" Soviet posture to take advantage of a weakened adversary.

That was not simply a theory; for Zhdanov's representative in Germany, Colonel S. I. Tiul'panov, as will be demonstrated, promoted rapprochement with Germans of almost all persuasions in the Soviet occupation zone, attempting to consolidate Soviet control, with a view toward gradual de facto incorporation of the area into the "progressive camp." Tiul'panov aligned himself closely with Walter Ulbricht, who had taken over K.P.D. leadership during his years in the USSR and had played a significant role in the establishment of *Freies Deutschland* (with its German nationalist overtones).

Tiul'panov's links to Zhdanov were both personal and institutional. He held three posts in the Soviet Military Administration in Germany, being in charge of agitation and propaganda, head of the Main Political Directorate of the Red Army, and representative of the CPSU in the Soviet occupation zone.[3] In his capacity as the chief *politruk* in the area, he was responsible to Colonel-General I. V. Shikin, another solid Zhdanovite. Shikin started his career as politruk in Gorkii,[4] Zhdanov's original fiefdom, being brought, subsequently, to Leningrad, where he served under Zhdanov during the war, becoming (political) deputy chief of the Leningrad Military District. When A. S. Shcherbakov, Zhdanov's brother-in-law[5] and boss of the Main Political Directorate,[6] died in May 1945, Shikin was chosen to succeed him.[7] Shikin was to be demoted during the Leningrad Affair, and did not gain rehabilitation until December 1954, after Beria's elimination, when Malenkov's star was waning and Abakumov, held responsible for the Affair, was executed.[8]

In his capacity as CPSU representative in the Soviet occupation zone, Tiul'panov often reported directly to Zhdanov.[9] Tiul'panov had been trained as an engineer in Leningrad, where he had risen through the city's political apparatus until being transferred to the Main Ukrainian Front in 1943. At one point, Tiul'panov revealed to a former member of the S.P.D., Erich W. Gniffke,* that he had been exiled to Siberia for "deviationism," but that Zhdanov, whom he knew personally from Leningrad, had intervened rapidly on his behalf. Subsequently, Zhdanov, together with Mikoyan, had arranged to bring Tiul'panov to the Soviet occupation zone.[10]

In contrast to the Tiul'panov-Ulbricht-Zhdanov approach (attempting to create a state along Soviet lines in at least part of Germany), the line supported by Malenkov† and Beria apparently meant resigning oneself to the expectation that the Soviet zone would be absorbed eventually by the much more populous Western portion, so that, at most, one could hope to keep a reunified Germany disarmed. Thus, the latter group preferred stripping the industrial infrastructure of the Soviet zone at breakneck speed, thereby obviating the possibility that a united Germany might pose a threat one day; this policy was intended, simultaneously, to contribute to the recovery of the Soviet Union from the economic devastation of the war through the massive "transfer" of German equipment to the USSR. Zhdanov, at one point, specifically criticized

---

*Gniffke had been identified with the left wing of the S.P.D. and supported the Tiul'panov-inspired "shot-gun marriage" between the S.P.D. and the K.P.D. that created the Socialist Unity Party (S.E.D.). Many of Gniffke's former S.P.D. comrades never forgave him for this act; see foreword of Gniffke's memoirs.

†Malenkov had been appointed chairman of the Committee for the Rehabilitation of the Economy of the Liberated Areas.[11] (This developed into the special committee, under the Council of People's Commissars, for the economic disarmament of Germany). Other members were Beria, A. A. Andreyev, and M. Z. Saburov (who was recalled from Germany in September 1945, because Malenkov needed his support against Voznesenskii on the home front, and eventually replaced the latter as chairman of Gosplan, in March of 1949).[12]

Malenkov's policy of dismantling East German industry, since it produced unemployment there and hampered the sovietization of the Russian zone.[13] As was shown earlier, in May of 1946 Zhdanov and Voznesenskii exploited the fiasco of Malenkov's and Beria's "transfer" of East German equipment to the USSR as one of the weapons to bring about Malenkov's (temporary) demotion from his position in the Secretariat of the Central Committee. The very fact that Malenkov was identified with the "reparations" approach provided additional incentive for the Zhdanovites to emphasize the opposite concept, East German "reconstruction."

Malenkov and Beria reportedly differed on one issue only, namely the tapping of Saxon uranium mines. Beria bore responsibility for development of nuclear weapons, and therefore was placed in charge of the extraction of Saxon uranium, code-named Operation Vismut.[14] Understandably, therefore, Beria favored this exceptional case of local "economic development," under the supervision of one of his deputies, M.G.B. Major General Andreii Mikhailovich Maltsev.[15] Generally, however, Beria cooperated with Malenkov[16] in supporting a policy based upon the assumption that the Soviet occupation zone would have to be abandoned eventually, an approach consistent with the cautious and minimalistic line on foreign affairs followed by both men. In Beria's case, this view persisted after the creation of the East German state. Subsequently (according to the March 11, 1963, *Süddeutsche Zeitung*), Khrushchev was to allege that "Beria wished to liquidate the D.D.R."[17] Malenkov and Beria were represented in the Soviet Military Administration (S.M.A.) by Vladimir S. Semyonov, Colonel General Ivan A. Serov[18] (an M.G.B. chief whose allegiance turned out to be flexible), and, briefly, Maksim Z. Saburov. Within the K.P.D., this group worked closely with Anton Ackermann, whose eclipse in the German Communist Party coincided with Beria's demise.[19]

Stalin appears to have preferred a middle road, viewing occupation as a chance to strengthen the USSR (through reparations) and to push Poland westward, while catering, up to a point, to German nationalism—contradictory as these aims might be.[20] Stalin, unlike the Zhdanovites, however, continued to look toward German reunification, rather than the creation of a separatist East German Soviet state.* In July 1947, Stalin addressed members of the S.E.D.:

In the question of the unity of Germany, we must proceed step

---

*In 1945–46, Stalin felt Germany would "recover and very quickly," stressing "all of Germany must be ours. . . Soviet," but, by 1948, he had concluded "the West will make West Germany their own and we shall turn East Germany into our own state." (Djilas, *Conversations*, pp. 114, 153–54).

by step. We must proceed despite all obstacles. However, we must not surrender to the illusion that the struggle concerning [German] unity can be won quickly. It may last five, six, or even seven years. The S.E.D. is a German party. We will support it, since it has to lead the struggle for the shaping of Germany from within. The purpose is to exclude reactionary forces from the economy and the administration and carry through genuine democratic reforms. The S.E.D. has to unify with the Communist Party in the Western zones. Sectarianism must not be permitted to spread among the working class parties. . . .The destruction in Europe is great. Reconstruction will demand much time. We have to reconstruct at home; we also have to help other nations. Germany needs its unity and its peace treaty. Only then will the struggle for a lasting peace be won. That is our most decisive aim. And for that reason, we have to remain longer in Germany than we ourselves would like. Comrade Grotewohl has raised the question of drawing frontiers. With respect to the eastern frontier, for instance, the S.E.D., as a German party, of course may adopt a different point of view than we [the USSR] or the Poles. With regard to the national question, the S.E.D. should not provide the other parties with reasons for agitating against it.

Gniffke, in reporting Stalin's words, comments that he appeared concerned to give the S.E.D. an appearance of independence.[21] Like Tiul'panov and other Zhdanovites, Stalin encouraged a "national" approach in the S.E.D., to the point of allowing "opposition" to the Soviet line! However, unlike Zhdanov, Stalin (on the same occasion) spoke, with characteristic caution, of a "step-by-step" policy, while Zhdanov fulminated against "dollar imperialism," which, he intimated, had to be confronted now, since it endangered Soviet wartime gains.[22]

Marshall G. K. Zhukov, the first commander in chief of the Soviet Occupation Forces and chief of the Soviet Military Administration, tended to reflect more accurately Stalin's gradualist approach, with a continued opening toward German reunification rather than East German separatism. Zhukov was replaced by Marshal V. D. Sokolov-skii in April 1946. There are indications that Zhdanov's associates had a hand in Zhukov's abrupt recall from his German command and in his subsequent relegation to some seven years of relative obscurity, first in Odessa and then in the Urals. As early as January 1946, Tiul'panov confidently told S.P.D. leaders that Zhukov's days in Germany were numbered.[23] (Presumably, Tiul'panov had been "tipped off" about this forthcoming change by his boss, I. V. Shikin, who is alleged to have been among those responsible for Zhukov's demotion—see fn. p. 31–32.)

Under Zhukov and his main assistant, Vladimir S. Semyonov, Otto Grotewohl, the head of the left wing of the S.P.D. in the Soviet zone, was influential to the point of permitting himself to be patronizing toward K.P.D. members. According to Erich Gniffke, before being demoted Zhukov had offered Grotewohl to oust Walter Ulbricht, Tiul'panov's ally, from the leadership of the K.P.D. if the Central Committee of the S.P.D. would lodge a complaint against him. For some reason Grotewohl failed to inform the Central Committee and thereby saved Ulbricht. Gniffke was informed about Zhukov's offer only years later, in 1948, whereupon he submitted a complaint about Ulbricht, in October of that year, as part of an open letter to the S.E.D.:

> Ulbricht's policy from the beginning was aimed at separatism [i.e., a separate communist state in East Germany]. . . .There is a two-track policy in the Eastern zone [of Germany]. One is the policy of reason and reality, which as early as 1945 had started on the track toward a "parliamentary-Democratic Republic," while the second track was initiated toward a "revolutionary policy with the final aim of splitting Germany." Representatives of the "policy of reason" were to be found not only among all the political parties, but also in the Soviet Military Administration. The outstanding representative of this policy was the first Chief of the Administration, Marshal of the Soviet Union, Grigorii [sic] K. Zhukov.[24]

Gniffke went on to contrast this "policy of reason" with the line of the "separatist" group, led by Ulbricht; he pointed out that "the representative of the revolutionary policy and supporter of Ulbricht was the representative of the CPSU(b) in the administration, Colonel Sergeii Tiul'panov's ally, from the leadership of the K.P.D. if the Central Committee of the S.P.D. would lodge a complaint against him. For some

While Tiul'panov had made it clear to Gniffke and others that he was pro-German (he had been educated at Heidelberg and had fluent command of the language), this did not change the basic fact that his task, as he saw it, was to consolidate Soviet control of the zone, and although he was more than willing to coopt obliging non-Communists into the regime, power would be monopolized by the K.P.D. leadership under his crony Ulbricht.

Once Sokolovskii took over command, Tiul'panov's influence was greatly enhanced, and correspondingly, the K.P.D. and particularly Ulbricht became more overtly dominant in the new regime. Eleven days after the recall of Zhukov, the S.E.D. was created through the forcible merger of the S.P.D. and the K.P.D. (the so-called "shotgun marriage"). This policy development was identified with Tiul'panov.[26]

Unlike Zhukov, Marshal Sokolovskii was not *the* great war hero, who, to some degree, could exploit his personal glory to further his own policy. Rather, he was a "desk general," who was familiar with Bolshevik party work, and he dealt with the problems of the zone from that perspective.

Sokolovskii's first public address in his new capacity could easily have been delivered by Zhdanov. It was a strident assertion of the two-camp theory, which Zhdanov was to promulgate the following year at the founding meeting of the Cominform, and Sokolovskii took pains to pay due homage to the importance of the party:

> Between the camp of socialism and the camp of declining capitalism there is no intermediate position. In this respect, a clear parting of the ways is taking place in all countries. An expression of this is the achievement of the unity of the working class as implemented in the Soviet occupation zone. The S.E.D. is the party called upon to fortify democracy in Germany. It is the guarantee for a successful struggle for peace and socialism. My experience, which I was able to gather also in work for the party [i.e., the C.P.S.U.], I place at the disposal of this struggle.[27]*

It is significant that Sokolovskii referred both to the CPSU and the S.E.D. as "the party," as if the latter were but another Communist party. Clearly the S.E.D. was to follow the lead of the CPSU as if it were merely one of its "fraternal" clients, rather than a new, merged "communist-socialist" party.

Immediately following Sokolovskii's speech, Tiul'panov symbolically moved up to Sokolovskii's side and delivered the next address. Thus, as Semyonov had been Zhukov's right hand man, Tiul'panov assumed this position under Sokolovskii.[28]

According to Gniffke, this marked the eclipse of Grotewohl's influence and, concomitantly, that of the S.P.D. Tiul'panov was to walk in and out of S.P.D. institutions at will. While under Zhukov's wing, Grotewohl had been most condescending, even to the venerable Wilhelm Pieck. This changed completely when Sokolovskii took over. Moreover, Tiul'panov began to bend and twist the structure of the S.E.D. to suit

---

*Whether this speech reflected Sokolovskii's personal views (or was drafted for him by Tiul'panov, representing his own approach and presumably that of the Main Political Administration under Zhdanov's protégé Shikin), remains a matter of speculation.

his needs. "He inspired Pieck to propose to the [German] Secretariat that it should 'appoint' Ulbricht as deputy chairman [of the S.E.D.], although this is actually contrary to the party statutes and, in fact, was not accepted at the time—no such job existed—which didn't prevent Ulbricht's wife, Lotte Kühn, from instructing the press to describe him as the 'vice chairman.' "[29] Thus, under Tiul'panov's protection, Ulbricht was flouting the pro forma structure of the S.E.D., which was itself Tiul'panov's artificial creation.

Following Zhdanov's lead, Sokolovskii opposed dismantling German industry; in fact, early in January 1947 he promised the S.E.D. leadership that he would try to put an end to this practice in the Soviet zone.

Sokolovskii and Tiul'panov invited the leaders of the S.E.D. to participate directly in negotiations concerning the termination of dismantling of industry. The result was the announcement of January 15, 1947, that "the request of the Socialist Unity Party of Germany to bring the process of dismantling to a final halt has been granted. When the dismantling of the war industries in particular is halted, there will be no further dismantling." Thus, Tiul'panov mobilized his own clients against the reparations policy of Malenkov and his surrogates within Eastern Germany.[30]

Since the special committee under A. I. Mikoyan (following Malenkov's demotion in 1946) had begun to investigate Malenkov's reparations policy during the previous summer and would reach its conclusion in May 1947, Tiul'panov's act clearly was a maneuver designed to give ammunition to the investigators in their search for "evidence" against Malenkov's dismantling practices.[31]

The antagonism in the Soviet occupation zone of Germany between the reparations officials and the Soviet Military Administration had been intense and overt almost from the beginning. Wolfgang Leonhard describes being driven through the Soviet zone of Berlin by an officer in the Red Army's political administration, who pointed to a building and declared, "That's where the enemy lives!" When asked if he was referring to a group of Nazis, the officer responded, "No, worse still—our own reparations gang!"[32]

The Zhdanov group's antidismantlement sentiment was the logical complement of the close ties established by Colonel Tiul'panov with the leadership of the K.P.D. Since, apparently, the Zhdanovites intended to consolidate the Soviet zone under Ulbricht's leadership, it would have made little sense to put their protégé in charge of a state which had been denuded of its industry. A "pastoralized" communist state was a contradiction in terms. The sanguine political expectations of the Zhdanovites simply left no room for Malenkov-Beria pessimism; they did not share the assumption that the Red Army eventually would have to evacuate Germany and that it was desirable, therefore, to leave behind a deindustrialized region. It was in Zhdanov's interest to set up a German communist leadership which, once in control, would be obligated to him (and other Zhdanovites) for gaining power in the zone and would have the local resources to avoid the necessity of constant recourse to (possibly hostile factions in) Moscow. Clearly, in addition to its fiefdoms in the USSR (Leningrad and Gorkii), the Zhdanov group was eager to establish factional outposts beyond the frontiers of the Soviet state itself.

During the Second Party Congress of the S.E.D., Sokolovskii apologetically stated that the continued Soviet exploitation of a certain sector of the German mining industry (which was crucial for Soviet nuclear development and, thus, had not been halted) was not to be regarded as new reparations, but simply as the completion of a previously initiated stage.[33] Anything that smacked of a holdover from the Malenkov-Beria dismantlement and reparations period clearly constituted an embarrassment for the Tiul'panov-Sokolovskii regime, calling for explanation or disavowal.

Late in the spring of 1948, Tiul'panov went so far as to assume a posture of penitence (implicitly for the extent of Soviet deindustrialization of Eastern Germany):

> Comrades, I am honored that our Comrade, Wilhelm Pieck, has such a high opinion of the Soviet occupying power, however, I would like to say that the Soviet occupation force in Germany has made incredible and...serious mistakes, which unfortunately can only be rectified with great difficulty. As the only excuse, I can only say that we never previously had to deal with a Socialist occupation. Perhaps I can give assurance that if in the future we should be compelled once again by our opponents to carry through another Socialist occupation then we will have learned from our experiences in Germany and will do it better.[34]

It is hardly characteristic of Soviet "procurators" to criticize their own state's policies; however, since dismantling of industry, in this case, was the policy of the "enemy," that is to say, the "reparations gang," led by Malenkov and Beria, Tiul'panov was being anything but self-critical.*

---

*By December of 1947 the "collegium" (administrative organ) in charge of Soviet property abroad was in the hands of Beria's associates, V. N. Merkulov and V. G.

The policy of winning over at least a portion of Germany, espoused by the Zhdanov group, led to a line of conciliation not only of German non-Communist adherents of the S.E.D., but, more remarkably, of ex-Nazis also, who were "rehabilitated" quite early and "legitimized" in 1948, under the banner of the National Democratic Party. In the spring of 1948, Tiul'panov delivered an address to the faculty of the Party Higher School, in which he announced the following policy:

> We, in the Soviet Military Administration, have initiated a series of investigations of former members and functionaries of the Nazi Party and have reached the conviction that very useful forces are to be found among them, which could be absorbed only with difficulty into the Mass and Party Organizations. Now we are preparing the release of former Nazi functionaries, and I have had detailed discussions with several of them. In order to activate these forces, we, on our part, have proposed the formation of a party in which these forces can be gathered, united and utilized for the further development of the [Soviet] Zone. This party will be called the National Democratic Party. These forces should be given greater possibility of development in the Zone.[35]

On June 16, 1948, the formation of the National Democratic Party (incorporating many ex-Nazis) was announced, about two months after Tiul'panov's address.*

Tiul'panov, it is noteworthy, was in the habit of sending New Year's cards that referred to the "great German people."[36] Even more remarkable was a statement, on November 6, 1947, by Marshal Sokolovskii to Ernst Lemmer (vice chairman of the Christian Democratic Union [C.D.U.]) and Jacob Kaiser (C.D.U. chairman), during celebrations of the thirtieth anniversary of the October Revolution. Sokolovskii, rather gratuitously, expressed the opinion that a somewhat stronger German armored force would have produced a different outcome for the last German offensive in the Ardennes (the "Battle of the Bulge"). According to Lemmer, it seems that the Soviet marshal would not have been displeased if the German High Command had thrown a few more Panzer divisions against the Western allies. Sokolovskii continued:

Dekanozov; see CIACR 76-12971, July 1976 (*Who's Who in Soviet Government*, January 1948), collected DSOs, 1948–66, unclassified, 1 and 2 of 39.

*Tiul'panov's approach seems to have reflected the tradition of German "National Bolshevism" of the 1920s and of Karl Radek's line.

The German offensive would have thrown the Amerikanski forces and their allies into the ocean, since the German soldier is a superb soldier, as superb as a Soviet soldier. As for the Frenchies. . . (he made a contemptuous gesture). . . . The Amerikanski are not good soldiers, but they have many machines and much technology. They don't want to fight or to die. They want to let the machines fight and die, but not the men. If the Ardennes offensive had had a little more power, the Amerikanski would have been thrown into the sea."[37]

Having expressed contempt for the American military apparatus, in typical Zhdanovite fashion, he went on to express the view that, among Western forces, the British soldiers had demonstrated the greatest fighting determination. Thus, Sokolovskii was true to the Zhdanovite line in that he expressed admiration for the Germans, contempt and antagonism for the United States, and some sympathy for the British.

A symbolic issue that sheds light upon the instinctive ideological inclinations of the Zhdanov group concerning German affairs was the choice of a flag to represent the German elements favoring the USSR. In mid–1943, when preparing for the formation on Soviet soil of the National Committee for a Free Germany* and its journal, *Free Germany (Freies Deutschland)*, the communist cadres involved found themselves at odds over which flag would represent the new organization on the masthead of its newspaper. While the German communist organizers took it for granted that the black, red, and gold tricolor would be hoisted (the revolutionary banner of 1848, behind which the left, including Marx and Engels, had rallied), Zhdanov's ally in the "Ghost Comintern," Manuilskii, vetoed this choice, insisting that "the black, red, and gold flag was reminiscent of the Weimar Republic—a period of weakness and crisis and mass unemployment; this would be a handicap to the movement. The black, white and red flag [i.e. the conservative emblem of Bismarck's Reich, based upon Prussia's colors, black and white] would be better, because it is popular with the officer's corps of the Wehrmacht, and, therefore, would contribute toward making possible the creation of a really broad movement."[39]†

---

*The main CPSU functionaries in charge of the Free Germany committee, were Zhdanov's brother-in-law, Shcherbakov, and Manuilskii, Zhdanov's "alter ego" in charge of the "Ghost Comintern," with a significant role being played also by the Hungarian Communist, Ernö Gerö.[38]

†See p. 95 fn.; in dealing with the emblem, once again the "National Bolshevik" tradition was evident.

Thus, the Zhdanovites were demanding that a banner be unfurled which stood for Bismarck, the Hohenzollern dynasty, and the Prussian officer caste, rather than for any "progressive" element in Germany. This controversy continued until May 1948 (with Zhdanov's allies in the bloc, Tito and Dimitrov, already under heavy fire from Moscow, and on the eve of Zhdanov's political and physical demise), when the Weimar tricolor received final official endorsement.[40]

The Titoists appear to have conformed to the pro-German orientation of their Zhdanovite allies. In the spring of 1947, the Yugoslav People's Youth constituted the first foreign youth delegation sent to Eastern Germany. While there, the leaders of the delegation endorsed the view that Ulbricht's Free German Youth should be accepted into the (communist-led) World Federation of Democratic Youth. At a later stage, this episode was to be used by Moscow against the Yugoslavs, who apparently spoke without first consulting the Soviet Komsomol (then controlled by N. A. Mikhailov, who emerged subsequently as an ally of Malenkov)[41] or high officials of the W.F.D.Y.[42] A delegation of members of Free German Youth was to tour Yugoslavia during the summer of 1948, but was abruptly prevented from doing so by Moscow in May.[43] It may be significant that it took the S.E.D. four days to welcome the 1948 Cominform resolution condemning Belgrade, a statement of support being released only on July 4, 1948, after considerable deliberations.[44]

If the Yugoslav communists backed Ulbricht's Germany, so, correspondingly, was Tiul'panov supportive of Tito. On April 18, 1948, with Belgrade-Moscow polemics already in an advanced (albeit secret) stage, Tiul'panov, discussing the transition from "people's democratic revolution" to "socialist revolution" presented the following hierarchy of regimes (resorting to the analogy of crossing a river from the bourgeois capitalist to the socialist bank):

> Yugoslavia has already reached the other bank; Bulgaria is taking the last few strokes to reach it; Poland and Czechoslovakia are about in the middle of the river, followed by Romania and Hungary, which have gone about a third of the way; while the Soviet Occupation Zone has just taken the first few strokes away from the bourgeois bank.[45]

This was a remarkably faithful reflection, of course, of the Zhdanovite pecking order, as established in Zhdanov's November 1946 address, during the Voznesenskii-Varga "debate," and, subsequently, at the founding meeting of the Cominform: Zhdanov's allies, the Yugoslav and Bulgarian regimes, head the list; the other "Slav" states follow; and the "non-Slav" countries, controlled primarily by other Soviet factions, trail behind. (The Soviet occupation zone of Germany, not yet granted "sovereignty" a mere three years after the end of the war, could not be promoted beyond it rear position; but it was significant that it was included at all in a list of "independent" states, and as one, moreover, that at least had embarked on the path to socialism, under Sokolovskii, Tiul'panov, and Ulbricht.) In typically Zhdanovite fashion, the Yugoslav fiefdom of Albania was not listed at all.

Moreover, in an article printed in *Démocratie Nouvelle* as late as June 1948, a mere few weeks before Yugoslavia's "expulsion from the Cominform," Tiul'panov spoke of the circumstances leading to the liberation of the countries of Eastern Europe from fascist rule. In the case of Yugoslavia, he described the primary role of the Red Army as having consisted of deterring the United States and Great Britain from intervening to affect the struggle against Nazi occupation; as far as Poland and Czechoslovakia were concerned, however, he asserted that the USSR, in addition to deterring Anglo-American intervention, also had prevented the consolidation of fascist forces within those countries. Conspicuously absent from Tiul'panov's analysis was any reference to the role of the Red Army in liberating Belgrade.[46] Since considerable significance was assumed in the Stalin-Tito dispute of those very weeks by the question of Yugoslavia's gratitude (or lack thereof) for Red Army aid during World War II (resulting subsequently in Belgrade's publication of Mosa Pijade's book, *La Faible de l'aide Sovietique a l'insurrection nationale Yugoslav*), Tiul'panov's article amounted to almost overt support for Zhdanov's Yugoslav allies.

It remains to ascertain the role played by Soviet factional conflict in precipitating the Berlin Blockade, the climactic event on the road to the partition of Germany. The question arises whether this episode constituted the last embers of the Zhdanovshchina or whether it developed from separate circumstances, manipulated by other elements. No conclusive response appears feasible, but the latter hypothesis cannot be ruled out entirely. The imposition of the blockade and the Cominform announcement of Tito's expulsion occurred within days of one another, and the cutting of communications between Berlin and West Germany was preceded by an unpublicized trip to the Soviet zone by Beria.[47] Thus, the blockade may have been intended to serve purposes unrelated to Zhdanov's "forward" strategy in Germany and elsewhere.

Tiul'panov, however, was to continue to serve in East Germany, in his various capacities, for about a year after Zhdanov's death; thus, inevitably, he played a role in the Berlin crisis. His speech of September 11, 1948, at the Congress of Victims of Fascism, contained one of the more stridently anti-Western statements made during this confrontation. In his address, he charged not only that "American monopolists" were calling for war, but also that they were restoring fascism in Germany, adding that the Soviet Union would "destroy all those who attempt to create a Fourth Reich."[48]

The abatement of the Berlin crisis was preceded by the sudden withdrawal from publication of another address by Tiul'panov that was to have appeared in the *Berliner Zeitung* of January 25, 1949. This speech, which assailed "Anglo-American imperialism" and voiced the Soviet Union's "full support" for the "honorable struggle" of the S.E.D., had been broadcast over the radio that morning; however, apparently at the instigation of his old antagonist V. S. Semyonov (reputedly averse to the "forward" line, who was to take charge in the fall of that year as ambassador to the new East German state) the presses were stopped at the last second and Tiul'panov's address was deleted.[49]

Two months later, Marshal Sokolovskii was replaced by General V. I. Chuikov, and although Tiul'panov remained on the S.M.A. staff until later in the year, he seems to have been deprived of influence.[50] On May 9, 1949, Chuikov officially lifted the blockade.[51] On November 7, 1949, the Soviet Military Administration was terminated, leaving in place only the Control Commission under Chuikov's command following the establishment of the "German Democratic Republic" under the titular leadership of Pieck and Grotewohl.[52] Tiul'panov's one-time ally Walter Ulbricht retained control of the S.E.D., but the Soviet presence in East Germany was no longer under Zhdanovite influence.

Years later, Tiul'panov was to reminisce about Soviet occupation and reparations policies.* He claimed that the USSR had not been exploiting (or drawing material advantage from) Germany—reparations were a question not of material compensation but of "reeducation." He discussed "reeducation" successes, even in the cases of German soldiers taken straight from the front. This, he stated, was an achievement of the *Germans themselves*, but was also a matter of "true and intimate collaboration of the victor and defeated, the liberator and the liberated."

This was rendered possible by the "unmasking of Nazi ideology and the development of a true German consciousness." He stressed that, later on, "after the Western powers, in conjunction with West German imperialism, divided Germany," a new task was added, "namely to raise consciousness concerning the organic unity between the social and

---

*Although he did not say so, his assessment pertained mainly to policies with which he had been personally involved. Thus, he chose to play down the whole question of deindustrialization, as implemented by his rival within the Soviet zone, M. Z. Saburov, who was carrying out the instructions of Zhdanov's adversary, Malenkov.

national questions, between democracy and the national interest of the German people, between the development of national consciousness and of fraternal linkage with all peace-loving forces."[53]

This summation was consistent not only with the policy of courting certain German elements that Tiul'panov had implemented, but no less so with the attitude on this question which had been expressed by Zhdanov at the first meeting of the Cominform:

> As is well known, the USSR favors the constitution of a unified, peaceable, demilitarized, democratic Germany. . . . *However,* this policy of the Soviet state with respect to Germany is coming up against the resistance of the imperialist circles of the U.S.A. and Britain. The session of the Foreign Ministers' Council in Moscow in March–April 1947, showed that the U.S.A., Britain and France were prepared, not only to work for disrupting the democratization and demilitarization of Germany, *but even for the liquidation of Germany as a unified state, for its dismemberment and for a separate decision on the question of peace* [emphases added]. The pursuit of this policy now takes place in a new situation, in which the United States has departed from the old course of Roosevelt and is going over to a new policy of preparing for new military adventure.[54]

Neither of these men was inclined to miss opportunities of making at least a ceremonial bow in the direction of German nationalism.

10 THE FOUNDING MEETING OF THE COMINFORM

The close cooperation of the Zhdanovites with Tito's Yugoslavs (and with Dimitrov's Bulgars) became unmistakable in September of 1947 at the secret founding meeting of the Cominform, in Szklarska Poreba, Western Poland—in many aspects the climactic event of the Zhdanovshchina. While both Zhdanov and Malenkov represented the Soviet Union* at the gathering, there can be little question but that this episode represented a major victory for the Zhdanovite forces. Zhdanov very obviously was in charge of the meeting and the major speaker on international affairs; he developed in far greater detail, and much more sharply, the line he first put forward publicly in November 1946[3] (a policy that Voznesenskii was simultaneously advocating in his book *The Economy of the U.S.S.R. during World War II*, the draft of which must have been circulating at that time).

Malenkov, on the other hand, was relegated to a secondary and most humiliating role, presenting a paper on domestic questions in the Soviet Union which, he was made to say, in essence, could be summed up best through the decrees on literature, culture, philosophy, and other areas, which had been issued by Comrade Zhdanov; in other words, it was Malenkov's task to act as a phonograph record of the Zhdanovshchina![4] Zhdanov's speech was reprinted two months after the gathering, when the existence of the Cominform was announced in the

---

*Another Soviet representative present, according to Reale, was Dimitrii Manuilskii, the veteran organizer and conspirator of the Comintern, whose task it must have been to help establish the new organization with the aid of the skills he had developed in running (and purging) its predecessor. Manuilskii had bloodied his hands in that purge, which included the decimation of the C.P.Y. Central Committee, *excepting Tito*. In other words, it is most probable that Manuilskii and Tito were linked by a tie "thicker than water." (For that matter, so were Manuilskii and Dimitrov, whose rise in the Comintern, indeed his release from a Nazi prison, was carried out with Manuilskii's aid.)[1] These factors make it all the more likely that Zhdanov, the Yugoslavs, and the Bulgars were not merely playing a highly visible role at the Cominform gathering, as some commentators believe, but were actually running it. If the meeting really was a Stalinite set-up, as the Yugoslavs would have us believe now, why, in addition to expelling Tito, humiliating Dimitrov, demoting (and apparently arresting) Zhdanov, as we shall see, (with both Zhdanov and Dimitrov dying conveniently of heart disease), did Stalin also imprison Manuilskii within a few months of this meeting, as Reale testifies?[2] Who was left then to spring Stalin's trap? Certainly not Malenkov, who, as will be demonstrated, was placed in a very humiliating position during the conference.

first edition of its official journal, *For a Lasting Peace, For a People's Democracy*, which lifted the veil of secrecy from the Szklarska Poreba meeting.[5] Malenkov's lecture was reprinted only in the second edition of the journal, two weeks later. In his address, moreover, Malenkov was made to perform as gravedigger for G. F. Aleksandrov, the one-time follower of Zhdanov who had gone over to the Malenkov faction and had become the object of a scathing Zhdanovite public attack some weeks before the Szklarska Poreba gathering. Malenkov's resigned announcement before key members of the international communist movement of his associate Aleksandrov's ideological and political demise (although, as it turned out, the obituary was highly premature) probably constituted the Soviet equivalent of a captive during a Roman triumph being dragged through the streets bound to the chariot of the victors.

It should be noted that, after Zhdanov disappeared from the scene and Malenkov made his political comeback, G. F. Aleksandrov, who, only three months earlier had lost his position as Agitprop chief (a position which, it may be recalled, he had gained as Zhdanov's replacement),* was to be promoted again. Thus, for instance, in 1950, he was given the honorific role of major official commentator on Stalin's writings concerning ideological matters. This occurred in connection with Stalin's attack on the work of Professor N. Ia. Marr, who had claimed that language was merely part of the societal superstructure and could be categorized according to class and socioeconomic development.[6] Thus, appropriately, during the period when Stalin attacked this leftist pseudoscientific theory from the "right" (in the sense that Marr was one of the dogmatic Marxist purists), Aleksandrov was chosen to help popularize Stalin's concepts.[7] Aleksandrov was to be promoted further in 1953–55, the period in which Malenkov enjoyed his brief ascent to the pinnacles of power; Aleksandrov became a member of the Presidium of the Academy of Sciences and then Soviet minister of culture. As soon as Malenkov was replaced as chairman of the Council of Ministers in 1955, Aleksandrov lost his ministerial post.[8] Thus, the fluctuation of Aleksandrov's career matched almost precisely the vicissitudes of Malenkov's political life. Such biographical linkages in Soviet affairs are hardly ever fortuitous.

Therefore, when Malenkov had to kowtow before Zhdanov in the presence of the international communist elite by describing the Zhdanovite humiliation inflicted on his own associate Aleksandrov as the very essence of Soviet domestic policy, one is forced to conclude

---

*In 1948–49, briefly, Aleksandrov tried to "atone" by courting Voznesenskii; his opportunism, on the eve of the Leningrad Affair, was mistimed. See Appendix B.

that this episode marked the nadir of Malenkov's fortunes.*

Meanwhile, the conference marked a high point in blunt, outspoken Yugoslav declarations on issues of international revolution.† At Zhdanov's bidding, or at least with his encouragement, according to some accounts, the two Yugoslav delegates, Kardelj and Djilas, opened fire "from the left" at the leaders of the "revisionist" Italian Communist Party (represented by Luigi Longo and Eugenio Reale) and also upon the French Communist Party (represented by Jacques Duclos and Étienne Fajon).[9] The Yugoslavs demanded revolutionary militancy in Western Europe. In response to Duclos' comments defending the P.C.F.'s past policy of participation in the French Cabinet (a policy supported, if not originated, by Stalin), Zhdanov screamed at the French Communist, "While you are fighting to stay in the government, they throw you out."[10]

Following Zhdanov's speech, Djilas concentrated his fire at the P.C.F., and Kardelj at the P.C.I. Zhdanov and the Yugoslavs admonished the two West European parties that their wartime and postwar policies of collaboration with socialists, liberals, and Christian Democrats had been wrong. Rather than cooperating with the bourgeoisie, the P.C.F. and the P.C.I. were informed, they should have pursued aggressive policies such as Tito's, designed to bring about rapid communist acquisition of power. After Kardelj concluded, Zhdanov chimed in again, insisting that "You Italian comrades are bigger parliamentarians than de Gasperi [the Italian Christian Democratic leader] himself. You are the biggest political party, and yet they throw you out of government."[11]‡

Not only did the gathering witness complete operational and ideological cooperation between Zhdanov and the Yugoslav delegates, but the Titoists were granted every possible courtesy. The Yugoslav delegation was mentioned first in the key resolution and in all communiqués. The official journal of the organization (*For a Lasting Peace, For a People's Democracy*) was to be published in Belgrade, which was to serve

---

*Such spectacles by no means are rare in Soviet history: Bukharin, at the Comintern's Sixth Congress, was compelled to act as one of the spokesmen for the new "leftism," signifying, in effect, the end of his own "rightist" period of power. However, while Malenkov's (like Bukharin's) statements at the meeting flagrantly contradicted the posture with which he was identified before and after the gathering, Zhdanov and the Yugoslavs operated at the gathering in complete consistency with their past performance.

†Just as the Yugoslavs were lecturing West European Communists how to act, Dimitrov's Associate, V. Chervenkov (according to Eugenio Reale), was laying down the law to the East European Communists on how to monopolize and consolidate power.

‡In the previous parliamentary elections, the Christian Democrats actually had won almost twice as many votes as the P.C.I.

as the headquarters of the new organization. Until Yugoslavia was expelled from the Cominform in the summer of 1948, all issues of the journal displayed the name "Belgrade" prominently at the top of the front page. It is noteworthy that the Communist Party of Albania, which Moscow clearly regarded — judging by Stalin's comments — as a Yugoslav colony, was the only European ruling Communist party not represented at the meeting, even though two nonruling parties (the Italian and French) were present. (Admittedly, the P.C.I. and the P.C.F. were partially "in power" during 1944–47.)

Moreover, in line with the position of the Zhdanovites during the Varga "debate" (that colonial independence could result only from revolutionary struggle), none of the Asian Communist parties then cooperating with bourgeois parties were invited. Even the Chinese Communist Party (which, despite Stalin's instruction to seek a *modus vivendi* with Chiang Kai-shek, had resumed fighting and made considerable progress in its struggle against Chiang) was excluded. The other major Communist parties of Asia had been playing passive roles, presumably in accordance with Stalin's (and perhaps even Malenkov's) policy preferences.* However, as early as January 1947, the activist Yugoslavs had been arguing that:

> The clash of interests between the U.S.A. and Great Britain in all parts of the world is obvious and should not be underrated.[15]
>
> American finance capital . . . has not only enslaved, from an economic point of view, practically the whole of South America, the Philippines, China, etc., but it is reaching for the "independent" capitalist countries, more especially for the British and French colonies, Dominions and spheres of influence.[16]

---

*Malenkov had been working on the Commission for the Far East of the Politburo, a body that included no known Zhdanovites.[12] Thus, the policy of inviting none of the Asian Communist parties may have been due to the Zhdanov group's understandable desire to keep Malenkov's clients away from this gathering. Another explanation for the absence of any representatives of the Chinese Communist Party at the founding meeting of the Cominform may be linked to the disdain for Zhdanov that Mao was said to have expressed openly, according to Wang Ming (Ch'en Shao-yü). The latter claims that, at the 1935 Seventh Comintern Congress, Dimitrov publicly repeated a statement by Zhdanov to the effect that Wang's political "arrow had hit the target." Since Wang, in his capacity as Soviet "Gauleiter" supervising Chinese communist affairs, was constantly sniping at his rival, Mao, the latter apparently took exception to this statement, exclaiming subsequently that "dogmatists discharge arrows without any target." According to Wang, "these words were aimed against Comrade Zhdanov's remark."[13] Just as significantly, Stalin told Kardelj explicitly, in 1948, that he had not authorized Mao's postwar military offensive and, although he admitted that Mao's insubordination might have been justified by the results, he regarded the Chinese case as exceptional.[14]

The Americans have gained a firm foothold in the Arab countries and in the Mediterranean.[17]

Colonial liberation movements. . . are heading not merely toward political liberation from foreign imperialism but also . . .the victory of people's democracy. . . . That is why the imperialist circles must seek to lean more and more on the national bourgeoisie and the other reactionary circles in the colonies. . . . It therefore occurs more and more frequently that certain colonial or dependent countries obtain so-called "independence."[18]

What they [the Americans] need is the world and not just certain colonies; what they need are free routes across all frontiers because they are everywhere able to oust their capitalist rivals from the markets, and gradually from all economic positions. That is why the United States looks upon the British and French colonial systems as impediments and. . .is. . . coming out in favor of the independence of colonial countries.[19]

Kardelj, like Voznesenskii and Zhdanov, concluded that the internal contradictions within the "Anglo-American camp" simultaneously made for international confrontation and weakened the camp itself during such a conflict:

As things now stand, however, the democratic forces and freedom-loving nations of the world are faced with the fact of a consistent anti-democratic and imperialist policy, which is all the more violent as the fissures within the present imperialist system widen.[20]

The contrast between the Yugoslav attitude toward the newly independent states and the views expressed by Varga on this topic could hardly have been greater. The position that American imperialism was operating in opposition to the "traditional" (that is, British) imperialists was also taken by Zhdanov in his speech at the opening meeting of the Cominform:

Although she succeeded in recovering her colonies after the war, Britain found herself faced there with the enhanced influence of American imperialism, which, during the war, had invaded all the regions that before the war had been regarded as exclusive spheres of influence of British capital (the Arab East, Southeast Asia). America has also increased her influence in both the Dominions of the British Empire and in South

America, where the former role of Britain is very largely and
to an ever-increasing extent passing to the United States.[21]

At the Szlarska Poreba meeting, Zhdanov went on to promulgate
his famous "two-camp" doctrine, with the additional implication that
revolutionary activity was feasible now all the more since the enemy
camp was weakened by division within its own ranks. Moreover, on top
of the "contradictions" between the U.S. and the declining European
imperialists, the adversary was losing his hold on the colonial areas,
with Indochina and Indonesia already being "associated with" the communist camp, and India, Syria, and Egypt (King Farouk's Egypt!) being
"sympathetic to" Moscow.[22] On this point, there was some evident confusion and contradiction. On the one hand, Zhdanov wanted to demonstrate how large a portion of the world already was on his side, so as
to magnify (at least optically) the chances of success of any communist
offensive in 1947; on the other hand, both the Zhdanovites and the
Titoists had stressed that the colonial national bourgeoisie remained
a puppet of the West, that the ex-colonial states were not truly
independent, and that insurrections were needed there to establish
"people's democracies." Asian Communists must have wondered which
was to come first: support for an Indian Cabinet "sympathetic to"
Moscow, or an uprising against that government to establish a people's
democracy. (In the case of Egypt and Syria, the issue was less prob-
lematic, since the local Communist parties were fragmented and obscure
and since both Zhdanov and Tito tended to sympathize with the Arab
states.)

The treatment of the colonial question at Szklarska Poreba is not
the only issue requiring clarification. The attack in 1945 upon a naive-
ly "revisionist" Earl Browder had made sense from a "leftist" perspective; however, the broadsides fired against the P.C.F. and P.C.I. in
September 1947 require some further explanation.* Clearly, the French

---

*There is room for speculation why the revisionist element among American Commu-
nists was singled out for attack, while the revisionist British Communists, led by Harry
Pollitt, were exempted from major criticism. As viewed by the Voznesenskii group, since
the United States was the primary antagonist, it would be in Russia's interest to diminish
British hostility toward the USSR. Thus, it would be useful to have a British Communist
Party which did not antagonize British society in general, or the left wing of the ruling
Labour Party specifically. In that case, the Soviet leaders could play off (against
Washington) the British "imperialists," who were supposedly engaged in a postwar
struggle with the United States over the dwindling world market—a classical instance
of "exploiting" the "internal contradictions" within the capitalist system. On the other
hand, since the United States could be assumed now to be fundamentally antagonistic
to the USSR, a Communist group which "accepted the American system" or cooperated
with the "reactionary" American labor unions would be of little use to the Soviet Union.
Consequently, a return would be required to the classical leftist "united front from

and Italian parties constituted powerful electoral forces, which could be useful to the USSR since they had secured important positions in their respective countries' postwar governments; however, their political fortunes appeared to be declining, and this may have been a contributory factor in the attack upon Duclos and Togliatti.

In May 1947, the P.C.F. had been eased out of the Cabinet, and the October 1947 municipal elections were about to produce, not unexpectedly, major Gaullist gains.[23] At the same time, the prospects of left-wing rule in Italy had declined sharply in January 1947, when Togliatti's allies, the Italian Socialists, had split into two parties: the P.S.D.I. (Social Democratic Party), led by Giuseppe Saragat, which allied itself with the Christian Democrats; and the P.S.I., led by Pietro Nenni, which maintained close relations with the Communists.[24] The P.C.I., like the P.C.F., lost its Cabinet posts in May 1947.

The Yugoslav attack upon the P.C.I. made considerably more sense, from Belgrade's point of view, than its criticism of the P.C.F. Duclos, after all, had spearheaded the attack on Browder and, in 1947 (speaking to Browder's rival, William Z. Foster, and to the Canadian Communist leader, Tim Buck), he had expressed himself as follows:

> The decisive question for individual parties and governments is "Where do you stand?" Two great bodies of opinion are competing for men's support. It is not true to say that this contest is between the Soviet Union and the United States, because it is going on in every corner of the civilized world. It is true, however, that the contest comes into sharpest focus and is more obvious between the struggle for the new democracy of which the decisive centre is as yet in Europe and the struggle to re-stabilize imperialism, of which the decisive center is now in the United States.[25]

Thus, Duclos clearly identified the United States as the primary antagonist and made obeisance to "new democracy" in Eastern Europe, sentiments that should have pleased Zhdanov and Tito. It is true, as William O. McCagg, Jr., notes, that Duclos went on to say:

> It is quite clear that the one means by which the danger of a third world war can be eliminated is by giving us in Europe sufficient time to show that the tremendous human advances achieved by the people of the U.S.S.R. on the ruins of Czar-

---

below"—à la Sixth Congress of the Comintern—with a tightly disciplined, doctrinaire Communist party in the United States, as opposed to a mere "political association," as initiated by Browder.

ism can be surpassed by the people of Europe building on the ruins of Hitlerism.[26]

While this comparison conceivably might have rubbed Soviet chauvinists the wrong way, substantively it focused on the point made by Tito himself to the same delegation: "It isn't the atomic bomb that worries the peoples of Europe today, but the need to restore our industries."[27]

Of particular significance to the Belgrade leadership, one might have assumed, was the stance of the French and Italian Communist parties regarding the Trieste issue. On this matter, the P.C.F. adopted a pro-Yugoslav position,[28] at one point even publishing an attack upon the P.C.I. for a statement made by Togliatti in *L'Unità* (May 16, 1945) in which he emphasized, "We Communists affirm the Italian nature of Trieste."[29] (After being condemned at the Szklarska Poreba meeting, Togliatti modified his stand on Trieste somewhat, announcing, on March 27, 1948, that "We will solve the Trieste question in the spirit of peaceful collaboration, in agreement with Yugoslavia. . . . It will not take us more than forty-eight hours, and we will solve it to the full satisfaction of our national aspirations."[30] Togliatti did not see fit to explain just how such an agreement with Belgrade, express delivery, could be made compatible with Italian "national aspirations.")

Why, then, did the Yugoslav delegates assail the P.C.F.? One interpretation is offered by Professor Stephan Dedijer, brother of Tito's one-time biographer, Vladimir Dedijer; he maintains that Yugoslav bluster at the Cominform's founding meeting may be explained, in fair measure, by Belgrade's eagerness to assume unquestioned leadership among European Communist parties, second only to the CPSU itself. This required both a very vocal role at the conference and the "demotion" of the two largest parties, the P.C.I. and the P.C.F.[31]

A further look at the Browder Affair, however, raises additional perplexing questions concerning the motives for the treatment of the P.C.F. at Szklarska Poreba. More than a year prior to Duclos' attack upon Browder,[32] William Z. Foster had sent a letter condemning Browder's "revisionist" interpretation of the Teheran Conference[33] to Dimitrov, who, it may be recalled, was operating de facto, under the direction of Manuilskii and Zhdanov, as the head of the "Ghost Comintern." Dimitrov wrote back "advising" Foster to withdraw his opposition at that point.[34] However, the following April, Duclos was given the green light to publish his condemnation of Browder's policy, although, in fact, Browder had already printed his views concerning the possibility of changing the C.P.U.S.A. to a mere "political association" as early as 1944.[35]

The Duclos article of April 1945 contains several references to debates within the Political Committee of the C.P.U.S.A. during January–February of 1945. According to Joseph R. Starobin, at that time a prominent member of the American party, details of these events had been communicated only to Dimitrov (presumably in his capacity as nominal head of the "Ghost Comintern"). Thus, the ammunition for Duclos' attack against Browderism had to emanate from Moscow, presumably from the men running the formally disbanded Communist International, Zhdanov and Dimitrov.[36] Not surprisingly, Duclos' article echoed a refrain that was soon to become the trademark of the Zhdanov group. He accused Browder of "underestimation of the deepening of the crisis of world capitalism by the war." Thus, there is reason to suspect that Duclos' publication was related to the postwar ascendancy, in Moscow and elsewhere, of a group espousing a "forward" position on international affairs.

As late as his November 6, 1946, address at the Bolshoi, Zhdanov stressed that "the victory of the Labour Party in Britain, as well as the defeat of the reactionaries and the victory of the left-wing party bloc in France, constitute an important shift of these countries to the left."[37] It would appear, therefore that, less then eleven months prior to the founding meeting of the Cominform and the onslaught upon Duclos, the P.C.F. was still in Zhdanov's good graces.

As a result of the tongue lashings received at the Cominform meeting, the French and Italian Communist parties initiated massive strikes, demonstrations, and riots late in 1947 and early in 1948. These attempts to create polarization did not work to either party's advantage. The April 1948 parliamentary elections produced a major victory for de Gasperi, a result that may have been caused in part by a sudden switch by Togliatti toward a somewhat more pro-Yugoslav stand on the Trieste question.[38] Presumably, the P.C.I. assumed from the proceedings at Szklarska Poreba that Belgrade was now a power center which had to be respected.

The Yugoslav assault upon the P.C.I. and P.C.F. was to be used later against Belgrade.

> The Conference of nine Communist Parties established that each Party has an equal right to criticize any other Party when the work of the Italian and French Communist Parties was subjected to stern Bolshevik criticism.
>
> It is a known fact that the Italian and French comrades did not oppose the right of other Parties to criticize their mistakes. They have, on the contrary, borne the brunt of Bolshevik criti-

cism and benefitted from its conclusions.* Moreover, the Yugoslav comrades, like all the others, took advantage of the opportunity to criticize the mistakes of the Italian and French
comrades and did not consider, any more than did others, that
by so doing they were infringing the equality of those parties.

Why then are the Yugoslav comrades making this radical
change and demanding the liquidation of already established
precedents in the Informbureau? Because they believe that the
Yugoslav Party and its leadership ought to be placed in a priv-
ileged position, and that the statute of the Informbureau does
not apply to them; that, having the privilege of criticizing other
Parties, they should not themselves submit to the criticism of
other parties.[42]

---

*In fact, the P.C.F. publicly adopted the Cominform line on October 29, 1947, only
after Zhdanov's report was made public on October 22, more than three weeks after the
end of the conference in September. Ronald Tiersky surmises that this delay was due to
the desire of the Soviet leadership not to prejudice the outcome of the French municipal
elections, scheduled for October 19–26.[39] However, with early election returns revealing
disastrous results, there was nothing further to be lost by going public. "Self-criticism"
by Thorez (along the lines of the Zhdanovite attack on the P.C.F. during the September
Cominform meeting) was published in *L'Humanité*, on October 30, 1947.[40] Duclos also
adopted the new "leftist" position.[41]

11 CALCUTTA, 1948, AND BELGRADE'S GLOBAL ROLE

At least as far as India was concerned, the Yugoslavs seem to have played a major role as Zhdanov's representatives in clarifying the message of Szklarska Poreba,[1] both at the Second Congress of the Communist Party of India (C.P.I.), held in Calcutta during February and March of 1948, and apparently also at the Southeast Asia Youth Conference of the World Federation of Democratic Youth held in Calcutta, virtually simultaneously with the C.P.I. congress. By this time, the Yugoslavs already were under severe attack by Stalin; early in February, Djilas, Kardelj, and Bakarić had been excoriated by Stalin in Moscow for their alleged role in planning the abortive Balkan Federation. That they were willing, nevertheless, to take a most active, indeed a leading, role at such an important international Communist gathering as the one in Calcutta indicates that the Yugoslav Communist leaders continued to be under the impression that, despite their clash with Stalin, they would be permitted to implement the tasks of militant international leadership that Zhdanov had assigned to them in September of 1947. This, in turn, implies that they felt they still had a protector in the Soviet leadership. (The Tiul'panov speech of April 18, 1948, discussed earlier in this study, indicates that they had some basis for this belief.) That protector presumably had to be Zhdanov.

Belgrade's representatives to the Asian gathering arrived with a reputation for radicalism on the issues central to the two Calcutta meetings. A militantly revolutionary piece by Edvard Kardelj, under the title of *Problems of International Development: A Marxist Analysis*, had been published in Bombay early in 1947.[2] It referred to the "national bourgeoisie" in the colonies as a "reactionary" agent of foreign imperialism and was "predicting" (that is, espousing) the victory of "people's democracy" (or Communist takeover) through "unrest and turmoil in which more of less sharp clashes between the imperialist reactionary forces and the democratic anti-imperialist forces will take place."[3] In other words, the Yugoslavs were calling for the forcible overthrow, as an imperialist agent, of the same Indian government that Varga had defended as being genuinely independent.

The Yugoslavs must have sounded particularly authoritative in view of Zhdanov's Szklarska Poreba declaration, in which he had asserted that "a powerful movement for national liberation has been brought about" in Southern Asia. (By way of contrast, Zhdanov admittedly had stated also that India—not just the Indian Communist Party—"sympathized with" the Soviet camp.[4] This implied that events on the subcontinent, just a few weeks prior to Szklarska Poreba, had cast doubt on the validity of Zhdanovite objections to Varga's thesis that India was genuinely independent. Zhdanov faced something of a dilemma: if the adversary camp was as weak as his friends claimed, it would be "capitulationism" to delay a "national liberation" revolution that could deprive the West of its colonial "reserves"; on the other hand, to launch a communist assault upon the new government of the Indian Dominion, a member of the British Commonwealth, might weaken a secondary rival—and the beneficiary would be America, the "main antagonist." Thus, in some Zhdanovite hearts, the question seems to have arisen whether to tolerate for a while the South Asian status quo.* If these uncharacteristic vacillations confused the Asian parties concerned, the Yugoslavs were quick to dole out advice that would encourage the adoption of the revolutionary path.)

It appears that a major porportion of the Indian delegates to the Calcutta C.P.I. meeting did regard Kardelj's words as constituting an authoritative interpretation of the Cominform line. After listening to a speech in which he asserted that the democratic and socialist revolutions must "intertwine" and that it was necessary for the bourgeoisie as a whole to be attacked, [6] the C.P.I. replaced its general secretary, P. C. Joshi, with B. T. Ranadive, the major exponent of immediate insurrection in India. The C.P.I. then proceeded to embark upon an adventuristic path which continued, with marked lack of success and tactical zigzags, until its termination in 1951. Subsequently, Ranadive was to be purged for his failures, and the Yugoslavs, whom Ranadive had praised originally for "showing us the correct Marxist revolutionary path,"[7] were saddled with much of the blame for the C.P.I.'s decision in 1948 to embark upon its disastrous policy.[8] Ajoy Kumar Ghosh, who had sided originally with Ranadive but later swung over to the Joshi group,[9] stated that, with the exception of some of the Communist leaders who questioned the tactical advisability of maintaining a monolithic party structure, "we swallowed all that the Yugoslavs told us."[10] Moreover, similar advice apparently was given by the Yugoslav delegates,

---

*Conflict in this area was already in progress. Representatives from India, Burma, and China had participated in the August 1947 International Youth Festival in Prague, where "the terrible exploitation of youth in the countries dominated by imperialism" was denounced. Preparations for the Calcutta Conference (originally scheduled to be held in Indonesia) were made at the Prague Festival.[5]

Vladimir Dedijer and Radovan Zogović, to the Southeast Asia Youth Conference.[11] (The "youth" sections of various Communist parties, and the W.F.D.Y. as an organization, served as a cover for the paramilitary and covert security apparatus of the communist movement). Insurrections, ultimately unsuccessful, erupted during 1948 in Burma, Malaya, and Indonesia, all of which had been represented at the conference, which was attended by Yugoslav delegates as well. Thus, it is widely believed that the Yugoslavs advanced the same adventuristic line here as at the C.P.I. conference a few days later, in which case they have to shoulder a part of the responsiblity for a series of counterproductive Asian revolts.

After the Calcutta conferences, the All-Burma Peasants' Congress met at Pyinmana, where, allegedly, 300 thousand persons gathered for the occasion. The Yugoslav delegation (along with representatives from the Viet-Minh) attended and expressed the highly provocative sentiment that, with such an impressive turnout, the communists could hardly fail to stage an uprising. Thereupon, the Burmese Communist Party prepared a revolt.[12]

Dedijer, himself a participant, admitted years later and with very little remorse that the Yugoslav delegation had given extremist counsel at the Calcutta conference(s): In answering the question whether the Yugoslavs had "doled out adventuristic advice in Calcutta,"[13] while he insisted that, of course, the seeds of revolution existed before the Yugoslavs appeared, and that the final decisions were in indigenous hands, he stated that:

> All Southeast Asia was suffering from poverty and injustice; a target of imperialist advances, the people had no recourse but to defend themselves with their bare hands. It is true that we did not conceal our opinions. We had just emerged from the revolution, we were young and full of enthusiasm. We wanted to help all the world's oppressed to liberate themselves as soon as possible.[14]

It is significant that there is no indication of any surprise or doubt on the part of the participating Asian Communists that the Yugoslavs were the spokesmen of the international movement (that is, of Moscow). Far from being regarded as nationalist "loners," the leaders of the C.P.Y. obviously were viewed as the most fanatical among the "faithful". Their leading role at Calcutta was to constitute the last moment of glory for the Yugoslavs during this period; soon, Zhdanov and Tito, as well as virtually all of their closest associates, would disappear from center stage of the international communist movement, victims either of death, banishment, or expulsion. It seems unlikely that these developments were unrelated, in view of the affinities and cooperation between Zhdanovites and Titoists suggested by the evidence discussed in this study.

Upon returning to Belgrade, Dedijer and Radovan Zogović, another Yugoslav delegate to the recently concluded Calcutta conference, were to find that an article they had written for the Cominform journal, *For a Lasting Peace, For a People's Democracy*, had been deleted by the editor of the journal, Pavel Yudin, reportedly an M.V.D. agent.[15] This article, in addition to stressing the praiseworthy role of the Yugoslav party in shaping the revolutionary line at the C.P.I. Calcutta conference, reiterated that gathering's call for India's secession from the British Empire and for the formation of a government which would oppose the "Anglo-American Imperialists" and "form an alliance with the democratic states."[16] Clearly, Yugoslav actions in dictating policy to the Third World did not sit well with some quarters in Moscow.

It appears that Yugoslavia did not confine its leftist advice to Asian Communists. In October 1947, a major strike took place in Chile's coal district, threatening to paralyze the country's entire industrial network. The Chilean government, under President Gonzalez Videla, asserted that the strike had been coordinated (in conjunction with local Communists) by two Yugoslav diplomats, who were expelled summarily.[17] The Chileans released a lengthy document covering alleged links between the activities of the two Yugoslav officials and General Ljubomir Ilitch, who, according to this official account, established contacts with local Communists during a visit to Chile in November 1946.*

Belgrade denied these charges and reacted harshly, not only cutting off diplomatic relations with Chile, but also accusing the Videla government of operating "in the interest of the expansionist tendencies of certain powers" (in other words, the United States).[18]

While the Chilean government conceivably could have publicized the alleged plot for domestic reasons,[19] subsequent Yugoslav behavior at Calcutta lends considerable credence to Chile's claims.

The Yugoslavs apparently also were propagating their radical approach within Eastern Europe. Edward Taborsky, a former personal assistant to Beneš and a Czechoslovak envoy to Sweden in 1945–48 reports that, even prior to Prague's short-lived willingness to accept the Marshall Plan,

> Tito and his aids in particular did not bother to conceal their
> contempt for what they considered a lack of revolutionary zeal

---

*General Ilitch had come for Videla's presidential inauguration, who included three Communists in his government, though he ousted them later.

and determination on the part of Gottwald. "What's the matter with you," one of the prominent Yugoslavs once barked at me, mistaking me for a Party member. "Why do you keep collaborating with these bourgeois parasites? Why didn't you twist their necks as we have done?"[20]

Moreover, Tito spoke openly of Gottwald's disgrace for the Marshall Plan episode. Taborsky links Tito's comments to those by Zhdanov at the Szklarska Poreba Cominform meeting[21] (only a couple of months after the Marshall Plan affair), where, in evident reference to Gottwald, Zhdanov asserted:

> Some comrades understood the dissolution of the Comintern to imply the elimination of all ties, of all contact between fraternal Communist parties. . . .The communists even of countries that are bound together as allies hesitate to establish friendly ties. . . . [The] need for mutual consultation and voluntary coordination of action between individual parties has become particularly urgent at the present junction when continued isolation may lead to the slackening of mutual understanding and, at times, even to serious errors.[22]*

Gottwald was summoned to Moscow for a summer trip in 1948, although many Czechs assumed that his stay would be of a more permanent nature. However, he was to return to Czechoslovakia coincidentally with Zhdanov's political decline. Slansky, his rival, who allegedly had links with Beria, was purged in November 1952, immediately preceding the announcement of the Kremlin "Doctors' Plot," with its sinister implications for the future of Beria (and, perhaps, of Malenkov).

---

*Not surprisingly, Gottwald did not attend the Cominform meeting; instead, Czechoslovakia was represented by S. Bashtovansky (Baštovanský) and Rudolf Slansky.

12 STALIN'S POLITICAL PREDILECTIONS
Other "Actors"

This study does not contend, of course, that the leadership of the communist movement consisted only of Zhdanovites and Malenkovites; even less does it wish to minimize the role of the man called Joseph Stalin.

It must be emphasized again that Stalin, unlike his various lieutenants, had no reason to engage in factional games, not being a contender for the succession (to himself!) or having to demonstrate his supremacy; he alone, therefore, could afford to deal realistically with "concrete factors." Thus, the tendency of the competing cliques to ignore Western words and deeds was characteristic far less of Stalin himself, who could remain above the "debates," at least for some considerable time, being content to manipulate the factions against one another (until one side waxed so strong and arrogant that he perceived a threat to *his own* power). Not being compelled constantly to "score debating points," he could focus on "the real world," or give vent to his genuine predilections.

To be sure, there is considerable room for speculation concerning Stalin's personal preferences, during this period on matters of international strategy and tactics. However, a certain consistency of approach, temperament, and "style" of operation can be noted in his published booklets, speeches, letters, and interviews in the post–World War II era. His evaluations and pronouncements indicate a more cautious and less ebullient mode of conducting international affairs than was espoused by the Leningrad group and its allies. It is true, of course, that Stalin's well-known February 9, 1946, "preelection" speech sounded some of the themes identified in this study with Voznesenskii's position. However, while this address presented considerably harsher propositions than the West had become accustomed to hearing from its erstwhile ally (presumably it played a role, together with increasingly truculent Soviet behavior, in prompting Churchill's Fulton, Missouri, "Iron Curtain" speech of the following month), it was a shade less sanguine that the Voznesenskii-Zhdanov theses. Closer study, for instance, reveals that Stalin did not view the "third stage in the general crisis of capitalism" as being at all *imminent* (even leaving the barest suggestion of doubt that it was *inevitable*):

> The war was the inevitable result of the development of world economic and political forces on the basis of modern monopoly capitalism. Marxists have declared...that the capitalist system...harbors elements of general crisis and armed conflicts and hence, the development of world capitalism in our time proceeds not in the form of smooth and even progress, but through crises and military crises.
>
> The fact is that the unevenness of development of the capitalist countries *usually* leads *in time* [emphases added] to violent disturbance of equilibrium in the world capitalist countries...the group of capitalist countries which considers itself less well provided than others with raw materials and markets usually making attempts to alter the situation and repartition the "spheres of influence" in its favor by armed force. The result is a splitting of the capitalist world into hostile camps, and war between them.
>
> Perhaps military catastrophes might be *avoided* if it were possible for raw materials and markets to be periodically redistributed among the various countries in accordance with their economic importance, by agreement and peaceable settlement. But that is impossible to do under the *present* [emphases added] capitalist conditions of the development of world economy.
>
> Thus, the First World War was the result of the first crisis of the capitalist system...the Second World War was the result of a second crisis.[1]

Thus, while Stalin certainly postulated that further conflicts should be anticipated because of the deepening general crisis of world capitalism, he avoided specifying when this might occur, although he seemed to think it would not be soon; moreover, he indicated that such conflict should be expected primarily between members of the capitalist camp. The very optimistic operational conclusions, therefore, drawn by Voznesenskii and Zhdanov for communist strategy in the immediate postwar years, based upon a contemptuous underestimation of the adversary's strength, could not be regarded legitimately as the logical culmination of Stalin's work. On the other hand, Stalin's address also provided little substance at this stage for Varga's concept that development of state planning in capitalist states would provide a mechanism for long-term postponement of the onset of major crises.

Soon afterward, Stalin came out with statements that may have been designed to temper the harsher implications of his well-publicized February 9 speech. On March 14, 1946, the Soviet leader published a response in *Pravda* to Churchill's Fulton address, and while attacking Churchill's statements, Stalin distinguished carefully between Churchill and Britain's Labour government. He concluded, moreover, that "it was not probable" that Churchill and his allies would "succeed in organizing a new military expedition against Eastern Europe after World War II."[2] In effect, therefore, he minimized any perception of threat, on the part of the USSR, resulting from the Fulton episode (which has been played up as a watershed in some Western "revisionist" literature).

Early in 1947, *Bol'shevik*, apparently apropos of nothing in particular, published a letter by the Soviet leader, ostensibly in response to an inquiry by Professor (Colonel) Razin of the Frunze Military Academy, concerning the contemporary implications of the work of the great nineteenth-century military theoretician, Karl von Clausewitz.[3] William O. McCagg, Jr., views this letter as part of a discussion within the CPSU regarding the role of *partiinost*. He speculates that Stalin was attempting to inject a greater degree of flexibility into party ideology.[4]

While this explanation may accord with the somewhat less dogmatic approach characteristic of Stalin's statements during this period (at least in comparison with Zhdanovite terminology), there are far more immediate and practical implications, which relate more specifically to Clausewitz's concepts and terminology.

Stalin supports Clausewitz for being correct in asserting that "in certain unfavorable conditions, the retreat is as legitimate a form of struggle as the offensive" and emphasizes that

> Lenin required the support of Clausewitz here in order, once more, to convict the "Left" Communists* who did not recognize the retreat as a legitimate form of struggle.
>
> It follows that Lenin approaches the works of Clausewitz, not merely as a military man, but as a politician, and was interested in those questions in Clausewitz's work which demonstrate the connection of war with politics.[5]

Stalin, however, goes on to attack German military theory as a whole, apparently because of its general inclination to favor offensive strategies, citing as negative examples such names as Moltke, Schlieffen, Ludendorff, and Keitel (at least the first three of whom were associated with theories of offensive warfare).

---

*Was this a thinly veiled warning to the contemporary "Left Communists?"

Moreover, Stalin also criticized Clausewitz himself, to the extent that, in his work,

> there is no section on the *counter-offensive* (not to be confused with the counter-attack). I am speaking of a counter-offensive after a successful enemy offensive, which, however, has not produced decisive results, and, in the course of which, the defensive gathers its forces, passes to the counter-offensive and inflicts a decisive defeat on the enemy.[6]

This last passage is transparently self-serving, in that it supports Stalin's "policy" of "allowing" the Germans to drive to the outskirts of Stalingrad before the Red Army made an effective stand and ultimately initiated its great "counter-offensive." However, there may have been more to this passage than an attempted *ex post facto* justification of Stalin's disastrous German policy from 1939 onward:

> So far as Clausewitz in particular is concerned, he is, of course, outdated as a military authority. Clausewitz was, in fact, a representative of the *manufacturing* period of war. But now we are in the *machine* period of war. Undoubtedly, the machine period calls for new military theoreticians. It is ridiculous to take lessons now from Clausewitz.[7]

Is this not a reference to the imminent development of a Soviet nuclear capacity? Did "machine period" have the same meaning for Stalin as the term "modern weapons" had for Chinese leaders during Peking's internal "debate" of 1965–66, when that euphemism was employed frequently to avoid direct reference to nuclear weapons? (It may be recalled also that, for a number of years, the name "Ministry of Medium Machine Building" was the public cover for Soviet nuclear work.) Clearly, caution (not the penchant for the offensive of Clausewitz, or of Zhdanov) was the sensible posture to adopt for a power which had not yet broken the adversary's nuclear monopoly, but was rapidly (if secretly) closing the gap. Once the weapon had been tested and deployed in considerable quantities, the USSR would be in a far better position to assert itself. However, until then (at least, so a Stalin was likely to reason), it would be foolish to provoke the other side.*

---

*This consideration may have contributed to Beria's apparent predilection for a "softer" foreign policy (for example with respect to postwar Germany); since the M.V.D. was ultimately responsible for nuclear development (the "Atomic State Trust Number I"),[8] it made sense for him to support a line calculated to avoid conflict until his weapons project could be completed successfully. (It must be recalled, in this context, that no sooner had the USSR achieved its first nuclear test in 1949 than the thermonuclear contest began; the Soviet Union tested *that* weapon only in 1953, with deployment taking longer still.)

It may be significant that the letter to Razin was signed "I. V. Stalin, February 23, 1946" (only two weeks after the "preelection" speech). Thus, the letter was suddenly released a year after its original composition, or else, it was deliberately backdated. It would appear that some development between February 1946 and February 1947 convinced Stalin that it was appropriate either to resuscitate a letter written in the previous year or to compose a new document under a spurious date from the period immediately following the "preelection" speech. The apparent ascendancy of the Zhdanovites during 1946, culminating in the ostentatious display of factional supremacy at the 1946 October Revolution anniversary parade, well may have constituted that development. Stalin apparently intended the publication of the letter to act as a red light to halt the rapidly accelerating process of Zhdanovite predominance by attacking one of its most characteristic attributes, namely an offensive strategy vis-à-vis the West. The letter's date (whether spurious or genuine), following so closely Stalin's February 9, 1946, address, signalled that this speech had *not* been intended to act as a catalyst, precipitating Zhdanov's and Voznesenskii's subsequent campaign in favor of a militant, "forward" policy.

In this connection, it is worth recalling once more the fact that Voznesenskii's adversary, Varga, was neither subjected to unqualified condemnation at the conclusion of the "debate" concerning his work nor eliminated physically or even just professionally (in glaring contrast with Vavilov, who lost his life for opposing Lysenkoism, or, for that matter, with Voznesenskii and most of his Leningrad allies, who were liquidated after Zhdanov's death). This would indicate that Stalin was interested in preserving "rightist" elements, like Varga, to keep the Zhdanov-Voznesenskii faction "under fire."

Nor were these the only occasions in this period when Stalin expressed policy predilections along such lines. In September 1946, he responded to written questions by the journalist and author Alexander Werth, intended for publication on September 29 in the *Sunday Times* of London. However, the Soviet news agency TASS uncharacteristically released the responses immediately, presumably indicating Stalin's view of their significance. The bizarre result was that the *New York Times* published the text on September 25, four days earlier than London *Sunday Times* itself![9]

As for the reason why Stalin desired prominent publication, the following passage from his answers may provide a clue:

> It is necessary to distinguish sharply between the noise about a "new war," which is being carried on now, and the real danger of a "new war," which does not at present exist.[10]

Asked if he believed in the "friendly and lasting collaboration of the Soviet Union and Western democracy, despite the existence of ideological discord, and in friendly competition between the two systems," he retorted, "I do, unconditionally." In response to a question regarding the future of Soviet-British relations, he stated, "I really believe in the possibility of friendly relations between the Soviet Union and Great Britain."[11] When asked if he felt that "the quickest withdrawal of American forces in China is vitally necessary for peace," he answered merely, "Yes, I do," as laconic an answer as could be given, in light of the Chinese civil war. The lukewarm nature of the response becomes more evident in the context of his subsequent statement in the same "interview" that, "I do not doubt that the possibilities for peaceful collaboration not only will not decrease but can even increase. 'Communism in one country' is fully possible, especially in such a country as the Soviet Union."[12] This was hardly a ringing endorsement of Mao's attempts to create a second major communist state, since Stalin seemed to assume the continuation of a situation in which only a single communist power existed.* (In Stalin's mind, the East European "new democracies" apparently did not count, any more than Outer Mongolia.)

When asked about the "threat" posed by America's monopoly of atomic weapons, he responded:

> I do not believe the Atomic bomb to be as serious a force as certain politicians are inclined to regard it. Atomic bombs are intended for intimidating weak nerves, but they cannot decide the outcome of war, since atomic bombs are by no means sufficient for this purpose. Certainly monopolist possession of the secret of the atomic bomb does constitute a threat, but at least two remedies exist against it:
>
> a. Monopolist possession of the atomic bomb cannot last long.
>
> b. Use of the atomic bomb will be prohibited.[13]

This statement does not appear to support the argument of some revisionist historians that the American monopoly of the A-bomb constituted a provocation of the USSR and one of the main causes of the "Cold War". On the contrary, it would seem to be consistent with this

---

*Given Stalin's comment to Djilas to the effect that Mao had defied Soviet instructions to reach a modus vivendi with Chiang Kai-shek, Stalin was apparently as unenthusiastic as he sounded; see Djilas, *Conversations*, p. 182. Admittedly, Stalin was discussing the attainment of a socioeconomic stage, but its international context was evident.

study's interpretation of Stalin's letter to Razin, namely, that the Soviet leader was peddling a "soft" line (at least, as compared with the approach of the Zhdanov group) so long as America's monopoly of nuclear weapons existed. The Razin document also foreshadowed an outgrowth of the November 1949 Cominform meeting, two years after the publication of the letter, namely, the Stockholm Peace Appeal and the "Ban the Bomb" campaign.[14]*

Just prior to the founding meeting of the Cominform, Stalin delivered an address on the occasion of the eight hundredth anniversary of the Russian capital. Aside from the fact that a paean to Moscow could be viewed as an attempt to counter the sizable number of articles praising Leningrad (particularly in party educational journals),[15] the substance of the "toast" to Moscow was significant, too:

> Finally, Moscow's service consists of the fact that it is the champion of the struggle for durable peace and friendship among nations, the champion of the struggle against the incendiaries of a new war. For the imperialists, war is a most profitable enterprise. It is not surprising that the agents of imperialism are trying to provoke a new war in one way or another.[16]

Stalin's statement that "the imperialists" were striving for a war "one way or another" left open the question whether armed force was to be used against the USSR, or whether, in line with Stalin's own concepts and the Leninist thesis regarding "the internal contradictions" among imperialist states, the Western powers would fight one another (perhaps to pry away colonies from each other, in an era of dwindling markets). By contrast, no doubt was left by Zhdanov, at the Szklarska Poreba meeting a couple of weeks later, that the Soviet Union and the "new democracies" were the main target of the threat of "imperialist war":

---

*This development made a great deal of sense from Stalin's viewpoint. The announcement of the Soviet test of a nuclear device was bound to cause anxiety in the West. Once it was known that the Soviet Union had mastered nuclear technology, but, in all likelihood, had not yet deployed an array of nuclear weapons, there would be considerable incentive for the West (so a Stalin would have thought) to launch a preemptive attack before Moscow could proceed with deployment. Consequently, the heavy moral and political weight of the Peace Appeal was brought to bear upon tender Western consciences. Moreover, given the quantitative superiority of Soviet theater forces in Europe after the "rush for the boats" of American troops at the end of the War, the elimination of the American nuclear umbrella (even had it been linked to the abandonment of the Soviet nuclear program) would have altered decisively the military balance, and resulting political perceptions, in Europe. For instance, if the United States had eliminated its nuclear arsenal, would Stalin still have hesitated to challenge the American airlift during the Berlin blockade of 1948–49?

The principal driving force of the imperialist camp is the U.S.A. Allied with it are Great Britain and France. . . .

The cardinal purpose of the imperialist camp is to strengthen imperialism, to hatch a new imperialist war, to combat socialism and democracy, and to support reactionary and antidemocratic, profascist regimes and movements everywhere.

In pursuit of these ends, the imperialist camp is prepared to rely on reactionary and antidemocratic forces in all countries, and to support its former adversaries in the war against its wartime allies.

The antifascist forces comprise the second camp. This camp is based on the USSR and the "new democracies."[17]

Even after the USSR joined the exclusive club of states with nuclear weapons, Stalin's doctrinal pronouncements remained cautious. His major work, *Economic Problems of Socialism in the U.S.S.R.*, published in the fall of 1952, has been interpreted by William O. McCagg, Jr., primarily as the assertion of a dogmatic Marxist position.[18] It seems, however, that a less theoretical problem concerned Stalin. One of the key sections of this (his last) work is part 6, which deals with "the question of the inevitability of wars between capitalist countries." It commences boldly:

Some comrades hold that, owing to the development of new international conditions since the Second World War, wars between capitalist countries have ceased to be inevitable. They consider that the contradictions between the socialist camp and the capitalist camp are more acute than the contradictions among capitalist countries; that the U.S.A. has brought the other capitalist countries sufficiently under its sway to be able to prevent them from going to war among themselves and weakening one another.[19]

These comrades are mistaken. . . . It would be mistaken. . . to think that these countries [Western Germany, Britain, France, Italy, and Japan] will tolerate the domination and oppression of the U.S.A. endlessly. [emphases added][20]

According to Stalin, "it follows from this that the inevitability of wars between capitalist countries. . . generally remains in force."[21]

He also asserts that:

the U.S.A. and Britain assisted Germany's recovery [from

World War I]. . .with a view to setting a recovered Germany against the Soviet Union, to utilizing her against the land of socialism. *But Germany directed her forces in the first place against the Anglo-French-American bloc* [emphasis added] and when Hitler Germany declared war on the Soviet Union, the Anglo-French-American bloc, far from joining with Hitler Germany, was compelled to enter into a coalition with the USSR.[22]

Unmistakably, Stalin's work indicated that the USSR was in no danger of attack by the West. On the contrary, when the imperialists turned upon one another, the Soviet Union would be in a position to choose which side to support.[23] The clear implication of Voznesenskii's work and of Zhdanov's speeches of November 6, 1946, and at the September 1947 Cominform session, by contrast, was that, despite the contradictions weakening the "Anglo-American camp" from within, the Soviet Union faced an unavoidable adversary in the United States, which would and indeed must be confronted. While nearly five years had elapsed since Stalin's September 1947 Moscow anniversary "toast," his last work seems to demonstrate that Stalin's imprecision on the earlier occasion concerning the nature and circumstances of a new war was "no accident".

Perhaps most significant among Stalin's public pronouncements during this period, viewed in the context of the factional struggle within the Soviet leadership, was the interview he granted to the Republican presidential aspirant, Harold Stassen, on April 9, 1947. The importance of this episode related to its substance only in part. Perhaps as significant as the gist of Stalin's responses was a subsequent controversy over the validity of the transcript released by Stassen, almost a month later, on May 3.[24] This text revealed Stalin playing a passive role, asking Stassen about the possibility of a postwar economic crisis in the West, with Stassen replying, "I believe we can regulate our capitalism and stabilize our production and employment at a high level without any serious crisis." Stalin pursued this line of questioning further: "Magazine analysts and the American press carry open reports to the effect that an economic crisis will break out." Stassen replied, "Yes, there were those reports. . . but they were wrong. The problem is one of leveling off at high production and stabilizing without having an economic crisis." Stalin requested clarification: "The regulation of production?" Stassen responded, "The regulation of capitalism. . ." Stalin asked, "What about businessmen? Will they be prepared to be regulated and restrained?" Stassen conceded that "some will have objections,. . . but they understand that the 1929 depression should not be repeated and they understand better, now, the necessary regulations concerning business. It requires a careful amount of fair regulation and wise decisions and prompt action by the government." Stalin concurred fully, "That is true."

Thus, the Soviet leader, by playing the role of interviewer rather than interviewee, elicited a response from Stassen that supported the essence of Varga's approach—rejected unequivocally by his critics in the Voznesenskii-Zhdanov faction—namely, the Hungarian economist's contention that as an outgrowth of wartime practices, state regulation of the capitalist economy had become feasible in the West.* Moreover, lest there be serious doubt that Stalin was condoning Varga's line, the Soviet leader himself, again in the form of a quasi-question, made bold predictions concerning the increase in America's exports to be expected during the postwar period (a key issue in the context of the "debate" whether the West would be affected soon by a classical capitalist crisis of overproduction). Stalin suggested that "about 10 percent of American production was exported before the war, and now South America is also a market. . . . So United States exports will increase to 20 per cent, is that not correct?" Stassen replied affirmatively, but added "I think 15 per cent,"27 thus downgrading somewhat Stalin's prognostication. In the previous year, Varga had stated that the United States "desired" expansion of its exports and, during the postwar period, would enjoy a "great advantage over Great Britain in the race for world markets,"28 a factor he cited as one reason why America's vast increase of production need not lead to a crisis. Stalin, therefore, was enlarging, in effect, upon Varga's predictions.

Following Stassen's release of his transcripts of the interview (pub-

---

*In a conversation with the United States ambassador to Moscow, Walter Bedell Smith, Stassen remarked that Stalin was very interested in the question of the possible approach of an American economic crisis. In reporting to Washington, Smith remarked that the answer to this question appeared to dictate "tactics regarding Germany, Austria, Korea, and other friction points."25 However, he appeared unaware that this question constituted a major point of contention in the rapidly developing ideological "debate" through which the factional struggle between two competing groups of Stalin's potential successors manifested itself. Thus, the response concerning this doctrinal issue could determine not only international strategy, but also *who* would be allowed to implement Soviet global policy. Had he realized that, in less than a month, a closed "conference" was to be held to "criticize" Varga's book (the Soviet version of the Stalin-Stassen interview was published in *Pravda* on May 8th, the day after the first session of that conference), Smith might have grasped the significance of this episode in terms of Soviet elite politics.

The State Department, in fact, did take note of the subsequent equivocation in the Soviet media regarding the authenticity of Stassen's text, but dismissed the matter, since "the versions, although differing, did not show serious discrepancy."26 However, American diplomats should have comprehended that it was precisely this lack of apparent substantive discrepancy which gave significance to the entire affair; why did Moscow quibble over mere semantic nuances, unless the whole issue had particular importance?

lished May 4, 1947), a peculiar sequence of events took place. For the next few days, there was no reaction from Moscow, which, in itself, was noteworthy. However, on May 8, *Pravda* released its version of the interview, in *paraphrased* form,* concluding with a paragraph which asserted that the text published by the American press was full of "arbitrary alterations and inaccuracies." This must have baffled the Soviet reader, since the American text of the conversation was not published, nor were the alleged inaccuracies specified in the *Pravda* comment.[29] On the same day, however, Moscow Radio broadcast a report (in English) which stated that "a number of *deliberate* alterations and unprecise [*sic*] points" were contained in the text released by Stassen. Moscow Radio gave several examples of alleged mistranslation, most notably claiming that the term Stassen and Stalin had discussed was not "regulation" but should have been translated more accurately as "control."[30]

Unless considered within the context of the "critique" that had been launched only one day earlier of Varga's view that bourgeois states had learned, in wartime, to *regulate* their economies and might be able to continue this practice during the postwar period, Moscow Radio's semantic distinction would seem a pointless exercise in pedantry. (At the time, only a small group of insiders could have known of the previous day's proceeding against Varga, which was not to be publicized for four months, with an actual transcript appearing in print only after six months.) The Russian term that Moscow Radio claimed had been mistranslated was *regulirovanie*, closely related to the German *regulierung*,† whereas the Russian word for "control" or "administration" in fact is *upravlenie*.

Stassen dismissed Moscow's charges, stating that he still had in his

---

*This contrasted with the treatment given to the other interviews Stalin granted during this period, which *Pravda* printed in *transcript* form; see Stalin's March 13, 1946, "interview with a *Pravda* correspondent," *Pravda*, March 14, 1946 (*Sochineniia*, vol. 16, pp. 35–43), or his December 21, 1946, interview with Elliott Roosevelt, appearing in *Pravda*, January 23, 1947 (ibid., pp. 66–74). Moreover, even when Stalin responded to a set of questions submitted by letter, the texts were printed in transcript form, with the Russian word for question, *vopros*, preceding each of the questions and with Stalin's responses preceded by the Russian word for reply, *otvyet*, thereby simulating the transcript of a news conference or interview. (See, for example, Stalin's response to questions by Eddy Gilmore of the Associated Press, *Pravda*, March 23, 1946, ibid., pp. 45–46; his response to Alexander Werth's letter of September 17, 1946, *Izvestia*, September 24, 1946, ibid., pp. 53–56; his response to Hugh Bailey's questions of October 23, 1946, *Pravda*, October 30, 1946, ibid., pp. 57–63; and his "response to a *Pravda* correspondent," *Pravda*, October 28, 1949, ibid., pp. 105–07.)

†The French Communist Party published the Stassen interview in transcript form, duly noting the controversy over the text, and taking care to translate the Russian word *regulirovanie* into the French *contrôle*, rather than *reglementation*, which would have been closer to the original term.[31]

possession the original notes of the interview, in Russian.[32]* Stassen certainly could have had no particular interest in tampering with the text, on an issue known to exist, at the time, only in the most exalted Soviet circles; indeed, had he really been to blame, why didn't *Pravda* follow the usual practice with Stalin interviews and publish the full transcript, rather than a vague paraphrase?

It seems suspiciously as if whoever handled the publication of the interview in the USSR was attempting to obviate the possibility that it might be viewed and quoted as "the gospel according to Stalin." Moreover, the editors of the English-language broadcast and the French translation actually went so far as to tamper with the text. This raises serious questions concerning Stalin's role in these curious activities. It would have been quite out of character for him to make statements, in an interview expected to be published, and not to say precisely what he wanted others to hear. Moreover, Stalin was renowned for saying no more than prudence dictated. In this respect, one should note Wolfgang Leonhard's startled comment, upon listening to Stalin's speech of July 3, 1941 (his first public statement after the German surprise attack), that it presented a shocking departure from the deliberate, measured manner in which Stalin habitually spoke.[33] This speech, coming during the biggest political trauma in Stalin's career, clearly was *the* exception; a very precise if somewhat stolid Stalin constituted the rule.†

Was it probable that a proverbially calculating Stalin, notorious for planning and scheming years ahead, changed his mind during the three-week interval following the interview, moreover on an issue we now know to have been of the greatest significance? If the Soviet leader, on the other hand, said precisely what he intended, as usual, and experienced no unaccustomed change of heart, then why the subsequent prevarication? Who was behind this maneuver? Why did the *Pravda* paraphrase differ from Moscow Radio's foreign-language broadcast and the French translation? Could anyone have presumed to

---

*The author of this book ascertained in telephone conversations (July 10, 1980) with Mr. Harold Stassen and Mr. Robert Matteson, who accompanied him in Moscow, that the English text of the interview was derived from Mr. Matteson's notes of the English translation provided during the interview by the *Soviet* interpreter, V. N. Pavlov. A brief meeting took place with Pavlov, subsequently, for the purpose of comparing notes. The author obtained that text (032/5-247, United States of America, General Services Administration, National Archives and Records Series); it confirms that the operative term, in face, was "regulation."

†The memoirs attributed to Khrushchev state emphatically that "right up to his very death, Stalin could express himself clearly and concisely. His formulations were short, comprehensible, and to the point. In this regard Stalin was possessed of a tremendous power. ...Everyone who knew Stalin admired this talent." Talbott, *Khrushchev Remembers*, p. 275.

"edit" Stalin for "foreign communist consumption," thereby tempering the pro-Varga implications of his interview? Was someone willing to take a chance by assuming that Stalin personally would not check on foreign language broadcasts and translations, particularly, if he had returned to Sochi after the May Day Parade? The same person(s), however, obviously could not risk actually altering Stalin's words in *Pravda* (where, consequently, even in paraphrase, one could not altogether avoid the term *regulirovanie*, thus weakening, in effect, Moscow Radio's assertion and the "corrected" French text).

Was there a group that had to fear—at the very time when it was assailing its adversaries through the device of a "critique" of Varga—being undermined and threatened by the publication of a statement from Stalin himself, not merely supporting Varga's main thesis, but, if anything, extending that thesis even further? Might not such a faction limit the "fallout" of this episode (including probable massive defections of supporters unwilling to speak up in apparent opposition to Stalin's own words), if it confined publication in *Pravda* to a mere paraphrase, so that Stalin could not be quoted verbatim (while also warning the cognescenti by adding a note to the effect that Stalin's statement had been distorted abroad)? The foreign Communists (Zhdanov's special bailiwick), who had been exposed to the *New York Times* text, however, had to be told much more specifically just which passages were taboo, a task that was accomplished quite simply by citing examples of "mistranslation." (This device obviously would not do for *Pravda*, printed in the language in which Stalin had given the interview.)*

*It may be objected that the thrust of the questions discussed here implies that a very dangerous game was being played by the Zhdanovites, indeed little short of a conspiracy. However, we do possess some material indicating that very possibility. In this context, it is useful to recall the passage, cited earlier, concerning Voznesenskii's reaction upon hearing that, in the aftermath of the Leningrad Affair, he had been sentenced to be shot: "Voznesenskii . . . spewed hatred against Leningrad. He cursed the day he had set foot in the city. . . . He said that *Leningrad had already had its share of conspiracies . . . from Biron to Zinoviev*" (emphasis added).

Voznesenskii had started on the ladder of promotion when appointed, through Zhdanov's influence, to the Chairmanship of the Leningrad City Planning Commission (see p. 28), and the quotation implies that this was when he became involved in the "conspiracies." The reference to Biron (held responsible for the supremacy of the "German Faction," which implemented a purge in the city on the Neva, during Empress Anna's reign, called the "Bironovshchina")[34] leaves little doubt *who* was being blamed for the "conspiracies." The mention of Stalin's old adversary, Zinoviev, indicates *whom* they were said to be threatening. No indication was provided that Voznesenskii's outburst was not spontaneous or had been the result of "physical measures."

While, admittedly, the source (*Khrushchev Remembers*) has not been fully authenticated, there are only two serious possibilities: either these are genuinely Khrushchev's "memoirs," smuggled out somehow, or they were "ghost-written" by the KGB, acting on behalf of the Brezhnev regime. Whichever is correct, Voznesenskii has been treated as

Whatever the precise circumstances of the affair, the interview given to Stassen appears to throw revealing light upon the question how Varga could survive an increasingly virulent campaign against him, without even being arrested at any stage, despite the status and power of his critics. (Indeed, it was the top stratum of his adversaries that ended by being shot.) The simple fact is that, at the very time when Varga was being assailed, Stalin demonstrated how close to Varga's thesis his own position was (irrespective of which "translation" one may see fit to accept).

In this context, particular significance is assumed by a tribute to Stalin that Malenkov published on December 21, 1949, on the occasion of the Soviet leader's seventieth birthday, three weeks after the November 1949 Cominform meeting that initiated the "Peace Movement."[35] Malenkov resuscitated the Stassen interview (at a time when the Leningrad Affair, that is, the annihilation of the Voznesenskii-Zhdanov faction, had just been concluded), citing a long passage *in transcript form* (complete with quotation marks), in which Stalin asserted that cooperation between peoples living under different systems was possible.[36] Despite *Pravda*'s publication, in 1947, of a mere paraphrase and its failure to produce the transcript of the meeting, Malenkov, two and a half years later, clearly saw no reason to refrain from citing the text. By publishing a direct quotation from the Stassen interview, Malenkov, *ex post facto*, removed the intentional ambiguity that had been created with regard to the validity of the text and the doctrinal propriety of citations from it. It seems reasonable to view Malenkov's move as a logical consequence of the elimination of the Leningrad group. He could feel unencumbered now to promote, however cautiously, the more circumspect, less sanguine, "rightist" Varga line sustained in the Stassen interview (and enjoying, it would

a hero, both by Khrushchev and his successor, and neither had the slightest reason to besmirch his reputation, as indeed the rest of the book shows quite clearly. Why, therefore, would either wish to include what is in essence an admission that there really may have been a Leningrad "conspiracy," organized by the Zhdanovites, especially since this implicitly eases the burden of guilt on Malenkov and Beria (both loathed by Khrushchev and Brezhnev alike) for having wiped out the Zhdanovites in the Leningrad Affair? While it is true that the impact of Voznesenskii's outburst is weakened somewhat by Khrushchev's comment that "obviously he had lost his sanity," this observation is related not to the "conspiracies," but, rather strangely, to the following "symptom" of irrationality: "It's nonsense to talk about Biron and Zinoviev in one breath." (Actually, as has been indicated, in Aesopian terms it made rather good sense.) Later in the same source (*Khrushchev Remembers*, p. 340), Khrushchev quotes a subsequent defendant, without questioning his sanity in any way, as using words almost identical to Voznesenskii's: "After his sentence had been announced by the court, Merkulov cursed the day and the hour when he first met Beria. He said Beria had led him to this end." Altogether, in the light of the considerations mentioned, one is left with the uneasy feeling that one cannot simply dismiss Voznesenskii's "last words."

appear, Malenkov's protection, perhaps from the end of the war onward).

In should not be inferred, of course, from this reconstruction of the Zhdanov-Malenkov contest, that there were no intermediate positions. Quite the contrary, there is no evidence that such personalities as Bulganin, Khrushchev, Mikoyan, Kaganovich, and Molotov were committed to one side or the other. Occasionally, it may have seemed to be in the interest of such "third parties" to tilt in the direction of one or another of the competing factions: for example, when Mikoyan backed Voznesenskii in attacking Malenkov's approach to reparations from Germany. The policies of these "independents" present highly complex questions. Illustrative of intermediate positions was Molotov's November 6, 1947, speech commemorating the thirtieth anniversary of the October Revolution.*

On the one hand, Molotov praised the efforts of the Leningrad leadership, both during the war, for its evacuation effort, and afterward, for its accomplishments in restoring the economy;[37] recognized the United States, in essence, as the principal antagonist;[38] and showed due deference to the "new democracies—Yugoslavia, Poland, Romania, Bulgaria, Czechoslovakia, Hungary, Albania."[39] (This order was not quite in line with the Zhdanovite position, since Bulgaria was listed fourth, behind Romania, a non-Slav country. The very mention of Albania, which had not been represented at the recent Cominform meeting—almost certainly as a favor to the Yugoslavs, who were in the process of taking over Albania—was enough to distinguish the list from the Zhdanov line.) However, while some of Molotov's points at least approximated the Zhdanovite line, he ignored the cultural purge being implemented under Zhdanov's aegis, repeatedly referred to Soviet (rather than Russian) patriotism, as distinct from the Great-Russian nationalist emphasis of the Leningrad group, and inveighed against the division of Germany into two embryonic states (although Colonel S. I. Tiul'panov, Zhdanov's man in the Soviet zone, was striving in effect to attain precisely that goal.[40]†

---

*This address is particularly significant since it was delivered soon after the founding meeting of the Cominform and well before the January 28, 1948 *Pravda* article attacking Tito's and Dimitrov's proposed East European federation. Thus, it coincided with a period when Zhdanov and his cohorts still were occupying a preeminent position.

†In fact, as the main Soviet representative at postwar Allied conferences dealing with Germany, Molotov had become identified publicly with a primarily reparations—oriented approach, which, this study has attempted to demonstrate, was opposed adamantly by the Tiul'panov-Zhdanov faction. The Soviet foreign minister repeatedly claimed ten billion dollars in reparations from Germany.[41] Moreover, he demanded major deindustrialization of that country, invoking the Potsdam formula of "fifteen per cent of such industrial equipment, in the first place from the metallurgical, chemical and

Thus, Molotov, to a limited extent, paid homage to certain aspects of the Zhdanov line, at that time still dominant, while managing on other issues to maintain a position that distinguished him clearly from the Zhdanovites without, however, appearing to join the camp of their opponents. This centrist approach reflected rather accurately Stalin's own maneuvers, as tended to be the case during most of Molotov's career.

Molotov, of course, was behaving with his usual degree of circumspection; an "independent" himself, he had navigated carefully between the two major factions for almost a decade. Between the fall of Paris and Hitler's invasion of the USSR, he, like Zhdanov, was increasingly treated as an obvious scapegoat for the miscalculation that the pro-German line was proving to have been. After June 22, 1941, however, he found ways of putting distance between Zhdanov and himself. According to Antonov-Ovseyenko's material, Molotov joined Malenkov and Beria during the period of Stalin's apparent breakdown to run the country and its defense, and it "was they who suggested to Stalin the idea of sending Zhdanov to Leningrad." At that time, "Molotov barely concealed his hostility toward Zhdanov. . . . For Zhdanov the fall of Leningrad would have meant the end of everything. If the city surrendered, the triumvirate of Molotov, Malenkov, and Beria would totally supplant him in the Master's favor." Later in the summer of 1941, Molotov joined Malenkov in heading a committee of investigation into the situation on the Northern Front; as a result of their adverse report, Zhdanov suffered a form of demotion. With Malenkov's decline and Zhdanov's ascent to brief hegemony in 1946–47, Molotov, as has been shown, maneuvered back into a more centrist position while avoiding the type of commitment to the Leningrad Group that would have brought him down with the Zhdanovites when finally they crashed (as was inevitable).

---

machine manufacturing industries, as is unnecessary for the German peace economy," to be shipped from the Western zones to the USSR, in exchange for various commodities, including food, coal, and petroleum, as well as an additional "ten percent of such industrial capital equipment as is unnecessary for German peace economy," to be shipped from the Western zones to the Soviet administration, "without payment of exchange of any kind at all."[42] To be sure, this was to be extracted at *West* Germany's expense; however, it would be *additional* to the de facto unrestricted removal of materials from the Soviet zone, to meet Moscow's demand for ten billion dollars in reparations (a figure not accepted by the West). Molotov, of course, was cleaving to positions developed from Stalin's claims at Yalta and Potsdam. Moreover, in line with Stalin's adage that "Hitlers come and go, but the German nation, the German state, remains, " Molotov's demands were pursued on the basis of the assumption that German economic and political unity would not be destroyed.[43]

13 THE "CROWN PRINCE"

Apart from the Zhdanovshchina itself, the 1946 celebrations of the October Revolution anniversary, the Varga affair, and the events surrounding the founding of the Cominform, there were other ostentatious displays of power by Zhdanov and his associates which would have been viewed as arrogant, provocative, and dangerous by a mind less suspicious than Stalin's (who, even if ailing and absent from Moscow for long periods, was very far from "retired," and understandably had a watchful eye kept on the activities of his "comrades in arms").

The Zhdanovites seem to have taken particular liberties concerning Finland, which apparently they regarded as Zhdanov's fiefdom. Zhdanov's emissaries there (in charge originally of supervision of the Finnish armistice), unabashedly began to refer to him as "our crown prince" in front of Western press representatives.[1] Soon, Zhdanov commanded almost as much attention in the Western press as Stalin himself, including an appearance on the cover of *Time* magazine (December 9, 1946). Moreover, in Finland, Zhdanov is reported to have acted almost completely on his own (taking little trouble to coordinate his activities with the other Soviet leaders) in encouraging attempts by the Finnish Communist Party (S.K.P.) to exploit the trials of alleged "war criminals" to seize power.[2] The Finnish Communists succeeded during April 1946 in forging the "Big Three Agreement" between the S.K.P., the Finnish Social Democratic Party, and the Agrarian Party. This development, quite unlike the coalition agreements in Western Europe, enabled the S.K.P. to establish a Cabinet based on a Soviet-oriented foreign policy and a domestic policy involving mass purges within the civil service, army, and police of persons deemed by Moscow to be responsible for Finland's wartime policy of military cooperation with the Germans.[3] Apparently in an effort to "restrain" Zhdanov (probably because Finland, since the Winter War of 1939–40, had been under watchful Western eyes, as a symbol of resistance to Soviet bullying), Stalin, in a show of "concern" over Finnish self-determination, sent the Leningrad leader a letter containing hints that Zhdanov may have been pressing for outright Soviet military intervention:

Finland cannot have the Communists in political power unless this is the wish of its workers and peasants. The Soviet army has no concern with the internal political conflict in Finland. This people has the right to complete and absolute independence.[4]

Thus, Zhdanov was not permitted to buttress his Finnish bailiwick by turning it into an overtly communist state.*

In 1948, Stalin accused the Yugoslav leadership of "unbounded arrogance" in one of his more credible charges (in the sense that it may have reflected genuinely what he felt).[5] This would not have been an unreasonable characterization of the Zhdanovite faction as a whole and, particularly, of its leader. The official United States representative in Finland, Maxwell M. Hamilton, reported to the secretary of state, for instance, that in a conversation on March 13, 1945, Zhdanov had told him "that, tactically, Leningrad's defense was more important than that of Stalingrad, and was principally responsible for the Red Army's ability to push into East Prussia."[6]

Such a boast, in front of a foreign diplomat, moreover, constituted an astounding indiscretion, since Stalingrad, of course, had been made *the* great symbol of Soviet determination and fighting capability, and because it was identified so closely with Stalin himself (and with Marshal Zhukov's planning). The protracted defense of besieged Leningrad, on the other hand, was linked with Zhdanov personally (although, in fact, here too Zhukov's military role had not been insignificant).

Zhdanov probably resented Zhukov's intervention, in September 1941, when the military leader descended upon Leningrad to reorganize its defenses. As mentioned earlier, in June 1945 at a press conference in Berlin, Zhukov referred proudly to his own role in the defense of Leningrad, at which point Andreii Vyshinskii added, "Yes it was Zhukov who saved Leningrad."[7] Perhaps (at Stalin's instigation?) Zhukov had been informed of Zhdanov's imprudent boasts and was attempting to ensure that he could not monopolize credit for ultimate victory in the north. This was a very serious matter for Zhdanov; as indicated in this study, his role in the defense of Leningrad provided a measure of atonement for egregious political errors in connection with the ill-fated Ribbentrop-Molotov Pact and the Winter War against Finland. (Zhukov, by contrast, had so many victories to his credit that reference to Leningrad was somewhat gratuitous, and he provided Zhdanov with a major incentive for having him removed from the public eye—perhaps part of the reason for Zhukov's sudden demotion in 1946.)

---

*A different interpretation of this episode is presented by Kevin Devlin (in Hammond, *Anatomy*, pp. 437–47).

Apart from indiscretions in front of Western representatives, Zhdanov apparently started to become altogether too boastful within the confines of the "communist family" itself. During one of Stalin's illnesses, Zhdanov reportedly translated a quotation from Schiller to a group of Spanish Communists: "The King is absolute when he does our will."[8] If this comment filtered back to Stalin, it does not require much insight to imagine what his reaction would have been. To be widely acknowledged as the "crown prince" of the Soviet Union was hardly a prescription for a brilliant and long future under Stalin, either politically or physically. Zhdanov's predecessor as party leader of Leningrad, Sergeii M. Kirov, who also had come to be regarded widely as Stalin's heir-presumptive, was killed under mysterious circumstances (with subsequent evidence suggesting collusion in his murder in the highest places),[9] just as Zhdanov was to die suspiciously soon after being demoted; a publication, five years later, stated in so many words that he had been murdered. In both cases, the persons accused of the murder (the "Left Opposition" and the "Kremlin Doctors," respectively) were not the culprits, but this in no way disproves that the victims *were* murdered. In both instances, the demise of the "crown prince" triggered a bloody purge of his friends, although the Leningrad Affair was less extensive than the purge of True Stalinists in the 1930s, which followed the annihilation of the Left and Right Oppositions. Kirov, unlike Zhdanov, however, was not involved heavily in international affairs. Zhdanov's intimate association with leaders of foreign Communist parties in all probability compounded his offense in Stalin's eyes.

14 Decline and Fall

The decline and fall of the Zhdanovites and Titoists, was part of a complex and protracted process. Its significance, in the context of this study, derives from the fact that the coincidence (in time) of their misfortunes was "no accident." Friction between a cautious Stalin and a militant Tito during World War II has been noted already. Stalin clashed with Djilas, early in 1945, over Yugoslav complaints concerning assaults upon Yugoslav citizens, including Partisans and their wives, by Red Army soldiers "liberating" Belgrade at the end of 1944. While Stalin periodically questioned Tito's provocative moves vis-à-vis the West, Soviet-Yugoslav relations would have to be described as amicable through most of 1946–47. In June 1946, Tito travelled to Moscow and was the only foreign dignitary allowed to stand with the Politburo members at Kalinin's funeral, despite the fact that other venerable guests, like Dimitrov, were also present.[1] Indeed, all other indications, from the Varga "debate" (and his recantation of his slurs on the "new democracies," headed by Yugoslavia) through the founding of the Cominform with headquarters in Belgrade, pointed to Tito being the Kremlin's favored protégé.

The first public sign that anything was seriously amiss appeared on February 12, 1948, when the Paris *Le Figaro* published a report that the Romanian Communist Party had ordered the removal of Tito's portraits from windows in which he was shown appearing in the company of Stalin, Groza, or Dimitrov. It also reported rumors circulating in Bucharest to the effect that Tito's position was not strong and that he had lost Moscow's confidence.[2] (It is likely that Romania had been within the jurisdiction of Malenkov's and Beria's organizations dealing with rehabilitation and reparations; at any rate, no sign of Zhdanovite influence has been discovered there.) Moreover, at a reception in Tirana, the Soviet chargé d'affaires replied to a proposed toast to Stalin and Tito by stating, "I drink to Tito, provided Tito is for unity in the democratic bloc."[3] On the day prior to the *Le Figaro* report, Molotov had unexpectedly presented Kardelj with a Soviet-drafted pact on mutual consultations in foreign affairs and requested his signature;

Kardelj complied.[4] Obviously, therefore, something more was at stake than obtaining complete Yugoslav submission to Soviet dictates, an objective that had been attained well and truly when Kardelj agreed to give his signature on February 11, 1948. In that case, it has to be assumed that the problem had aspects more complex than a purely one-dimensional conflict between two parties, the CPSU and the C.P.Y.

In fact, Robert Conquest has pointed to evidence that the rift had interfactional aspects within the Soviet capital: in January of 1948, a Yugoslav delegation headed by Djilas met with Stalin and his associates, including Zhdanov and Voznesenskii, but excluding Malenkov. On January 22, 1948, *Pravda* printed a Dimitrov statement enthusiastically advocating an East European Federation; on January 28, 1948, *Pravda* strongly denounced the same statement. Following this development, on February 10, 1948, Stalin summoned the Yugoslavs and the Bulgars to a meeting with him and his colleagues, this time excluding Voznesenskii, but including Malenkov, as well as M. A. Suslov (who later was to denounce, in public, Voznesenskii, his book, and all those who praised him). Suslov had been brought into the Secretariat a short time before, and Conquest argues that this promotion and Malenkov's return to a major position in the conduct of the CPSU's international relations were intended to neutralize the influence of the Zhdanovites.[5] The evidence presented in this study would tend to bear out Conquest's thesis.

In this context, it is by no means unlikely that Stalin was less than pleased with Zhdanov's apparent attempt to establish a power base outside the USSR in the Soviet East European empire, by means of control of the new Cominform organization which was being established in Belgrade, the capital of Zhdanov's and Voznesenskii's Titoist friends. At Szklarska Poreba, Zhdanov and the Yugoslavs had exhibited a degree of arrogance that bordered on hubris. Their display of near omnipotence there, however, may have been precisely what convinced Stalin that they had to be disciplined. This is not to imply that Zhdanov had failed to check with Stalin before his Cominform manipulations. However, a full report of the precise flavor and color of the transactions at Szklarska Poreba may have aroused Stalin's suspicion that a very significant gap separated what he had authorized from what actually transpired. As to the source of the report, was Malenkov not a humiliated eye-and ear-witness of developments at that gathering? Of course, this is speculation, but what follows is not.

Svetlana Alliluyeva informs us of a peculiar exchange between Stalin and Zhdanov at the dictator's Black Sea resort during the fall of 1947 (presumably shortly after the September 22–27 Cominform meeting). Stalin, "angered by Zhdanov's silence at the table, suddenly turned on him viciously: 'Look at him sitting there like Christ, as if nothing was of any concern to him!' "[6] One interpretation of this strange episode might be that Stalin was telling Zhdanov not to sit there sanctimoniously, as if he had been up to no mischief, because the Georgian was "on to him." Significantly, he was not the only Zhdanovite in trouble. Stalin's daughter goes on to describe another incident, at about the same time, when Stalin was told that A. A. Kuznetsov, Zhdanov's crony and Beria's rival, would be in attendance at dinner that evening and voiced no objection. However, when Kuznetsov appeared in the evening and approached him, smiling, Stalin refused to shake his hand and dismissed him with, "I didn't summon you." Svetlana, although admittedly not the most astute political observer, surmised that perhaps the Leningrad Affair already was brewing then.[7]

Stalin displayed the same degree of anger toward the Yugoslav and Bulgarian Communist parties as toward the other "heroes" of Szklarska Poreba. Early in February of 1948, Dimitrov, with two of his associates and the Yugoslavs Kardelj and Bakarić, arrived in Moscow, having been summoned in effect.[8]* They came to discuss a number of issues, including the proposed Balkan Federation and Belgrade's agreement with Xoxe permitting Yugoslav intervention in the Shqiptar state "to defend Albania from possible attack by the Greek monarchofascists"[10] (which did not preclude Yugoslav troops being used to assist Xoxe in his struggle against Hoxha). Since Stalin originally had offered to let Yugoslavia "swallow" its small southern neighbor, it was strange that he would take umbrage at this now. Nevertheless, Stalin suddenly exclaimed, "Albania is an independent state!" and demanded to know why the USSR had not been consulted on this matter.[11]

The main topic during the January–February 1948 Moscow meetings, of course, was the issue of the proposed Balkan Federation, which has been described many times by Yugoslav sources and does not require detailed reiteration here. However, some aspects are noteworthy. When Stalin demanded to know why the USSR had not been sent a draft of the Bulgarian-Romanian agreement, one of the building blocks of the prospective federation, prior to its signing, one of the Bulgarians, V. Kolarov, responded that the draft, in fact, had been sent to Moscow. Stalin turned to Molotov, asking whether this was correct, and the Soviet foreign minister confirmed that Kolarov was right.

---

*The Russians had wanted Tito himself to come, but he chose not to. However, Djilas, who was already in the Soviet Union, was added to serve as a third senior member of the Yugoslav delegation.[9]

Nevertheless, Stalin continued to lambast the Bulgarians, as if Molotov had denied that the draft had been submitted.[12]

At this point, certain difficulties have to be resolved, since the Yugoslav version of the manner in which the quarrel with Stalin developed at that meeting, as published from the 1950s through the 1970s, has been contradicted now on one significant point by revelations the Yugoslavs released in 1980. The traditional accounts had agreed, more or less, on the sequence outlined below:

Kardelj, on his part, defended the Yugoslav-Bulgarian agreement made at Bled (another building block toward federation), which the contracting parties had also submitted to the USSR for comments and changes, and he claimed, according to the older version, that the Soviet Union suggested only one change, which the parties, in fact, accepted. Kardelj then said to Stalin, "Except for that comment, which we incorporated, there were no differences." Stalin interrupted him, exclaiming, "Nonsense! There are differences and grave ones!"—yet he gave no examples and quickly changed the subject to Albania.[13] However, during the exchange with Kardelj, Stalin was observed "glancing silently and not without reproach at Molotov who hung his head and with clenched lips in fact confirmed Kardelj's claim."[14] Certainly, had the Soviet foreign minister known of any differences between the Yugoslav draft and a Soviet text, there is no reason why he would have refrained from supporting Stalin with the aid of examples. He must have realized already that his failure to deny that Kolarov had been right would not make Stalin very happy with him.

It would appear, therefore, according to the traditional accounts, that the Soviet foreign minister actually had approved the Balkan agreements with a single modification. (Incidentally, Stalin's supposed ignorance on these topics seemed to confirm that his ailments and prolonged absences for rest and recuperation had left him with a very loose grasp of the daily conduct of affairs.) Stalin, therefore, obviously was "looking for faults" over which to assail the Yugoslavs and Bulgarians. This raises the question whether the ostensible apple of discord, the Balkan Federation plan, was the real matter at issue at all. One might even ask why, if Romania and Bulgaria had made arrangements without Soviet consent, as was alleged, a Romanian delegation was not summoned to Moscow? Was it because, unlike Tito's and Dimitrov's followers, the Romanians had no Zhdanovite taint and, thus, were not suspect? Was the real issue Stalin's concern that the Zhdanovite-Titoist alignment, after using the Cominform meeting to create an *ideological* bloc based in Belgrade, was attempting now to give this bloc *state-organizational* form as well? Dimitrov's words, a day after the meeting at Stalin's villa, are most noteworthy: "What is involved here is not criticism of my statement [concerning federation] but something else."[15]

In its internal logic, and in the conclusions drawn, this version appears to be reasonably coherent. However, a somewhat different presentation was released in 1980, following Kardelj's death, in the form of a volume of his memoirs, *The Fight for the Recognition and Independence of the New Yugoslavia, 1944–57.* (Moreover, a newspaper report appeared at that time, revealing that Kardelj's new account, on an essential point, confirmed an interview given somewhat earlier by Bakarić, who had participated in the crucial 1948 Moscow meeting.)

According to the newly published interpretation, Stalin's behavior at the stormy session had not been quite as capricious as the earlier accounts had suggested. The Yugoslavs now confirm that Stalin, in fact, was quite right in saying "Nonsense! There are differences and grave ones!" with regard to the proposed Yugoslav-Bulgarian Federation. The new presentation emphasizes that the quarrel at that meeting quite openly revolved around Stalin's demand that the federation should consist of a "one-on-one" association; that is, it had to be bilateral, with Yugoslavia and Bulgaria each being an equal partner. The Yugoslavs, however, insisted on a basic law that would reduce Bulgaria to the status of one of seven constituent republics, on a par with Slovenia or Bosnia (and, it appears, they had cajoled Dimitrov into concurring).[16]

It had been known, of course, for many years that such differences existed over the framework of the proposed new state, with some of the Bulgars insisting on parity as early as the initial discussions at the end of the war, while Stalin originally supported the Yugoslavs but later changed his mind.* Until recently, however, Yugoslav sources had omitted reference to this substantive question as the overt issue that precipitated the acrimony of the fateful 1948 Moscow session. The new version, of course, does not necessarily contradict the logic of the conclusions that could be drawn from the earlier accounts; namely, that Stalin may have exploited an issue of this type as a pretext to break up a Zhdanovite fiefdom in the bloc. However, it does not square with the implication that Stalin acted capriciously by insisting that there were genuine differences that he refused to spell out (the existence of which supposedly was refuted by Molotov's behavior). The new publications indicate that there was no reason at all for bewilderment

---

*Antonov-Ovseyenko states, "In May 1946 [Stalin] tried to provoke a clash between Dimitrov and Tito." (*Time of Stalin*, p. 286).

on anyone's part, since both sides knew precisely what was the real bone of contention.

The simplest explanation of this episode may be that, in order to disrupt the coalition of Zhdanov's various friends in the bloc, Stalin utilized the existence of profound national differences, not so much perhaps between Tito and Dimitrov as between Bulgars like Chervenkov and the "Macedonian" members of the C.P.Y. It was suspected in Sofia that one of Belgrade's reasons for refusing Bulgaria constitutional "parity" was to create "fluidity" in the international frontier between the two countries, so that Bulgarian Pirin Macedonia might be annexed to Yugoslav Vardar Macedonia.* Stalin knew very well that, if this particular aim were sabotaged by ensuring "fifty-fifty" status in the putative federation for Bulgaria, the Yugoslavs would lose interest in the scheme (as happened, in fact).[17]

Stalin's concerns, of course, extended beyond the two south Slav states. He objected to the extension of Tito's and Dimitrov's influence to other East European countries through the series of interlinking agreements suggested by the Bulgarian leader. Stalin's comments are highly revealing:

> A customs union, a federation between Romania and Bulgaria—this is nonsense! A federation between Yugoslavia, Bulgaria, and Albania is another matter.[18]

> Federation between Yugoslavia, Bulgaria, and Albania. . . should be created, and the sooner, the better. . . right away, if possible, tomorrow!. . . Agree on it immediately. . . a federation ought to be formed between Romania and Hungary, and also Poland and Czechoslovakia.[19]

The Machiavellian elegance of Stalin's preferred system of linkages was to be admired: while a single, all-embracing East European federation might pose problems for Soviet dominance over the region, each separate pairing proposed by him just happened to couple states with an on-going history of mutual antagonism (Czechoslovakia and Poland over Teschen, Romania and Hungary over Transylvania, Yugoslavia and Bulgaria over Macedonia, Yugoslavia and Albania over Kosmet).

Much has been made of other irritants in the relationship between Stalin and C.P.Y. leaders, such as Djilas's complaints concerning the numerous instances of rape and murder of Yugoslav citizens (including Partisans) committed by Red Army soldiers.[20] However, Wolfgang

---

*For further discussion of the impact of this issue on the Bulgarian leadership, see pp. 147–48.

Leonhard has revealed that S.E.D. representatives voiced almost identical charges late in 1947, receiving, in fact, very similar responses from the Soviet side: quotation of an old Russian proverb that "in every family there is a black sheep"[21] and reminders that the honor of the Red Army should not be impugned. Nevertheless, Moscow did not criticize the S.E.D. officially for its complaints.[22]*

That all of these irritants were side issues, and that Dimitrov's hint to his Yugoslav friends ("What is involved here is. . . something else") went to the core of the matter, seems to be borne out by a trip to Leningrad taken by part of the Yugoslav delegation during the middle of the traumatic January–February 1948 meetings with Stalin. Djilas states, in his *Conversations with Stalin*, that his journey "brought some relief" and goes on to note:

> Our encounter with Leningrad's officials added human warmth to our admiration. . . .we got along with them easily and quickly. . . .Though it never occurred to us to complain about the Soviet leaders, still we observed that these men approached. . .life. . .in a simpler and more human way than was the case in Moscow. . . .I could very quickly arrive at a common political language with these people. . . .I was not surprised to hear two years later that these people, too, had failed to escape the totalitarian millstone just because they dared also to be men.[24]

Quite apart from the significant contrast drawn between the Kremlin and the Leningrad fiefdom of Zhdanov, why would it occur to anyone that the Yugoslavs might conceivably "complain about the Soviet leaders" to the Zhdanovites? Is this not significant in itself? Dedijer also records the warm reception the Yugoslav delegates received in Leningrad and quotes them as saying, "Somehow, in Leningrad one feels different than in Moscow."[25]

To underline the significance of this episode, Stalin himself took due note of the Yugoslav trip to Leningrad, as indicated in his angry letter of May 4, 1948, to the Yugoslav leaders, in which he discusses the journey in the context of Belgrade's complaints about recruitment of Soviet agents within Yugoslavia:

> It must be emphasized that Yugoslav comrades visiting Moscow frequently visit other cities in the U.S.S.R., meet our

---

*It is noteworthy that Lev Kopolev, who subsequently became a prominent dissident, was arrested for the first time on April 5, 1945, while a major in Red Army Counterintelligence, for the "crime" of attempting to end acts of pillaging and rape by Soviet troops in Eastern Europe. He was found guilty of "anti-Soviet activities."[23]

people and freely talk with them. In no case did the Soviet Government place any restrictions upon them. During his last visit to Moscow, Djilas went to Leningrad for a few days to talk with Soviet comrades.

According to the Yugoslav scheme, information about Party and State work can only be obtained from the leading organs of the C.C. of the C.P.Y. or from the Government. Comrade Djilas did not obtain information from these organs of the U.S.S.R. but from local organs of the Leningrad organizations. We did not consider it necessary to enquire into what he did there, and what facts he picked up. We think that he did not collect material for the Anglo-American or French intelligence service but for the leading organs of Yugoslavia. Since this was correct we did not see any harm in it because this information might have contained instructive material for the Yugoslav comrades. Comrade Djilas cannot say that he met with restrictions.[26]

Stalin* appears to be saying that, if Tito were going to become embroiled in Soviet factional disputes and to send off his emissaries to a conclave in Zhdanov's bailiwick, he saw no reason why Tito should feel aggrieved if the Soviet Union backed its own factions in Belgrade, such as pro-Soviet elements like A. Hebrang and S. Žujović. In view of subsequent events, a very sinister chord is struck by Stalin's reference to an information-transfer link between the Leningrad group and the Titoists, bypassing Moscow. Stalin says, in his silky way, that he is not suspecting the Yugoslavs of giving this information to foreign intelligence services—yet. Soon, of course, he was to claim precisely that, with obvious implications for the Leningraders who had supplied the information. The May 4 letter almost certainly constitutes a link between the Tito Affair and the Leningrad Affair.

From late March of 1948 until late May of that year, the Central Committees of the Yugoslav and Soviet Communist parties conducted a secret correspondence of which this excerpt is a vital part, exchanging claims and counterclaims. By late May, there was no question but that Tito had been ostracized from the international communist movement. On Tito's birthday, May 25, Dimitrov was the only Communist leader to send him a congratulatory telegram.[27] Under the circumstances, the bravery and loyalty displayed by Dimitrov, ailing and aging, was commendable.

---

*The letter is signed in the name of the CPSU Central Committee as a whole, but no one has contended that, in this case, the author was anyone but Stalin himself.

A week earlier, on May 17, the Yugoslavs sent a letter to the CPSU, declining to come to a Cominform meeting (summoned to meet, not in Belgrade, the established headquarters, but in Bucharest), on the grounds that the Soviet Union and all its satellite parties had committed themselves already against Yugoslavia and, in the cases of Hungary and Czechoslovakia, had even insulted the Yugoslavs. While not about to attend a gathering that was stacked against them, the Yugoslavs were nevertheless conciliatory in their concluding paragraph:

> We desire that the matter be liquidated in such manner as we prove, by deeds, that the accusations against us are unjust. That is, we will resolutely construct socialism and remain loyal to the Soviet Union; remain loyal to the doctrine of Marx, Engels, Lenin, and Stalin. The future will show, as did the past, that we will realize all that we promise you.[28]

In its reply, perhaps sarcastically, the CPSU Central Committee referred to the willingness of the French and Italian Communist parties to let "other parties" criticize them. This statement appears to have a double meaning: the only way to survive is to submit to utter humiliation, if the Kremlin so wishes; moreover, since the "other parties" criticizing the P.C.I. and P.C.F. had been led, most stridently, by Zhdanov and the Yugoslavs, there was also an *ad hominem* element— How does it feel to be the accused rather than the prosecutor, you high and mighty Titoists? Moscow also stated that it considered the decision of the Yugoslavs not to appear in Bucharest as tantamount to an admission that their acts were indefensible.[29]

Zhdanov, within an arm's reach of Stalin, obviously was no longer in a position by May to make sentimental gestures to help his South Slav allies (although, as will be seen, this was not yet the case during the previous month). In June 1948, the second Cominform gathering took place in Bucharest and, while Dimitrov was absent, the Soviet delegation included Malenkov, Suslov (Voznesenskii's adversary—see p. 164). . . and Zhdanov. The meeting passed a resolution condemning the Yugoslavs for having pursued an anti-Soviet foreign policy and other heinous crimes, and it was published over the names of all the delegates attending, including Zhdanov's.[30] Thus, precisely as, in 1928, Bukharin had been forced to denounce "rightist" deviations, and in 1947 Malenkov had been made to join in the condemnation of G. F. Aleksandrov, Zhdanov, in the following year, had to see his name affixed to a document condemning Tito.

Evidence of continued ties between Zhdanovites and Titoists is available even for the first few weeks following the initiation of the March–May 1948 secret polemic between Tito and Stalin. In his previously discussed address to the East Berlin Party Academy in April, Colonel Tiul'panov, Zhdanov's and Shikin's protégé in the Soviet zone of Germany, ranked the East European states in the following pecking order: Yugoslavia, Bulgaria, Poland, Czechoslovakia, Romania, Hungary. . . . This was precisely the Zhdanovite hierarchical order, of course, as laid down during the Varga-Voznesenskii debate and the founding meeting of the Cominform: the list was headed by regimes allied to Zhdanov and descended via "neutral" areas to countries controlled almost entirely by other Soviet factions, with Slavs taking precedence over non-Slavs. Thus, it is evident that some Zhdanovites were still backing Tito strongly a month after the secret Soviet-Yugoslav polemic exchanges began.

The impact of the vicissitudes experienced by the Zhdanov faction upon its Bulgarian allies, particularly Dimitrov, is noteworthy. When he returned home after the tongue-lashing he received in Moscow during January–February 1948, Dimitrov tempered his previous line concerning the inevitability of war. Late in 1947, he had implied that it would be difficult, at least, to avoid a conflagration:

> The imperialists, more particularly the American imperialists, are trying to find a way out of their post-war difficulties and the threatening economic crisis in the economic enslavement of as many countries as possible and in the preparation of a new aggressive war, above all against the most important and powerful guardian of and fighter for peace — the Soviet Union. . . . They are trying in every way to clear the deck for their crusade for world domination, which, of course, they cannot imagine without a new world war. . . .
>
> The great historical task is to achieve what we failed to achieve on the eve of the last war — the setting up of a powerful anti-war united front of democratic people and countries against the fomentors of new wars to frustrate and foil the aggressive plans of the imperialists and, in the first place, of the American capitalist monopolies.[31]

From this alarmist, Zhdanovite position shortly after the founding meeting of the Cominform, Dimitrov had moved, within six months, to a much more circumspect posture, playing down the threat of armed conflict:

> All this noise, steady propaganda, and incitement to new wars have their definite aims and purposes, which are harm-

ful for our peoples and can only benefit our enemies.

We should know and remember, however, on the basis of a careful study of the actual international situation, the balance of power in the different countries and on an international scale, of what is actually going on and not, what is represented as happening without actually taking place; we should know that a new war is neither inevitable nor imminent. . . although there are imperialists and adventurers interested in kindling the conflagration of a new war.[32]

Thus, suddenly, Dimitrov was denouncing alarmist talk as harmful; the elements interested in conflict were limited to unnamed "imperialists and adventurers" ("adventurers" in the communist movement also?), in significant contrast to Dimitrov's previous statement which accused "the imperialists, more particularly the American imperialists. . ." of actual "preparation of a new aggressive war. . . against. . . the Soviet Union." Among the many reasons cited by Dimitrov for his newly found confidence that a great war was not about to be unleashed was that,

No masses would stake their life, shed their blood, expose their homes to destruction, their families to ruin and annihilation, for the interests and enrichment of the imperialists. How now, after the Second World War, could the peoples be roused—the American workers and farmers, peasants and other working peoples in so-called Western Europe—and sent to shed their blood in the Balkans or in Czechoslovakia?[33]

This statement represented a "rightist" revisionist position; not only could one wean away the British, a secondary adversary, from the Americans, as Varga hoped, but American workers *and farmers* (hardly the most progressive element in Marxist terms) could be relied upon to resist the element among imperialists "interested" in conflagration. It appears that Dimitrov was bending over backward to make up for recent errors in the ideological and other realms. (Only a few months earlier, Stalin had accused Dimitrov and Tito of having authored a statement that, in the Soviet leader's view, meant "preventive war—the commonest Komsomol stunt; a tawdry phrase which only brings grist to enemy mills.")[34] Nevertheless, Dimitrov did stand by his ally Tito for some time longer. In fact, the Yugoslavs have claimed that he even encouraged Tito to remain firm against the Cominform.[35].

As late as May 4, 1948, *Rabotnichesko Delo* published an address by Dimitrov, made a few days earlier, in which he referred to "progressive mankind, including our people, the peoples of Yugoslavia, Czechoslovakia, Romania, Hungary and Poland."[36] Thus, Yugoslavia was still receiving top billing on Dimitrov's list of progressive countries, nearly two months after the announcement by General Barskov, the head of the Soviet mission in Yugoslavia, that Soviet advisers would be withdrawn from that country (March 18, 1948).

Although the names of Bulgarian Communist Party leaders were published as signatories of the June 28, 1948, Cominform resolution condemning Tito's regime, there is little doubt that the break with Yugoslavia was not supported unanimously in Sofia. The Bulgarian names affixed to the resolution were those of Traicho Kostov and Vulko Chervenkov.[37] As was mentioned earlier, Tito's old collaborator Dimitrov had sent the Yugoslav leader birthday congratulations on May 25, 1948 (the only East European personality to do so).[38] Moreover, on June 30, 1948, the Bulgarian government newspaper, *Otechestven Front*, published an editorial stating that "the sound foundations of our relations with Yugoslavia are unshaken. . . [and] cannot be affected by a temporary crisis in the Yugoslav Communist Party." The press department of the Bulgarian government followed this editorial with a release stating that the recent Cominform condemnation did not change Yugoslav-Bulgarian relations and stressing that "the Bulgarian government will honestly and sincerely collaborate with the Yugoslav government" in the spirit of mutual assistance existing between them. Moreover, "Bulgaria will abstain from interference in Yugoslav internal affairs." At the same time, however, the Bulgarian Fatherland Front's National Council published a statement calling upon the government of Yugoslavia to move back into line with Communist principles.[39]

On July 2, 1948, Dimitrov announced publicly that union between the two countries continued to be a historic necessity. Clearly, he had not given up on close relations with Bulgaria's Yugoslav neighbor. Opposition to his line within the ruling group in Bulgaria emanated apparently from either (possibly both) the "Muscovite" element, consisting of V. Chervenkov, V. Poptomov, G. Damianov and General Panchevski, or the Bulgarian "nationalists," led by T. Kostov.[40] As a result, when the Bulgarian Workers Party's Central Committee met on July 12, Dimitrov (not acting of his own volition, one presumes) accused the Yugoslavs of encroaching upon Bulgarian rights in Macedonia, as established in previous agreements. The Central Committee also seized this occasion to declare that the CPSU played an "incontestably predominant role in its leadership of the struggle against fascism, and in defense of peace and socialism."[41] Any possibility of an autonomous Bulgarian approach thus was precluded.

Subsequently, at the Fifth Party Congress of the Bulgarian Workers Party (held December 18–25, 1948), Dimitrov, uncharacteristically, was to launch an onslaught upon Tito:

> The treachery of the Tito group. . . also found expression in the attitude of the group to the matter of the South Slav Federation and the Macedonian question. This group is sliding down the slippery road of nationalism and today stands in the position of the Greater Serbian chauvinists, who strive for hegemony in the Balkans and for the annexation of Macedonia to Serbia and Yugoslavia.[42]

It may not have been a coincidence that the USSR was represented at this congress — to witness, as it were, Dimitrov's belated adherence to the anti-Tito line — by Mikhail Suslov,[43] who had been added to the Soviet delegation at the fateful June 28, 1948, Cominform meeting (along with Malenkov, thus leaving Zhdanov in a distinct minority), and who was to direct the November 1949 Cominform session that condemned the C.P.Y. for being "in the power of murderers and spies."[44] spies."[44]

Although additional material has appeared, dealing with the immediate postwar period,* not much is known about Dimitrov's last few

---

*Interesting (if accurate) assertions concerning Dimitrov's views of Tito appeared in the January 1979 issue of the Bulgarian Writers' Union's Journal, *Septemvri*, which contained the memoirs of Tsola Dragoycheva, a member of the Politburo of the Bulgarian Communist Party.[45] This account presents Sofia's basic line on Bulgarian-Yugoslav relations during the immediate postwar period, particularly with regard to the Macedonian question. She contends that the Tito-Dimitrov relationship was far less smooth than the Yugoslav versions (particularly the publications of Djilas and Dedijer) would seem to imply. Specifically, she asserts that, in 1945, Dimitrov was confronted with a Yugoslav attempt to make the Sofia leadership acquiesce to Bulgaria's incorporation into the proposed federation as merely one of seven constituent republics. She cites a January 13, 1945, letter from Dimitrov to Traicho Kostov, stating:

> The new project [for federation] of the Yugoslav comrades cannot be accepted in its present form. The basic problem is that *it sets the trend that Bulgaria will be absorbed by Yugoslavia.* The Yugoslav comrades do not take into account the fact that it is not a question of simply including Bulgaria into the Yugoslav Federation (with the same rights as enjoyed by Serbia and Croatia), but to set up [between] today's Federal Yugoslavia and Bulgaria a bilateral allied (Federal) state [based] upon the equality of rights principle. [Dragoycheva's emphasis][46]

Dragoycheva goes on to assert that the August 1, 1947, Bled Agreement between Tito and Dimitrov established that:

> there should be no steps aimed at immediate unification of the Pirin [Bulgarian Macedonia] Region with the [Yugoslav, Vardar] Macedonian Republic. [This could only be] carried out after the establishment of the union between the People's Republic of Bulgaria and the Federal Republic of Yugoslavia — that is, after the Federation (of the two states), when the borders between the People's

months. He "retired" from active leadership early in 1949 and was ordered to Moscow on the pretext that his ailments were best treated there (however, reportedly, he was made to bring all his belongings with him, clearly implying that he would not be coming back).[50] Like Zhdanov, he died soon after his removal from power. Like Zhdanov (and Kirov) he died a "hero," and was given a state funeral.[51] However, it is quite possible that it was less embarrassing for Moscow to arrange a natural death than to execute the world-famous figure who had hurled defiance at Göring in the Reichstag Fire Trial. Stalin might have brought about his death, as was implied by the Yugoslavs[52] (in the same fashion as Zhdanov's and Maxim Gorkii's deaths,[53] both of whom were reported later to have been executed medically). Antonov-Ovseyenko states that "Stalin succeeded in removing Dimitrov. . . without much trouble."[54] Precisely the same five doctors signed Dimitrov's death certificate as had signed Zhdanov's in the previous year.[55] Three of these physicians ultimately were to be accused in the "Doctors' Plot."[56]

There is some evidence that Finnish Communists remained loyal to Zhdanov and, perhaps, to Tito until Zhdanov's death. Interestingly enough, Finnish Agrarian Party newspapers alleged, shortly after Zhdanov's demise, that he had been murdered (with one paper speculating that Stalin had a role in the affair).[57] Since the Agrarian Party had been a government coalition partner of the Communist Party, it is just conceivable that Finnish Communists, still in shock over the sudden disappearance of their "protector,"* had leaked the rumor to their partners. It is noteworthy that only at this point, on September 8, 1948, did the Finnish Communist Party condemn Tito publicly, apparently for the first time.[59] The condemnation resolution was supposed to have been passed at the party's congress, which was held between August 28 and 30[60] (just prior to the announcement of

---

Republic of Bulgaria and the People's Republic of Macedonia already would have been deleted. [Dragoycheva's emphasis][47]

However, she goes on to claim that the Yugoslavs unilaterally attempted to bring about such "unification" of the two Macedonia regions without first achieving federation between Bulgaria and Yugoslavia, thus causing Dimitrov, at the December 1948 Fifth Congress of the Bulgarian Workers Party, to exclaim: "We were betrayed."[48] The authenticity of Bulgarian *ex post facto* revelations concerning Dimitrov's attitude has to be viewed with a grain or two of salt, of course, given the history of relations with Yugoslavia since Zhdanov's death.[49] (For recent Yugoslav revelations dealing with the issue of federation, see pp. 139–40.

*Although the (Zhdanov-controlled) Allied Control Commission had been abolished in 1947, the Zhdanovite presence probably still was felt among Finnish Communists, particularly since in January 1948 Zhdanov's deputy on the Control Commission, Lt. Gen. Zavonenkov, returned to Finland as ambassador of the Soviet Union.[58]

Zhdanov's death), yet this development was not publicized until after Zhdanov's demise. Perhaps, the Finnish party realized that Zhdanov and his supporters were being purged and that it had better dissociate itself publicly from the Leningrad faction. This may not have stopped some Finnish Communists, however, from expressing their real sentiments privately.

Also noteworthy, perhaps, was the reaction of Belgrade to the death of the man whose name, after all, had been among the signatories of the Cominform resolution condemning Yugoslavia only two months previously. The Central Committee of the C.P.Y. sent a telegram to Moscow stating that it "deeply regretted the heavy loss suffered by the Central Committee of the Bolshevik Party — the death of the worthy collaborator of Stalin, Comrade A. Alexandrovich Zhdanov."[61] Not only were the Yugoslavs praising Zhdanov, but perhaps they were also implying that he was Stalin's equal, not his subordinate, by employing that term "worthy collaborator." To be sure, the episode of the telegram is open to different interpretations.

It is of interest that, during the Danubian Conference (held in Belgrade in mid-August of 1948), intimates of Anna Pauker, the Romanian foreign minister and a key party figure, were reported to have quoted her to the effect that Zhdanov had incurred Stalin's wrath as a result of the Yugoslav affair.[62] If Zhdanov's relations with Tito caused the former's purge or even death, conversely it may have been Tito's link with Zhdanov that was the real cause of Yugoslavia's expulsion.

Zhdanov was eliminated soon after the June 1948 Cominform meeting. A month prior to his death on August 31, 1948, he was no longer signing messages in the name of the Central Committee; Malenkov was.[63] Even more noteworthy was the publication in *Pravda* on August 7 of a letter (dated July 10, 1948) addressed to Stalin personally and signed by A. A. Zhdanov's son, Yurii A. Zhdanov, apologizing for having adopted anti-Lysenkoist positions (see pp. 59–60).[64]

Given the Soviet (indeed the general Communist) penchant for attacking surrogates, this public humiliation of a Zhdanov could not but be interpreted as a loud signal that Zhdanov himself was in severe trouble. The prominence given to the apology by the younger Zhdanov, which, after all, dealt with a highly esoteric subject, leaves very little doubt that this was a message to the Soviet élite.

Of course, Zhdanov's downfall and death did not end the matter. The notorious Leningrad Affair was to ensue a year later, causing the demotion or disappearance (in many cases the death) of most of the surviving Zhdanovites, including persons as prominent as N. A. Voznesenskii and A. A. Kuznetsov, plus A. A. Voznesenskii, P. S. Popkov, I. V. Shikin, M. I. Rodionov (Zhdanov's friend in charge of the Council of Ministers of the R.S.F.S.R.),[65] and G. M. Popov (a complex case; see p. 30), to mention only the best known. A factional rivalry that could lead to such a bloody denouement surely may have sufficed to contribute, at the very least, to the conflict that led to the break with Tito.

That Zhdanov died in disgrace and that his passing was not due to natural causes is confirmed by the material in Antonov-Ovseyenko's work:

> With the help of Beria...Malenkov managed to *discredit Zhdanov, accusing him of a plot against the party.* Zhdanov fell ill and died suddenly on August 31, 1948. Zhdanov's appointees in Leningrad held high positions in the party and state—men like Aleksei Kuznetsov, Pyotr Popkov, Mikhail Rodionov, and Aleksandr Voznesensky [*sic*]. They couldn't be left where they were. The Leningrad affair cost the lives of thousands of party workers, military men, and industrial workers. They were accused of plotting [to proclaim Leningrad] the capital of the country once again, in place of Moscow....What was unusual was [that the charges were] not publicized in the press. In the Central Committee resolution of February 1949, Kuznetsov, Popkov, and the other Leningrad leaders were accused of violating state discipline....On Abakumov's direct orders, *testimony against the late Andreii Zhdanov was extracted from these officials*....Who were the men that died....Kuznetsov was the party's provincial secretary. Popkov was the chairman of the province's Soviet executive committee. All the secretaries of the party's district committees also went. Voznesensky was the rector of Leningrad University and brother of the former chairman of the State Planning Commission. Rodionov had been premier of the Russian Republic. In addition, two thousand military men were rounded up within a few days. *No sooner had Zhdanov been buried———than all traces of his days in Leningrad were destroyed,* including material on the nine hundred days of Leningrad's resistance....Stalin ordered the Museum of the Defense of Leningrad closed and arrested its director, Major Rakov....Books dealing with achievements by Leningrad scientists and cultural figures were banned....Zhdanov's death belongs to a series of mysterious incidents....Trotsky 1940, Zhdanov 1948, Dimitrov 1949. This brief martyrology could be lengthened....

[Beria] might have taken a hand in Zhdanov's premature death even without Stalin's special orders from on high. [emphases added][66]

It is clear from the context that such orders *were* given—Antonov-Ovseyenko is commenting merely that, in this instance, they were received gladly. The author's adjective "mysterious" is meant to be sarcastic, since, of course, the world has known for decades who ordered Trotsky killed, and Antonov-Ovseyenko's own book leaves little doubt that Dimitrov—and others on his list of "martyrs"—were killed at Stalin's behest.

A. N. Kosygin's survival of this purge poses interesting questions. The memoirs attributed to Nikita S. Khrushchev contain a pointed reference, which, to a cynical eye, reads as if Kosygin may have "fingered" his comrades during the Leningrad Affair:

> The accusations against him cast such a dark shadow over him that I simply can't explain how he was saved from being eliminated along with the others. Kosygin, as they say, must have drawn a lucky lottery ticket.[67]

It should be noted that Kosygin was prominent among Politburo members who, in publishing tributes to Stalin on the occasion of his seventieth birthday, felt called upon to insert a condemnation of Yugoslavia. His denunciation of the Belgrade leadership (written at the time of the macabre finale of the Leningrad Affairs, the victims of which had welcomed the Yugoslavs so cordially to the city on the Neva despite Stalin's displeasure with Tito, barely two years earlier) was hardly appropriate for a birthday greeting:

> The working people of Yugoslavia have been plunged into unheard of poverty and ruin. The Fascist Tito-Ranković band has turned the country into a colony of Anglo-American Imperialism.[68]

Was this gratuitous polemic meant to demonstrate conspicuously that Kosygin, once a Zhdanovite, had "reformed" truly and was eager now to espouse the line, even beyond the call of duty?

Although Khrushchev and Beria also published passages that were highly critical of the Tito leadership,[69] Malenkov, Zhdanov's long-time rival, refrained from provocative declarations, either concerning the Yugoslavs or the West. As noted previously, Malenkov's message on this occasion resuscitated Stalin's more "rightist" (that is, nonmilitant and low-key) statements about the United States, including the interviews Stalin had given to Stassen, Werth, and Elliott Roosevelt.[70]

Molotov, whose bailiwick, after all, was foreign policy, in contrast to Kosygin, did not refer to the Yugoslavs at all, except by omission; he listed the "people's democracies" as "Poland, Czechoslovakia, Hungary, Romania, Bulgaria, Albania, Korea," thus not only deleting the Yugoslavs but demoting post-Dimitrov Bulgaria to a position lower than non-Slav countries like Romania and Hungary.[71] Mikoyan, whose responsibilities, like Kosygin's, lay in the realm of economics, did not presume to deal with foreign affairs at all.[72]

As pointed out earlier, Wolfgang Leonhard has revealed that Voznesenskii was still very popular in Belgrade after March 1949, when Leonhard arrived in the Yugoslav capital. Copies of his works were widely available there. By contrast, Zhdanov was resented in Belgrade after June 1948,[73] presumably because he had failed to hold up under pressure and had submitted to the charade of "presiding" over the expulsion of his Yugoslav allies from the Cominform, shortly before his death in the summer of 1948. If his sudden fall from power left the Titoists of Southeastern Europe without a powerful protector in the USSR, it proved fatal for most of the Zhdanovites themselves.

According to one version, Voznesenskii's eventual liquidation, more than a year after Zhdanov's demise, was the culmination of developments in which a role was played by the fact that the Gosplan chief questioned Stalin's decision to sever economic relations with Yugoslavia.[74] Assuming that the Yugoslav leadership was aware of the circumstances of Voznesenskii's downfall, as presented in that account, Belgrade's sentiments toward him as late as 1949 (described by Leonhard) become readily understandable. Their relations had been mutually supportive, in any case, until June 1948, as this study has attempted to demonstrate. Whatever may be the correct interpretation, that is, the precise contributory causes, there is no convincing reason for dissociating Voznesenskii from the Leningrad Affair, the downfall of the Zhdanovite faction as a whole. It is doubtful whether a man of Stalin's temperament really needed the additional incentive of being "provoked" by Voznesenskii's reported intercession on Yugoslavia's behalf to liquidate a member of this "leftist" faction, although admittedly, unlike the other victims of the post-Zhdanov purge, Voznesenskii, being of Politburo rank, had been almost equal in status to Zhdanov himself. The memoirs of Veljko Micunovič, Yugoslav ambassador to Moscow, 1956–58, indicate that Voznesenskii's death was associated clearly with the Leningrad Affair and that Khrushchev assailed Malenkov for his role in this matter, including specifically the deaths of Kuznetsov and Voznesenskii (this contention is in line with the version presented in the memoirs attributed to Khrushchev himself).[75]

15 Post-Zhdanov "Zhdanovism"

It should be noted that after their expulsion from the Cominform Tito and his associates were to continue for some time to espouse a "leftist" position. On December 29, 1948, Edvard Kardelj, Yugoslav vice premier, delivered a stridently anti-American address, consistent with the Zhdanov-Voznesenskii line:

> The rich monopolistic groups of American finance capital began to dream of world domination, of domination over markets, over the sources of raw materials, with respect to the export of capital, with respect to the industrial development of other countries, etc. Of course, the monopolistic groups in other major capitalist countries, primarily in England and France, while supporting, on the one hand, the action of the American monopolists, are, on the other, pursuing their own aims in the struggle for markets, for the export of capital, for sources of raw materials, etc. . . . A fierce campaign is being whipped up against the USSR and countries of people's democracy. . . . Instead of economic cooperation on the basis of equality. . . different forms of "aid," with definite political aims. . . that in practice amount to substantial restriction of independence, is given. Such is the case with what is called the Marshall Plan.[1]

While Kardelj took time out to refute Soviet charges against his country, his speech went on to propagate, once again, the basic revolutionary line of the Calcutta conference:

> In the East, immense revolutionary and creative energies of oppressed colonial and semicolonial peoples are awakening. Despite. . . the Cominform resolution, the united front of the socialist and people's democratic countries, headed by the Soviet Union, remains unshaken in the struggle against the enemies of peace, against imperialist expansion and the attacks of the enemies of socialism. The forces of imperialism are handcuffed.[2]

Similarly, in his address to the C.P.Y. Fifth Congress, July 21, 1948, Tito, stressing repeatedly that the Yugoslav party had remained loyal to the CPSU, reminded the Soviet Union that its main accusation against the Yugoslavs had been that they were too revolutionary:

> Further, it is claimed that we are building socialism too quickly, that we are issuing decrees and laws overnight, etc. Therefore, they are making the same insinuations that Milan Grol and all the reactionaries inside the country and outside of it have already made.[3]

At the same congress, it will be remembered, Kidrič attacked Hebrang and Žujović, who had been purged, because of their concept that possibilities were limited at this juncture for "the construction of socialism" in Yugoslavia. Kidrič's argument received further backing, subsequently, from Edvard Kardelj's article in the Belgrade *Kommunist* of July 1949 attacking Varga.

Milovan Djilas presented a report concerning agitation and proganda work in the party to the same congress of the C.P.Y., in which he boasted that the Yugoslavs had purged "the social-democratic rightist" elements among their cadres. He went on to assert that the following constituted priorities ini the area of Agitprop:

> First, to unmask all attempts and schemes by the imperialists directed against the independence of our country; secondly, to fight resolutely for a democratic peace, to unmask the warmongering campaign, to unmask the imperialist policy of oppression and enslavement of other peoples and their democratic rights, in which American imperialism must be kept in mind as the main bearer of imperialist enslavement and the warmongering campaign; thirdly, to extend comprehensive support to the struggle of the Soviet Union and the democratic camp which it heads.[4]

The Yugoslavs, during this period, were obviously at great pains to stress not merely that they were strictly loyal Marxist-Leninists (a point made repeatedly by Djilas), but that they would leave no room to be "outflanked to the Left."

As far as the USSR itself is concerned, it is noteworthy that, at the time when Stalin was presiding over the "operational implementation" of the Leningrad Affair (V. M. Andrianov was sent to Leningrad on February 24, 1949, to succeed P. S. Popkov as first secretary of the local party apparatus),[5] he was willing to allow ideological positions identified with the Zhdanov-Voznesenskii group to persist. As was posited earlier in this study, after the outcome of a factional struggle has been determined, it is "safe" for the victor to adopt the loser's platform.

Late in 1948, a session of the council of the Economics Institute of the Academy of Sciences of the USSR condemned several members (most of whom clearly were Jewish) of the previously disbanded (Varga) Institute of World Economics and World Politics and of its journal, *Mirovoe Khoziaistvo i Mirovaia Politika*, accusing them of cosmopolitanism, bourgeois objectivism, servility to foreign interests, and glossing over the contradictions of American imperialism.[6] This session was chaired by K. V. Ostrovitianov (see Appendix E).* At a time, therefore, when the March 13, 1949, announcement of Voznesenskii's "release" from his ministerial and state planning posts,[8] and the virtually concurrent purge of the Zhdanovites in Leningrad, were barely months away, Ostrovitianov was continuing to play a role typical of the Zhdanovshchina,† and its antisemitic, chauvinistic, Great-Russian, and anti-American characteristics.

Varga, however, was still resisting his persecutors and was not to recant fully, strangely enough, until after the Leningrad Affair was in full progress and his opponents were being exterminated (see Appendix E).

In his concluding remarks, at the Economic Institute's session late in 1948, Ostrovitianov condemned Varga for continuing "stubbornly to deny his gross errors of *principle* which were characterized in our Party press as errors of a reformist nature. [emphasis added]."

Once more Varga was condemned, this time for espousing a "reformist, more exactly, a [presumably British] 'Labourite' thesis."[9]

Nevertheless, on March 15, 1949, *Pravda* printed a letter to the editor, signed by Varga, in which he defended himself against those

---

*According to Professor Aron Katsenelinboigen (who corresponded with the author of this study), Ostrovitianov, whom he knew, was not a man of strong views, and in that sense was not a firmly committed Zhdanovite.[7] Nevertheless, after presiding over the 1947 conference that condemned Varga, he was put in charge of the new Institute of Economics, which incorporated Varga's old Institute of World Economics and World Politics, in January of 1948; in this capacity, Ostrovitianov came under Voznesenskii's aegis and would have to be regarded as part of Zhdanov's coalition.

†According to Dr. Katsenelinboigen, in 1966 a Soviet economic delegation was sent to Yugoslavia under Ostrovitianov's leadership, the first such visit, it seems, at least since 1948. Apparently, "the Yugoslavs still remembered him . . . as the acknowledged head of Soviet economics . . . as . . . [had been the case] under Stalin" (Katsenelinboigen manuscript, p. 32.) It may be assumed that Belgrade remembered Ostrovitianov's 1947 role in helping to place Varga in the dock, among other reasons for his somewhat contemptuous underestimation of the importance of the "new Democracies," especially Yugoslavia. Consequently, and it seems correctly, Ostrovitianov was deemed to be the appropriate personality to lead a group of economic experts, presumably sent to inject a note of cordiality into Soviet-Yugoslav relations.

who were "slandering" him and denied ever having said that 1949 would not see an American crisis of overproduction or that he ever had supported the Marshall Plan (in fact, he cited a lecture he delivered on August 27, 1946, as showing that he was "the first scientist in the Soviet Union to oppose the Marshall Plan"). Moreover, he sharply rejected assertions that he was "a man of Western orientation."[10]

Yet at the same time, having been disciplined, Varga now published works refuting most of his old themes. He stressed that he had been wrong concerning Britain, that it was not making "progress in the direction of democracy of a new type";[11] moreover, despite his previous assertion, Britain had not become a genuine debtor to India after the war:

> In amount of capital, India is England's creditor, but in income from capital, England is even now the exploiter of India . . . . [however] India is able to maneuver between England and the United States, utilizing the discord between English and American Imperialism.[12]

More importantly, he reversed himself and confessed that "to call war-regulation of the economy 'planned economy'. . . is of course wrong."[13] Moreover,

> It was absolutely erroneous to examine the rise of the countries of people's democracy only as a political phenomenon . . . .The breakoff was undoubtedly one of the most important social-economic results of the Second World War and signifies a deepening of the general crisis of capitalism.[14]

Subsequently, while criticizing London for its anti-Soviet line, he was to add that "Britain has not only failed to preserve her position as a world power but, on the contrary, is more and more declining to the position of satellite of the USA."[15] He proceeded to state that the British attempt at

> political domination over Western Germany, which Britain thought to carry out with the help of Social Democracy, has also collapsed. The American-oriented Catholic Party has prevailed in Western Germany. . . . Britain's effort to strengthen her positions in the Near East by turning Greece and Turkey into her satellites proved unsuccessful. . . . Both countries fell under the sway of the USA.[16]

Varga had come around to the (Zhdanovite) view that Soviet moves (for instance, in the Berlin Crisis or the Greek civil war) were to be directed primarily not against Britain, the influence of which in these regions had long since been overtaken by American dominance. Indeed,

the Anglo-American contradiction—the basic contradiction of the Capitalist world—is becoming more and more aggravated and is making itself felt in literally all parts of the globe.[17]

Varga now had adopted Voznesenskii's old line: encourage the secondary antagonist (Britain) to turn upon the primary adversary (America).* Precisely when the Zhdanov-Voznesenskii faction had been liquidated entirely, therefore, Varga was "persuaded" finally to become the spokesman, de facto, of all the pet theses of the Zhdanovshchina, disavowing his own views on the possibility of regulating postwar bourgeois economies, on the role of the "new democracies," on the economic status of ex-colonial areas, and on the identity of the principal adversary.

It would seem, therefore, that Stalin was allowing certain aspects of the Zhdanovshchina to continue well after the elimination of its authors, perhaps as a signal to members of the victorious "rightist" faction, particularly Malenkov and Beria, that they would not be allowed to fill the void left by the demise of Zhdanov, Voznesenskii, and their associates. The memoirs attributed to Khrushchev state:

I . . . began to suspect that one of the reasons Stalin had called me back to Moscow [in 1949] was to influence the balance of power in the collective and to put a check on Beria and Malenkov. . . . Stalin . . . gave me support. . . . I was constantly running up against Beria and Malenkov.[19]

Of course, a change in the "objective circumstances"—that is to say, the unavoidable conclusion that the United States had emerged as the leader and the material and ideological basis of the resurgent Western Alliance and that Soviet international objectives could not be attained without overcoming this obstacle—also may have played a role in the regime's decision to enforce Varga's final "conversion," in 1949, to significant portions of the Zhdanovite creed. (It must be remembered, moreover, that in the same year the USSR became a nuclear power.) That Varga was allowed to resist until after the Leningrad Affair already had commenced could be accounted for by Stalin's

---

*Not surprisingly, in a conversation with Carl F. Norden, the American representative in Belgrade, as early as February 3, 1945, Tito had expressed the belief that British domination in the Mediterranean was a phenomenon of the past.[18]

desire to ensure that, during the several months following Zhdanov's death, such powerful remaining Zhdanovites as N. A. Voznesenskii, I. V. Shikin (with his influence in the political administration of the armed forces), and A. A. Kuznetsov (with his growing foothold in the security services), should not be perceived by other cadres to be waxing in strength because of Varga's symbolic submission. Once the Leningrad Affair was well under way, Varga could safely be pressured into full recantation.

Comparable developments could be noted in the realm of political philosophy. There was a delay of about a year between the publication of the second and third editions of *Voprosy Filosofii*.[20] The journal, which had been established as a result of Zhdanov's attack upon Aleksandrov, had been edited initially by B. M. Kedrov, concerning whom there are data that indicate deep antagonism toward Beria, and, conversely, support for Zhdanov (see Appendix C). The third edition of the periodical, edited at that stage, by D. I. Chesnokov, attacked Kedrov and his associates editorially for the same, essentially "rightist," deviations that Zhdanov had pinned upon Aleksandrov*—namely, lack of *partiinost'*, bourgeois objectivism, and cosmopolitanism (a strange experience for a former Zhdanovite). Moreover, Kedrov was denounced for having been oriented insufficiently toward *Soviet* philosophy, precisely Zhdanov's charge against Aleksandrov. Thus, just as *Voprosy Ekonomiki* continued to espouse Voznesenskii's policies even while the former chief of Gosplan, himself, was being stripped of his titles, so *Voprosy Filosofii*, long after Zhdanov's death, followed in the tracks of the Zhdanovshchina (paradoxically employing Zhdanov's characteristic invective to persecute some of his supporters).

It would seem, therefore, that Stalin's wrath was not aroused primarily by the Zhdanov-Voznesenskii faction's ideological posture— remembering, however, that the Zhdanovites wielded ideological polemics as a weapon in the power struggle and that Stalin, personally, found their "style" uncongenial, since his own policy predilections habitually tended toward caution† and a far less "forward" line than was propagated by the Leningrad group. Since factions were outlawed,

---

*Aleksandrov was mentioned also in that editorial, but only in marginally critical terms: "So too Aleksandrov's article in *Voprosy Filosofii*, Volume I, 1948, contains an apathetic, academic treatment of the historical conditions of the rise of Marxism."[21]

†That Stalin allowed the Berlin blockade to be attempted is not necessarily an example of the pursuit of an adventuristic policy. After all, Berlin was an isolated city, enveloped by the Soviet zone. His attempt at consolidation of power in that zone was less significant than his unwillingness to challenge the American airlift to the city. Moreover, the decision of January 1949 to overrule the postulates of Tiul'panov's speech, and the consequent formal termination of the siege in May 1949, would appear to indicate that the Berlin blockade was more of a probe than a serious challenge.

of course, at least theoretically, the preliminary bout for the succession to an aging Stalin required a "decent" cloak, in the form of a "debate" on international strategy (and related "domestic" issues), buttressed heavily by disputations over subtleties of doctrinal interpretation. This provided a convenient opening, moreover, for scoring points against rival contenders, "unmasking" them as deviationists or even heretics, an elegant way of delegitimizing them as candidates. When all is said and done, however, the "debate" constituted a means toward an end, rather than being at the core of the issue itself. One is led to assume, therefore, that Stalin resorted finally to "administrative measures" against the Zhdanovites because of suspicion triggered by the increasing number of key fiefdoms, inside the USSR, the bloc, and even beyond, that they created, staffed, and controlled, and by the consequent boastful self-assurance, indeed presumption, that they displayed. Until the Leningrad faction was decimated, however, holding a sheltering hand over courageous opponents who were willing to criticize the Zhdanovite platform provided a useful avenue for undermining the influence of the "crown prince" and his allies.

Once the faction had been annihilated, however, there was no tactical reason for Stalin to refrain from picking up those of its fallen banners that had become more relevant with the passage of time. No danger remained at that point that such action could be interpreted as a manifestation of continued Zhdanovite strength. In fact, *then* it became tactically useful for Stalin to allow portions of the Zhdanovshchina to continue, if only as a signal to would-be adherents of the victorious Beria-Malenkov group that the "rightists" would not be permitted now to replicate the ascendancy achieved by Zhdanov and his allies in 1946–47 (as represented by the composition of the leadership on the dais while reviewing the November 1946 parade, the cultural Zhdanovshchina, the attack on Aleksandrov, and the September 1947 Cominform meeting).

It is not at all uncommon in Soviet history for the victor in a factional "ideological" struggle to turn around after defeating his opponents and to adopt their "platform". Khrushchev, for example, attacked Malenkov for having asserted that nuclear war would destroy civilization, yet, once he had overcome his rival, Khrushchev propounded views rather closer to Malenkov's position than to his own previous statements.[22] Similarly, having demanded priority for the development of heavy industry, in opposition to Malenkov's "New Course" (which emphasized increased production of consumer goods), Khrushchev, after emerging victoriously from the contest, himself adopted the role of consumer advocate.[23]

Stalin, in an earlier instance, had denounced the party's left wing as "superindustrializers." Yet once he had secured his political ascendancy vis-à-vis the "left," Stalin identified with the extreme industrial objectives of the First Five-Year Plan.[24]

16 FINALE

The limited flow of information from totalitarian states is not conducive to absolute and dogmatic conclusions. Yet, the "footprints" that the Soviet political process leaves in the open literature, as this work has attempted to demonstrate, are neither too few nor so insignificant as to preclude meaningful efforts to retrace the convoluted paths beaten by the (factional) protagonists in CPSU decision making. This study does not claim that Tito's apparent involvement in the "domestic" conflict and the intrigues between the Zhdanovites and their opponents in the Soviet élite constitute the entire story. However, for all the reasons discussed, and in view of the highly suggestive evidence analyzed, it seems probable that this element at least contributed significantly to the outcome.

This is not to say that the many factors enumerated in the more traditional accounts of this episode (and summarized in the closing paragraphs of the Introduction) did not play an important role in the exacerbation of relations that led to Stalin's break with Tito. Nevertheless, the primarily bilateral problems (the role and behavior of the Red Army upon reaching Yugoslavia in 1944-45, Soviet attempts to infiltrate the C.P.Y. and the "joint" companies, for example) in some cases were matters of the past or in the process of solution; even cumulatively, taken together with the more recent question of a Balkan federation, they should not have sufficed, under normal circumstances, to precipitate such a drastic outcome. Stalin, himself, implied strongly that, in Dimitrov's phrase, "something else" was behind this denouement when he pounced angrily upon a section in the Yugoslav-Bulgarian agreement that demanded "support" for "all action directed . . . against all hotbeds of aggression." Stalin exclaimed, "this is preventive war—the commonest Komsomol stunt; a tawdry phrase which only brings grist to enemy mills."[1]

Thus Stalin left little doubt that his problems with Tito and Dimitrov were linked integrally to the overall question of the "general line" of Soviet international policy. It was precisely in this wider arena, however, as this study has attempted to demonstrate, that a major factional "debate" had been taking place for approximately two years prior to the clash with the Yugoslavs; the Zhdanovites and their Titoist associates had been pushing the very same line that Stalin now denounced, perhaps with some exaggeration, as "preventive war."

Of course, the term "Titoist," after Yugoslavia's expulsion from the Cominform, was to evoke entirely different connotations: to wit, the image of a "rightist," nationally assertive deviation. However, as the evidence examined here implies so strongly, prior to the break the "Titoists" were almost indistinguishable from the Zhdanovites — militant, ultraleftist, and inclined toward moves, in Europe and Asia alike, deserving the pejorative "adventuristic."

It is for these reasons, that this work has viewed the Soviet-Yugoslav relationship in the wider context of the factional conflict within the Soviet leadership over the direction of international policy as a whole.

Perhaps the most difficult question to resolve concerns the personal role of Stalin himself. It may be objected that, in this presentation, it seems as if his subordinates were dominating the arena of conflict, while he appears only at long intervals, mysteriously *ex machina*, to bring affairs to a logical denouement. Admittedly, this does not square with what is known about Stalin prior to the defeat of the Germans. However, our evidence indicates that, during the years on which this study has focused, he suffered from recurrent bouts of a dangerous and debilitating ailment, reduced his work-load significantly, and absented himself from Moscow for prolonged periods, on doctors' orders. At least partially as a result of this development, his grasp of the daily conduct of policy is shown to have become somewhat discontinuous and superficial. These were precisely the developments that made Stalin's associates believe, it seems, that the time had come to open the battle for the succession.

The more fierce (and desperate) this struggle became, the more overt the traces it left, and that, in all probability, is the reason why so substantial a portion of the "debates" over Soviet international policy (1946–47) is available to us from open sources. Of course, under such conditions, the principal antagonists are likely to overreach themselves, and there seems little question but that the Zhdanovites and Titoists were guilty of that error during 1947. This development, however, may have been exactly the factor that induced Stalin finally, late in that year, to intervene and "behead" a faction which, in its hubris, seemed to be acting as if it were in power already, thus alarming his suspicious mind. Prior to these events, it is highly probable that he had not been entirely displeased to see the contenders for the succession at each other's throats, so long as one faction was not about to attain complete and final victory. In any case, Stalin appears to have learned his lesson, since, after the Tito affair and until the last months of his life, he took great care to maintain a balance between mutually antagonistic subordinates and avoided further prolonged absences from the center.

17 POSTSCRIPT
The Battle Revived, 1952–53

In the winter of 1952–53, echoes of the Varga-Voznesenskii polemic were to be heard once more, following the appearance, on the eve of the Nineteenth CPSU Congress, of Stalin's pamphlet *Economic Problems of Socialism in the U.S.S.R.*, his last major work. This publication contained the ominous phrase: "[Denying] the existence of objective laws of economic activity. . . [leaves us] at the mercy of 'economic' adventurers."[1] At the congress itself, Malenkov, presenting the main report of the Central Committee, stressed this theme, saying, "Denial of the objective character of economic laws is the ideological basis of adventurism.[2]

Precisely who was the target of such vehement denunciation ("adventurism," after all, being one of the most damning pejoratives in the Bolshevik dictionary, used habitually against "leftists") did not become clear until December 24, 1952, more than two months after the congress, when *Pravda* published an article by M. A. Suslov—who had gained prominence, it will be recalled, through his role in Tito's expulsion from the Cominform. Suslov stated that there had been "a group of philosophers and economists" who did not believe in the objective nature of economic laws; that Stalin, in his recent work, had condemned such views as "dangerous"; and that a particularly bad example of this heresy had been "the anti-Marxist booklet by N. Voznesenskii, *The Wartime Economy of the U.S.S.R. during the Great Patriotic War* . . . [which] represented a hotch-potch of voluntaristic views."[3] (This was the first indication published in the Soviet Union that Voznesenskii might have met an untimely end.)

In this connection, Suslov saw fit to reveal that the Central Committee had passed a decree secretly, on July 13, 1949 (during the period of the Leningrad Affair), under the title "On the Journal *Bol'shevik*." In that decree, the editors of *Bol'shevik* were accused of having "permitted a serious mistake when [the journal] opened its columns to sycophantic praise of the booklet by N. Voznesenskii." The personalities who had been guilty of this "serious mistake" were revealed to have been P. N. Fedoseev, M. T. Iovchuk,* D. T. Shepilov (later to become

---

*M. T. Iovchuk, unlike G. F. Aleksandrov, appears to have been a whole-hearted Zhdanovite; over two decades later, he was to publish an article in *Kommunist* (the

Khrushchev's foreign minister), and. . .G. F. Aleksandrov![5] (Having been Zhdanov's client, Aleksandrov had replaced his patron in 1940 as head of Agitprop, was promoted to the Orgburo, and became a Malenkov supporter and the target of one of Zhdanov's most vitriolic attacks in 1947. Aleksandrov was apparently intimidated and changed sides once more in a display of singularly poor timing, since he decided to win his way back into grace through "sycophantic praise" of Zhdanov's ally Voznesenskii, who just then became a victim of the Leningrad Affair!)*

These developments, coinciding with what amounted to Malenkov's anointment as Stalin's successor at the Nineteenth CPSU Congress and continuing, as will be seen, into January and February of 1953, might be viewed, not unreasonably, as an *ex post facto* attempt to justify Malenkov's role in the Leningrad Affair (which could provide eventual ammunition against the new "crown prince," even though it had not been publicized at that date) by portraying one of its main victims as an "anti-Marxist." Suslov's *Pravda* article was followed by the publication of an apology, signed by Fedoseev,[6] and a whole series of further articles denouncing certain economists for "adventurist" and "subjectivist" views, similar to the heresies propounded by Voznesenskii.[7] Early in January of 1953, the USSR Academy of Sciences (Economics) held a well-publicized conference at which K. V. Ostrovitianov, Varga's old nemesis, was compelled to criticize himself and others for having "propagandized and praised" Voznesenskii's "anti-Marxist" work.[8] This session was followed by a general meeting of the academy, January 30–February 2, 1953, at which Pavel F. Yudin delivered a report on Stalin's latest work and denounced Fedoseev for insufficient self-abasement over his "mistake" concerning Voznesenskii.[9] (This was the same Yudin who had edited the Cominform journal, played a major role in the expulsion of Yugoslavia from that organization in June 1948, and, together with Suslov, had replaced the late A. A. Zhdanov in the Cominform apparatus; Yudin was one of the organizers of the Cominform's third general meeting, on November 27, 1949, at which the Yugoslavs were condemned for being "in the power of murderers and spies."[10] Thus, Voznesenskii, appropriately, was denounced in 1952–53 by the bureaucrats who had been Tito's and Zhdanov's adversaries.)

If these were all the data available concerning the period of Stalin's

---

successor to *Bol'shevik*), paying tribute to Zhdanov on the occasion of the eightieth anniversary of his birth.[4]

*As indicated in Appendix B, Aleksandrov was to change sides once again, becoming a strong supporter of Malenkov for the second time, rising to become minister of culture at the apex of Malenkov's fortunes, to be demoted finally, together with his patron.

last months, one would be justified in assuming that the "rightists" under Malenkov had won the final battle and were simply "mopping up" isolated pockets of the Zhdanovshchina (and whatever shreds of reputation it had left). Unfortunately, the picture is not that simple. We now know that, early in November 1952, some weeks after the Nineteenth Party Congress, a group of doctors, most of them Jewish, had been arrested; they were to be vilified on January 13, 1953, in the frame-up that has become known as the "Doctors' Plot." They were alleged to have murdered (by medical means) A. A. Zhdanov and A. S. Shcherbakov, as well as having attempted to kill Marshals A. M. Vasilevskii, L. A. Govorov, and I. S. Konev, and others.[11] Since the alleged victims (and would-be victims) of the "terrorist" doctors included four of the more prominent participants in the Zhdanovite "parade of the (temporary) victors" taking the salute on November 7, 1946, plus Zhdanov's old ally and brother-in-law, Shcherbakov, this sensational announcement could not bode well for the two personalities who had most to gain from Zhdanov's liquidation, Beria and Malenkov. Even more ominous was the commentary in *Izvestia*, on the day the "plot" was publicized, pointing the finger at one of the two, at least:

> The wrecker-doctors were able to function over a considerable period, because some of our Soviet organs and their executive officials lost their vigilance and were infected with gullibility. . . .The State Security organs must be specially vigilant. However, these organs did not promptly discover the terrorist organization of the wrecker-doctors.[12]

This allegation of lack of "vigilance" threatened Beria's very existence; it dated back to Shcherbakov's demise in May 1945, when (prior to A. A. Kuznetsov's incursion into the security domain) Beria undoubtedly still was the "executive official" ultimately responsible for supervision of "State Security organs." (Moreover, with the decline of the Zhdanovshchina, Beria again exercised predominant control of these "organs" in 1948–51, at the very time of Zhdanov's death.) At least one of his predecessors, Yagoda, lost his life after a similar charge.[13] It sounded ominously, therefore, as if at least one-half of the Beria-Malenkov duumvirate might be decapitated.

Material that has become accessible with the appearance of Antonov-Ovseyenko's book (as well as the Khrushchev "memoirs"), leaves little room for doubt that Beria and some of his associates actually were in severe jeopardy from 1951 onward and that the "Doctors' Plot" was fabricated in part to eliminate the Beria group:

The Bip Pope no longer trusted the Little Pope, Beria. Stalin promoted him in order to deprive him of direct control over the secret police. Stalin constantly shuffled the Lubyanka pack. He. . . grew sick of Abakumov. . . .The Master hunted up a replacement for him in the Central Committee apparatus, and in 1951 the Organs got a new chief, Semyon Ignatyev. . . .The case of the Kremlin doctors brings us back to the circumstances of Zhdanov's death. Zhdanov had suffered from hardening of the arteries, in the opinion of the Kremlin professors. To their misfortune, however, the X-ray technician Lydia Timashuk, after studying Zhdanov's electrocardiograms, had diagnosed his difficulty as coronary thrombosis. Meanwhile Zhdanov had not been alerted by anyone and had not taken proper care of himself. When, some years later, the Organs heard about Timashuk's diagnosis, they had her write an official statement refuting the opinion of the Kremlin doctors. . . . Abakumov was the minister of state security at that time. When the head of the investigations division showed up with the materials for the doctors' case, *Abakumov chased him out of his office*. . . . Stalin called in Abakumov. The minister returned from the Central Committee building *to the Lubyanka as a prisoner*. [emphasis added][14]

S. D. Ignatiev [*sic*] a man very close to Khrushchev, had replaced Beria's supporter, Abakumov, as Minister of State Security. In 1952 *he was actively engaged in a savage purge of Beria's men in the security services*. [emphases added][15]

Abakumov, as was pointed out earlier, had played an executioner's role in the Leningrad Affair.

The Gensek had decided that the time had come to part with. . . Beria. . . . Not long before the Gensek's demise, Beria admitted to Mikoyan that he expected to be arrested any day: "He's going to wipe us all out."[16]

However, upon closer analysis, the other half of the Beria-Malenkov axis appears to have been no less imperiled, since *Pravda*, on the same day, suddenly shifted gears after repeated attacks upon deviations of the *left* ("adventurism," "subjectivism") and denounced *"Right* [emphasis added] opportunists standing on the anti-Marxist point of view of the 'damping down' of the class struggle."[17] This phrase seemed to cover not only Malenkov's evident lack of enthusiasm for the Zhdanovshchina, and the priority he had accorded to productivity (over Zhdanov's *partiinost'*) ever since the Eighteenth CPSU Congress, but also the fundamental opposition he had expressed, barely three months earlier, to Khrushchev's ideologically motivated (almost "Maoist") scheme to create "agrotowns" at the expense of private allotments. Malenkov, characteristically, stressed that the author of the plan had forgotten the "production tasks" of agriculture.[18]

If any additional element was required to personalize the sudden shift in Moscow's political winds from "antileftist" to "antirightist," it was the sudden reemergence from obscurity of Zhdanov's son, Yurii, three days after the Kremlin doctors were denounced, as the signatory of an article in *Pravda* actually dealing with economists—a topic rather remote from his own branch of the sciences.[19] His last bow on the political stage, it will be recalled, had been taken some three weeks before the announcement of his father's demise, when he published an abject apology in *Pravda* for his anti-Lysenkoist heresies, addressed to Stalin personally. At that time, his peculiar form of self-abasing public correspondence on a rather esoteric topic was viewed, correctly, as sounding the death knell of the Zhdanovite ascendancy and of the elder Zhdanov himself.

His *Pravda* article of January 16, 1953, however, was not at all apologetic or humiliating for him. Coming three days after the announcement that the enemies of the Soviet Union had murdered his father, who, by inference, therefore was one of the great heroes of the fatherland, the reappearance of Yurii A. Zhdanov signaled a form of canonization of the Zhdanovite cause and its supporters, as a whole. However, one deceased member of that faction had to be excluded specifically from this return to glory, N. A. Voznesenskii. The reason was simple: Zhdanov himself, whether he was actually murdered or not, had never been disgraced officially, publicly or, as far as we know, secretly. Like Kirov, the previous "crown prince," he had been given the funeral and eulogy of a "hero." Voznesenskii, on the other hand, had been denounced in an originally secret decree of the Central Committee, and, what was worse, that decree had been published less than a month earlier. Consequently, while the younger Zhdanov could be permitted to reemerge "on the side of the angels" as the signatory of a *Pravda* broadside against certain deviations, without any inference of culpability on his or his father's part, the victim of that attack, at least by inference, was Voznesenskii. (The article denounced scientists, particularly in economics, who "denied the objective nature of scientific laws.")[20]

It is not the task of this study to resolve the mysteries surrounding the last months of Stalin's life. It does seem, however, as if the old tyrant, after finally anointing his successor in October 1952, was beset, once more, by the same suspicions and fears with which he had come to view his earlier "crown princes," Kirov and Zhdanov. Consequently, having initially allowed attacks to be launched against the reputation of the leftists whom Malenkov had removed about three years earlier, particularly Voznesenskii, probably as a way of legitimizing the succession, Stalin, at the end of 1952, apparently hastened to "restore the balance." No sooner had the developments of October–December 1952 seemed to ensconce Malenkov and Beria in power than the events of January 1953 posed a threat to their positions, perhaps even their lives, as far as can be judged from the data available. The ghosts of their old adversaries, Zhdanov and Shcherbakov, were conjured up, so to speak, to haunt them. That both Beria and Malenkov viewed matters in this light is indicated by their haste in denouncing the whole affair of the Doctors' Plot as a crude fake within weeks of Stalin's death; moreover, they removed from power the official in charge of the "case," Minister of State Security S. D. Ignatiev (subsequently protected by Khrushchev), and packed off Yurii A. Zhdanov to an obscure post in Rostov.[21]

Appendix A
The Beria-Zhdanov Rivalry

The conflict between Beria and Zhdanov may be viewed, to some extent, as rivalry between Yezhov's associates and elements that were promoted to play a role in liquidating the nominal perpetrator of the Yezhovshchina.

Less than two years after taking over the (murdered Kirov's) Leningrad organization, Zhdanov and Stalin co-signed a decree asserting that Yagoda's N.K.V.D. had fallen behind by four years in its quota of political arrests. Their telegram containing this allegation signaled Yagoda's end and his replacement by Yezhov.[1]

Somewhat over a year later, at a well-publicized commemoration ceremony of the twentieth anniversary of the Cheka/O.G.P.U./ N.K.V.D., Zhdanov and Yezhov were featured, side by side at the center of the dais, with Kaganovich, Andreyev, Dimitrov (aligned with Zhdanov and Tito, as this study has indicated), and Voroshilov on the right, and Bratanovskii, Molotov, and Khrushchev on the left.[2]

Yezhov had been a member of the Special Secret Political Department of State Security,[3] which is believed to have "arranged" Kirov's murder (the direct beneficiary being Zhdanov, who took over the victim's Leningrad bailiwick). Other participants in that sinister outfit were A. N. Poskrebyshev, Ya. D. Agranov, and M. F. Shkiriatov (who was to be one of the only 2, out of 154, Leningrad delegates to the 1934 Seventeenth Party Congress to be "reelected" to the 1939 Eighteenth Party Congress).* Thus Zhdanov, having obtained his Leningrad

---

*Since the two delegates, Shkiriatov and A. A. Andreyev, both were also members of the Party Control Commission, a body represented at the Congress irrespective of geographical criteria,[4] one cannot be certain that Shkiriatov owed such prominent survival to the new Leningrad boss, Zhdanov, as a reward for favors rendered. Shkiriatov became Yezhov's assistant in the N.K.V.D.; however, together with Zhdanov, he was to be among Yezhov's accusers at the Eighteenth Party Congress[5] — how voluntary such a role was, in view of the fact that Stalin had chosen Yezhov to be the scapegoat for the Great Purge, is another question. In any case, Shkiriatov was one of the participants, subsequently, at a high point of the Zhdanovshchina, on the famous rostrum "packed" with Zhdanovites, taking the salute during the November 1946 parade, when such personalities as Malenkov, Beria, Molotov, Khrushchev, and Stalin himself were noticeable by their absence (see pp. 28–35). It may be, therefore, that Zhdanov and Shkiriatov were tied to one another, perhaps sharing skeletons in the closet going back to Kirov's assassination.

fiefdom, thanks to services rendered by Yezhov, in return helped to pave Yezhov's path to power by collaborating in the document that marked Yagoda's downfall. Yezhov himself benefitted no less than Zhdanov from Kirov's death, since he replaced the murdered Leningrad leader on the CPSU Secretariat.[6] Moreover, Zhdanov's protracted effort to place his protégés in key positions hardly would have been feasible but for the vacancies created by Yezhov's enormous purge, particularly of Kirov's appointees (a blood bath, the dimensions of which were reflected in the turnover of Leningrad representatives between the two party congresses).[7]

Thus, when Beria took over the N.K.V.D. and purged most of the perpetrators of the Yezhovshchina, he was depriving Zhdanov of allies, to whom the Leningrad leader owed a great deal and who, in turn, were indebted to him.

The Evolution of the Political Relationship between G. F. Aleksandrov and A. A. Zhdanov

According to Dr. Mark Kuchment, Aleksandrov should be viewed as a bon vivant, very bright, but basically cynical and extremely lazy. His rise in the bureaucracy was due primarily to the close personal relationship he managed to develop with Stalin himself. His political pronouncements, it seems, resulted more from expediency than from any personal predilections.[1] Certainly this description indicates his "flexibility" and throws light upon his repeated switches from one faction to another, a behavior that may have precipitated Zhdanov's highly publicized onslaught upon him in June 1947.[2]

Aleksandrov, like Varga, was to survive his critics (unlike Vavilov, for instance, whose heresies pertained to relatively esoteric issues). Both apparently enjoyed the personal protection of an "arbiter" in the very highest of positions, probably Stalin himself.

Kuchment's account lends credibility to Ilya Ehrenburg's assessment that he was attacked by Aleksandrov in 1945 upon someone else's instigation* and that Aleksandrov was trying to signal "Do not take it personally" by approaching Ehrenburg at a Panslav Committee meeting on the day before the attack was published.[3] Ehrenburg himself may have been under Beria's wing, at that stage, since the Jewish Anti-Fascist Committee, of which he was a prominent member, appears to have been established under N.K.V.D. sponsorship.

Alexander M. Nekrich believes that Zhdanov may have viewed with apprehension Aleksandrov's rapid rise as a possible threat to the Leningrad leader's predominance in matters concerning theory, particularly the party's attitude to the arts and sciences.[4] This explanation is quite plausible. Aleksandrov, after all, took over the Central Committee's Agitation and Propaganda Department in September 1940, when Zhdanov appears to have been in trouble; although Zhdanov retained overall supervision of these topics, one may suspect

---

*At that time, Aleksandrov presumably acted under instructions from Zhdanov, who had resumed his supervisory functions in Moscow when the siege of Leningrad was lifted.

that Aleksandrov obtained his position at someone else's initiative. Whatever may be the correct interpretation of developments in 1940, or of their personal relationship when Zhdanov came back from Leningrad at the end of the siege, by 1946 Aleksandrov attained increased prominence. He had already become a member of the Orgburo[5] and, on January 21, 1946, he was chosen to deliver the ceremonial address on the occasion of the twenty-second anniversary of Lenin's death—quite an honor for the young (then 38 years old) chief of Agitation and Propaganda, who spoke on topics directly relevant to the Zhdanovshchina, which was to be unleashed some days later. Zhdanov, with undoubted seniority, particularly on such issues, would have seemed to be a more obvious candidate to shoulder this task. Significantly, the style, tenor, and substance of Aleksandrov's speech all differed to some extent from the approach that came to be identified with the Zhdanovshchina. Zhdanov appears unlikely to have sponsored this address, which dealt with the great war effort but failed to mention Leningrad, spoke of the *Soviet* (as opposed to the *Great Russian*) people as "the conscious creator of a new social regime," referred to the "enlargement" and blossoming of workers' democracy, and discussed the "just resolution of the national question,"[6] a phrase more easily identifiable with Beria's than with Zhdanov's line.[7] If the political sentiments expressed in this speech did not suffice to annoy Zhdanov, then perhaps the very fact that Aleksandrov was chosen to deliver it may have had this effect. Soviet leaders do not take kindly to being over-shadowed in their own special domain by former protégés.

Early in 1947, Aleksandrov's book *The History of Western Philosophy* was awarded a Stalin Prize.[8] Just prior to this event, on December 4, 1946, he had delivered a major address to the Academy of Sciences. This lecture was given great prominence, appearing first in *Pravda* (December 5 and 6). On January 6, 1947, it was decided that the Publishing House for Political Literature, of the Union of State Publishing Houses, would print two hundred thousand copies of the address under the title *Concerning Soviet Democracy*. Aleksandrov's lecture paid lip service to some of the Zhdanov-Voznesenskii positions, referring, for example, to the "subordination of English economy and policy to American economy and policy." However, Aleksandrov added that "great historic consequences. . .will follow in the world economic, political, and diplomatic arena in coming *years or decades*, as the result of the supplanting of England by the United States of America and the subordination of England to the interests of the United States [emphasis added].[9] Zhdanov and Voznesenskii, unlike Varga, asserted, of course, that the effects of postwar developments in the West, in the form of a crisis that would follow America's assumption of leadership, would be felt much more imminently than in "years or decades." Aleksandrov praised "the construction of democratic states in Yugoslavia, Czechoslovakia, Poland, Bulgaria, and other states,"[10] but failed to draw Zhdanovite conclusions from this development, in terms of an anticipated reversal in the correlation of forces between the Eastern and Western blocs.

Like his Lenin anniversary address of some ten months earlier, Aleksandrov's lecture stressed Soviet as opposed to Great Russian achievements, for example in World War II,[11] as well as praising the accomplishments of the Soviet state rather than of the party.[12] Moreover, also in a manner quite alien to the customs of the Zhdanovshchina, he actually spelled out the substance of Western critiques of Bolshevism (by Max Weber, Max Lerner, Harold Laski and others), concerning such delicate issues as the totalitarian nature of Soviet rule, the "Oriental" character of the Soviet people and state, the inability of Marxism (not just the Soviet brand) to consider "irrational" elements in human motivation, the single-party structure of Soviet government, absence of freedom of the press or of toleration within the Soviet system, and even the pervasive influence of the Soviet security apparatus.[13] Although Aleksandrov, of course, attempted to rebut such attacks, the very fact that they were spelled out at all in a publication with wide circulation presented a strange contrast to the prevailing patterns of the Zhdanovshchina.

Thus, when Zhdanov launched his personal attack upon Aleksandrov on June 20, 1947, there is reason for believing that he was tackling a former protégé, who not only was beginning to rival his sponsor in the latter's special area of responsibility and reputation, but also, if he had not actually endorsed the line of the Malenkov-Beria opposition, at any rate had moved in a direction incompatible with Zhdanovite tenets.

The explanations suggested by Nekrich and Kuchment both are revealing in this context, since they indicate that Aleksandrov, no dogmatist, was precisely the kind of man to attempt establishing his own fiefdom by switching factional allegiance, opportunistically, presumably relying upon the protective shadow of his relationship with Stalin. It seems that, as he began to establish his independence vis-à-vis Zhdanov, he required additional support (particularly in view of Stalin's prolonged absences from Moscow during the immediate postwar period), and this factor led to linkage with Malenkov, of one kind or another, as a counterweight to Zhdanov. That Malenkov joined in condemning Aleksandrov, belatedly, at the founding meeting of the

Cominform, *three months after Zhdanov had done so* (in a gathering
that was dominated overwhelmingly by Zhdanov and the Yugoslavs),
could not but be perceived by observers of the increasingly deep rift
between the two factions as a sign of Malenkov's weakness, indeed
humiliation.

Aleksandrov himself apparently viewed the episode in this light
and drew characteristic conclusions. Intimidated, he seems to have
switched sides once more, in a display of singularly poor timing, since
he attempted to win back his way into grace through "sycophantic
praise" of Zhdanov's ally Voznesenskii (Zhdanov himself having died
in the meantime), who was about to become a victim of the Leningrad
Affair! Consequently, Aleksandrov brought down upon his own head
a Central Committee decree of condemnation on July 13, 1949.[14]
However, by 1950 he had managed already to bounce back into Stalin's
favor.

Buffeted, like most other bureaucrats, by the vicissitudes of the
terminal period of Stalin's life, Aleksandrov earned his passage back
into Malenkov's good graces, rising, during Malenkov's rather brief
reign after Stalin's death, to become Malenkov's minister of culture in
1954. In March 1955, a few weeks after Malenkov was deprived of the
Chairmanship of the Council of Ministers, Aleksandrov lost his post
as minister of culture,[15] ostensibly because of his involvement in a sex
scandal.[16]

It is noteworthy that five days after Aleksandrov was fired, on
March 27, 1955, his demotion was linked publicly to accusations that
were being levelled simultaneously against Malenkov, concerning economic issues. Appropriately, the author of this revelation was the same
K. V. Ostrovitianov who had replaced Varga early in 1948, taking over
the newly formed Institute of Economics, and who had been the target
of criticism for his pro-Voznesenskii posture during the tumultuous last
months of Stalin's life.[17]

Appendix C
B. M. Kedrov

There seems to be little doubt that B. M. Kedrov enjoyed Zhdanov's support, although few details are known of their political relationship. Both Kedrov's father (Mikhail S. Kedrov) and his brother (Igor M. Kedrov) had been high-ranking security service officials under Yezhov (with whom Zhdanov also had close ties, see Appendix A), who were tortured and killed after Beria replaced Yezhov.[1] In fact, the Kedrov family had been at daggers drawn with Beria ever since 1921,[2] and their enmity had become a blood feud with the liquidation of two of the Kedrovs. Consequently, B. M. Kedrov was a logical choice as Zhdanov's candidate for promotion over Aleksandrov, once the Leningrad leader realized that his erstwhile protégé was "playing factional games" (see Appendix B). Presumably, that is why Kedrov was made editor of *Voprosy Filosofii* when that journal was established following Zhdanov's verbal assault upon Aleksandrov. Kedrov, unlike Aleksandrov, could not conceivably look to Beria and Malenkov for support; thus, he could be relied upon to remain Zhdanov's client.

The attack upon B. M. Kedrov in 1949, when his journal had come under the editorship of D. I. Chesnokov, very likely was the work of Beria, who had reason not only to purge yet another Zhdanovite, but who could not afford to let a bitterly hostile Kedrov remain in a prominent position.[3] One of the charges against Beria published in December 1953, when his name was pilloried in a *Pravda* editorial, was that he had killed the elder Kedrov.[4] It appears that Khrushchev was attempting to enlist the support of surviving Zhdanovites by exploiting the "Beria case." B. M. Kedrov himself, in the Khrushchev period, was to be promoted to the rank of director of the Institute of History of Natural Science and Technology of the USSR Academy of Sciences.[5] During his "Secret Speech" to the Twentieth Party Congress, Khrushchev again resuscitated the case of the elder (Mikhail S.) Kedrov, claiming that he had been tortured under Beria.[6] Given the senior Kedrov's own shameful career in the secret police,[7] it was a peculiar name to invoke, unless Khrushchev, now attempting to annihilate Malenkov (at least politically), with Beria long since shot, was reviving memories of Zhdanov's associates, who were anathema to the

Leningrad leader's main surviving adversary, Malenkov. While Kedrov senior had confronted Malenkov only indirectly (in as far as Malenkov and Beria apparently were linked closely in the post-Yezhov period), his younger son had been involved in a more obvious adversary relationship, since he seems to have owed his editorship of *Voprosy Filosofii* to Zhdanov, benefitting directly from Zhdanov's onslaught upon Malenkov's ally (at that time) and subsequent minister of culture, G. F. Aleksandrov. Khrushchev apparently knew how to exploit anti-Malenkov sentiments among Zhdanovites who had managed to stay alive during the Leningrad Affair. (It is true that Khrushchev did not dare, until 1957, to charge Malenkov openly with instigating the Affair and that, earlier, V. S. Abakumov was made to bear the blame; Malenkov's role was hardly a secret from the cognescenti, however, almost from the time the victims disappeared.)

APPENDIX D

Stalin, 1945–52: Possible Limitations on His Activities; His Appearances, Statements, and Publications

Whether because of ill health and related prolonged absences from Moscow, or other reasons, Stalin seems to have been considerably less active than normally during the period between the fall of 1945 and the culmination of the Leningrad Affair. A useful index of Stalin's low profile is the relative sparsity of writings in his name appearing during the greater part of the period in question. Between February 23, 1945, and September 5, 1945, no fewer than eighteen major published statements were attributed to Stalin. Subsequently, there was a gap of some three months without any publications signed by him. In fact, there is reason to believe that he was in Sochi, recovering from cardiovascular problems, during this period. The Soviet leader had a series of interviews and letters printed during February–March 1946 (plus the important February 9 "preelection" speech). However, between March 27 and September 24, 1946, the only noteworthy publication to bear his name was the May Day order of the day. From September 24, 1946, until the spring of 1950, only thirteen publications worth noting appeared in Stalin's name, or fewer than one every three months.[1] Most of these were quite brief, and many were not substantive.

Suddenly, in 1950, Stalin's pen was pressed again into action; from then on, he published his lengthy and important writings on Marxism and linguistics (summer of 1950),* his *Economic Problems of Socialism* (fall of 1952), and many letters and interviews. Between the spring of 1950 and his last published work, a letter to James Reston, on December 26, 1952, he published some twenty-one pieces, several of considerable substance and length.

These statistics would seem to substantiate accounts asserting that Stalin was repeatedly incapacitated because of health problems during

*The biting critique of this work in Aleksandr I. Solzhenitsyn's *The First Circle*, (Chapter 19), is inspired literature, but does not devote attention to its significant political implications.

179

the first half of his seven to eight postwar years.

Of course, if, as Dr. Alexander Nekrich believes, Stalin was helping to promote conflict between Malenkov and Zhdanov, he might have wished, in any case, to maintain a low profile as an incentive for his lieutenants to "slug it out" in a battle for the putative succession. Nevertheless, there is evidence concerning Stalin's health problems in this period (see pp. 27–28, 36). Moreover, as this study has indicated, the peculiar circumstances surrounding the interview he granted to Harold Stassen in the spring of 1947 would seem to reveal traces of other hands than Stalin's alone in manipulating delicate issues (see pp. 124–29). That raises questions of his ability, at the time, to deal with the management of day-to-day affairs. Just the fact that he took extended vacations late in 1945 and 1946 (missing the October Revolution ceremonies in both years) would be out of character, unless Stalin was seriously incapacitated. A man who disposed of an uncounted number of domestic adversaries (real or potential), many of them top level cadres, hardly would have been so trusting as to leave Moscow unattended, were it not absolutely necessary. Stalin is unlikely to have forgotten the specific circumstances that made possible his initial victory over Trotsky, namely, the latter's absence from Moscow at the crucial juncture immediately following Lenin's death. (So, too, was Khrushchev to lose his position in 1964, while he was resting near Stalin's vacation area on the shores of the Black Sea.)[2]

Appendix E
Varga's Publications After Zhdanov's Death

In one of the great survival stories of Soviet history, Varga managed to continue publishing his material, without having to renounce fully (until mid-1949) the allegedly erroneous positions for which he had been censured since the meeting held in the spring of 1947. In the second half of 1948, another conference gathered, again under the direction of K. V. Ostrovitianov, this time focusing on positions adopted by Varga's now defunct journal *Mirovoe Khoziaistvo i Mirovaia Politika* (World economics and world politics). In his opening report, Ostrovitianov criticized Varga for not yet having admitted his "reformist" mistakes (either during the initial conference or in his writings since then). Once again, Varga managed defiantly to hold his ground on most issues:

> Of course, it is painful that I, a party member, should be berated, in my old age, in the organs of the press. . . . I cannot follow the advice and admit all the criticism of my work to be correct. This would mean that I am deceiving the party, hypocritically saying, "I am in agreement with the criticism" when I was not in agreement with it.[1]

Varga did concede, however, that he had erred with respect to two issues, land reform in the "new democracies" and the amount of time it would take for an economic crisis to break out in the United States; he now stated that such a crisis might take even *longer* to develop than he had anticipated. If Varga had been too bold (or "leftist") in his original prediction of the date of such a crisis, where did that leave a real "leftist" like Voznesenskii? Varga noted, moreover, that his had not been an error of "principle."[2]

He insisted steadfastly that he had been correct regarding both the impoverishment of the belligerent powers (excepting the United States) and the importance of Britain's debtor status vis-à-vis India ("What sense is there in trumpeting that India is now the same colony of England as before. . . ?").[3]

Regarding his position with respect to the ability of bourgeois states to plan their economies, while qualifying slightly his earlier statements, he reasserted:

The usual function of a state as an instrument for plundering the working people can come into conflict with its function as an institution for the defense of the country. A situation can arise, and has arisen in time of war, in which the state in the interests of conducting the war, in the *general* interests of all monopolies...has been compelled to act against the interests of the *individual* monopolies.[4]

On March 15, 1949, Varga was allowed to publish a lengthy letter to the editor in *Pravda*, strongly defending himself and concluding:

I request the editor to publish this letter so that no doubts about my attitude may arise among the workers, and in general among honest people abroad, under the influence of the slanderous propaganda of the enemies of the working class, the instigators of a new war.[5]

Thus, although he was being berated publicly, his defense also was provided with a prominent forum. It appears that Stalin may have been protecting him, at least until the Leningrad purge was implemented (Varga's letter was published only two days after the announcement that Voznesenskii was being demoted).[6] Somewhat later in the year, however, Varga was forced to capitulate. With respect to his accusers, he stated:

This criticism was necessary and correct. My mistake was that I did not recognize at once the correctness of this criticism as other comrades did. But better late than never.[7]

This rather flippant *mea culpa* ("better late than never!") revealed that Varga perhaps was less than totally stricken with remorse over his past "heresies." Moreover, rather tendentiously, Varga referred to Lenin's work "Left-Wing Communism, an Infantile Disorder."[8] This may have been Varga's way of saying, "Yes, I have been forced to revise my previous pronouncements, but the 'Left-Wing Communists' of the 1940s are no longer in a position to publish anything!" Varga pointed out that "he is wise who does not make very substantial mistakes and who is able to correct them easily and quickly."[9] After all, *his* mistakes were merely ideological; *their's* had been factional and operational.

In fact, Varga managed to remain on the editorial board of *Problems of Economics (Voprosy Ekonomiki)*[10] and continued to publish in that and other journals.[11] However, during the subsequent few years he had to cleave closely to the line he had adopted grudgingly in his *mea culpa*, published in the third 1949 issue of *Problems of Economics*. His new orthodoxy was reflected in the following paragraph, published in 1952:

> A certain group in the Conservative Party, Lord Amery Wooton and others, have repeatedly opposed American loans under existing oppressive conditions. The Bevan group in the Labour Party, reflecting the dissatisfaction of broad strata of the population, is raising the question of lowering the excessive military expenditures dictated by the American aggressors.[12]

Posthumously, therefore, the Voznesenskii-Zhdanov group had at least one of its propositions accepted by its former victim, Varga, namely that one should lure away the secondary (British) antagonist from the primary adversary (the United States). The fact remained, however, that Voznesenskii and Zhdanov were dead, while Varga was very much alive.

NOTES

Chapter 1

1. For a concise analysis, see Uri Ra'anan, "Some Political Perspectives Concerning the U.S.-Soviet Strategic Balance," in *The Superpowers in a Multi-Nuclear World*, ed. Geoffrey Kemp, Robert Pfaltzgraff, Jr., and Uri Ra'anan, pp. 18–19.
2. Ibid.

Chapter 2

1. Robert Conquest, *Power and Policy in the USSR*, p. 295.
2. Jonathan Harris, "The Origins of the Conflict between Malenkov and Zhdanov: 1939–41," *Slavic Review* vol. 35, no. 2, June 1976, pp. 291, 292.
3. Leonard Schapiro, *The Communist Party of the Soviet Union*, p. 407.
4 Harris, "Origins," pp. 291–92 n., 293 n. 15, 294 n. 18.
5. Schapiro, *Communist Party*, p. 436.
6. Harris, "Origins," p. 292 n.
7. Harris, "Origins," pp. 290–92.
8. Ibid., pp. 292–93.
9. Harrison E. Salisbury, *The 900 Days*, p. 163.
10. Harris, "Origins," pp. 296–97; Boris Meissner, "Schdanow (II)," *Osteuropa*, vol. 2, no. 7, April 1952, p. 95.
11. Salisbury, *900 Days*, p. 165.
12. John Erickson, *The Road to Stalingrad*, p. 30; Meissner, "Schdanow (II)," p. 94.
13. Harris, "Origins," p. 297 n. 76.
14. Erickson, *Road to Stalingrad*, p. 96, and see n. 75.
15. A. A. Zhdanov, *Pravda*, June 29, 1939, as cited in Jane Degras, ed., *Soviet Documents on Foreign Policy*, vol. 3, p. 352.
16. Admiral N. G. Kuznetsov, "Before the War," *International Affairs* (Moscow), no. 1, January 1967, p. 100; Albert Seaton, *Stalin as Military Commander*, p. 94.
17. Harris, "Origins," p. 291.
18. Edgar Tomson, "The Annexation of the Baltic States," in Thomas T. Hammond, ed., *The Anatomy of Communist Takeovers*, p. 224; "Communist Takeover of Estonia," Special Report No. 3 of the Select Committee on Communist Aggression, U.S. House of Representatives, 1954, including emigré eyewitness accounts.
19. Martin Van Creveld, *Hitler's Strategy 1940–1941 — The Balkan Clue* pp. 69–71; Georg Von Rauch, *A History of Soviet Russia*, pp. 297–98.

20. Barry A. Leach, *German Strategy Against Russia, 1939–41*, p. 67; S. Goliakov and B. Ponizovsky, *Le Vrai Sorge*, trans. M. Matignon, pp. 242–43.

21. Goliakov and Ponizovsky, *Le Vrai Sorge*, pp. 242–43; F. W. Deakin and G. R. Storry, *The Case of Richard Sorge*, p. 223.

22. For whatever it may be worth, according to the "controversial" writer David Irving, German intelligence learned of an August 2, 1940, meeting at which, despite the assurances of Molotov and Marshal Voroshilov regarding the strength of Soviet defenses, there was discussion of "certain information [which] indicated that after her victory in the West, she [Germany] would start a war against Russia." In addition to indicating perhaps that Molotov had a personal stake in the pact with Germany, beyond merely having implemented orders to negotiate with Ribbentrop—an assumption consistent with his apparent downgrading the following month—Irving's account appears to indicate that Sorge's warnings were being taken very seriously in Moscow. See David Irving, *Hitler's War*, p. 162.

23. A. M. Vasilevskii, *Delo Vsei Zhizni*, p. 105, as cited in Albert Seaton, *Stalin as Military Commander*, p. 92.

24. Alan Clark, *Barbarossa, The Russian-German Conflict, 1941–45*, pp. 278–80.

25. Zbigniew Brzezinski, ed., *Political Controls in the Soviet Army*, pp. 5–6.

26. *Pravda*, September 7, 1940, p. 1: "Ukaz," Prezidiuma Verkhovnogo Soveta SSSR Ob obrazovanii narodnogo komissariata gosudarstvennogo kontrolia SSSR (signed) Predsedatel' Prezidiuma Verkhovnogo Soveta SSSR M. Kalinin, Sekretar' Prezidiuma Verkhovnogo Soveta SSSR A. Gorkin. Moskva, Kreml', 6 sentiabria 1940g; John Erickson, *The Soviet High Command*, pp. 557, 840–41; Robert Conquest, *The Great Terror*, pp. 645–49; Anton Antonov-Ovseyenko, *The Time of Stalin, Portrait of a Tyranny*, pp. 282–83; Roman Kolkowicz, *The Soviet Military and the Communist Party*, p. 63; Brzezinski, ed., *Political Controls*, p. 5. It should be noted, however, that Mekhlis may have been penalized for trying to blame the Finnish fiasco on "mistakes by the People's Commissariat of Defense and by K. E. Voroshilov personally" for which "Mekhlis was sharply rebuked." See N. G. Kuznetsov, "Pered voinoi," *Oktiabr'*, 1965, no. 9, pp. 188–89, in Seweryn Bialer, ed., *Stalin and His Generals*, p. 136.

27. Vasilevskii, *Delo Vsei Zhizni*, p. 106, in Seaton, *Stalin as Military Commander*, p. 92.

28. See n. 26. As was pointed out above, Mekhlis, until that point, had been deputy people's commissar of defense and chief of the Main Political Administration of the Red Army. See also Bialer, *Stalin and His Generals*, p. 634.

29. *Pravda*, September 7, 1940, p. 1. Ukaz—Prezidiuma Verkhovnogo Soveta SSSR—O naznachenii tov. Mekhlisa L.Z. narodnokom komissarom gosudarstvennogo kontrolia SSSR i zamestitelem predsedatelia SNK SSSR-(signed) Predsedatel' Prezidiuma Verkhovnogo Soveta SSSR M. Kalinin, Sekretar' Prezidiuma Verkhovnogo Soveta SSSR A. Gorkin, Moskva, Kreml', 6 sentiabria 1940 g.

30. *Pravda* September 7, 1940, p. 1. Ukaz-O naznachenii tov. Vyshinskogo A. Ya. zamestitelem narodnogo komissara inostrannikh del.

postanovlenie Soveta Narodnykh Komissarov Soyuza SSSR- (signed) Predsedatel' Soveta Narodnykh Komissarov Soyuza SSSR V. Molotov, Upravliaiushchii Delami Soveta Narodnykh Komissarov Soyuza SSR M. Khlomov Moskva, Kreml', 6 sentiabria 1940g.

31. "V Tsentral'nom Komitete VKP (b)," *Pravda*, September 7, 1940, p. 3; Percy E. Corbett, "The Aleksandrov Story," *World Politics*, vol. I, no. 2, January 1949, p. 162; Associated Press, "Vishinsky Named as Molotoff Aid," *New York Times*, September 8, 1940, p. 28; Harris, "Origins," pp. 299–300.

32. A. S. Iakovlev, *Tsel'zhizni*, pp. 208–36, in Bialer, *Stalin and His Generals*, pp. 116–22.

33. Colonel-General B. L. Vannikov, "Iz zapisok narkoma vooruzheniia," *Voenno-istoricheskii zhurnal*, 1962, no. 2, pp. 78–86, in ibid., pp. 153–54; General of the Army A. V. Khrulev, "Stanovlenie strategicheskogo tyla v Velikoi Otechestvennoi," *Voenno-istoricheskii zhurnal*, 1961, no. 6, pp. 64–80, in ibid., pp. 368–77; A. M. Nekrich's *June, 1941*, sparked a major controversy in the USSR, during which Zhdanov's role and that of his close collaborator, N. G. Kuznetsov (at that time commander in chief of Soviet Naval Affairs) were discussed. See "Extracts from the book by A. M. Nekrich, 22 June 1941," in *Survey: A Journal of Soviet and Eastern European Studies*, no. 63, April 1967, pp. 170–73; "Discussion of the Book," *Survey*, no. 63, pp. 173–80; Maury Lissan, "Stalin the Appeaser," *Survey*, no. 76, Summer 1970, pp. 53–63.

34. N. G. Kuznetsov, "Voenno-Morskoi Flot nakanune Velikoi Otechestvennoi voiny," *Voenno-istoricheskii zhurnal*, 1965, no. 9, pp. 73–74; Kuznetsov, "Pered voinoi," *Oktiabr'*, 1965, no. 11, pp. 146–47, 162–71, in Bialer, *Stalin and His Generals*, 189–200 (esp. pp. 190–91). A serialized version of Kuznetsov's memoirs appears in English in *International Affairs* (Moscow), from May 1966 to March 1967.

35. *Pravda*, May 7, 1941, p. 1: Ukaz, Prezidiuma Verkhovnogo Soveta SSSR- Ob osvobozhdenii tov. Molotova V.M. ot obiazannosti predsedatel' soveta narodnykh komissarov SSSR- (signed) Predsedatel' Presidiuma Verkhovnogo Soveta SSSR, M. Kalinin, Secretar' Presidiuma Verkhovnogo Soveta SSSR A. Gorkin. Ukaz, Presidiuma Verkhovnogo Soveta SSSR- O naznachenii tov. I.V. Stalin predsedatelem soveta narodnykh komissarov SSSR- (signed) Predsedatel' Presidiuma Verkhovnogo Soveta SSSR, M. Kalinin, Sekretar' Presidiuma Verkhovnogo Soveta SSSR A. Gorkin. Ukaz, Prezidiuma Verkhovnogo Soveta SSSR- O naznachenii tov. V.M. Molotova zamestitelem predsedatel' soveta narodnykh komissarov SSSR- (signed) Predsedatel' Presidiuma Verkhovnogo Soveta SSSR M. Kalinin, Sekretar' Presidiuma Verkhovnogo Soveta SSSR A. Gorkin.

36. Kuznetsov, in Bialer, *Stalin and His Generals*, p. 101.

37. Harris, "Origins." p. 302.

38. Salisbury, *900 Days*, pp. 169–70.

39. Antonov-Ovseyenko, *Time of Stalin*, pp. 266–67, 282.

40. Svetlana Alliluyeva, *Only One Year*, p. 420.

41. Alliluyeva, *Only One Year*, p. 258 fn.

42. Erickson, *Road to Stalingrad*, p. 188.

43. Antonov-Ovseyenko, *Time of Stalin*, p. 267.

44. Salisbury, *900 Days*, p. 258. See also Appendix A.

45. Ibid., p. 256.

188   *Notes to pp. 20–25*

46. Alexander Werth, *Russia: Hopes and Fears*, p. 82.
47. Strobe Talbott, ed. and trans., *Khrushchev Remembers*, pp. 256–57.
48. Antonov-Ovseyenko, *Time of Stalin*, pp. 267, 282.
49. Salisbury, *900 Days*, pp. 308–09.
50. Clark, *Barbarossa*, pp. 141–42; Salisbury, *900 Days*, 311; B. V. Bychevskii, *Gorod-front*, pp. 92–95, 98–100, in Bialer, *Stalin and His Generals*, p. 437.
51. N. N. Voronov, "Podvig sovetskogo naroda," *Istoriia SSSR*, 1965, no. 4, pp. 21–22; idem, *Na sluzhbe voennoi*, pp. 194–95, in Bialer, *Stalin and His Generals*, p. 458; Salisbury, *900 Days*, p. 645 n.
52. Erickson, *Road to Stalingrad*, pp. 352–53; Salisbury, *900 Days*, pp. 605–12.
53. Antonov-Ovseyenko, *Time of Stalin*, p. 282.
54. Franz Borkenau, *European Communism*, p. 283. This particular assertion has not been supported by other sources. Soviet biographic sources published at a relative high point in Malenkov's career, early in 1954, contain no reference to his work in the International Department. (See Conquest, *Power and Policy*, p. 470.) Indeed, such authorities as Fainsod imply that a Foreign or International Department in the Secretariat of the C.C. was not re-established until the postwar period. Others believe that the International Department inherited the functions of the Comintern prior to the termination of the war.
55. Enrique Castro Delgado, *Mi Fe Se Perdió*, pp. 229–31.
56. Wolfgang Leonhard, *Die Revolution Entlässt Ihre Kinder*, p. 242.
57. Castro Delgado, *Mi Fe*, pp. 229–31.
58. Ibid., p. 221.
59. Schapiro, *Communist Party*, p. 512.
60. Ibid., Conquest, *Power*, p. 80.
61. Salisbury, *900 Days*, p. 341.
62. Vladimir Rudolf, "The Execution of Policy, 1945–57," in Robert E. Slusser, ed., *Soviet Economic Policy in Postwar Germany*, pp. 36–41. This is a valuable series of firsthand accounts by former Soviet officials in the Soviet occupation zone of Germany. See also Vladimir Aleksandrov, "The Dismantling of German Industry," in Slusser, ibid., pp. 14–17.
63. Rudolf, in ibid., pp. 41–42; Schapiro, *Communist Party*, pp. 512–13.
64. N. S. Patolichev, *Ispytaniye na zrelost' [Test of maturity]*, pp. 280–84 — see T. H. Rigby, "How the Obkom Secretary Was Tempered," in *Problems of Communism*, March–April 1980, pp. 59–60.
65. Solomon Volkov, *Testimony, the Memoirs of Dmitri Shostakovich*, pp. 269–70.
66. Antonov-Ovseyenko, *Time of Stalin*, p. 298.

Chapter 3

1. Interview with Alexander M. Nekrich at the Russian Research Center of Harvard University, February 6, 1979.
2. George K. Schueller, *The Politburo*, p. 68. Very little is known of the activities of this or other committees of the Supreme Soviet.

3. J. V. Stalin, "Report on the Work of the Central Committee to the Seventeenth Congress of the Communist Party of the Soviet Union, January 26, 1934, Section I—The Continuing Crisis of World Capitalism and the Position of the Soviet Union," in Stalin, *Works*, vol. 13, pp. 288–388, particularly pp. 288–312; Stalin, "Report on the Work of the Central Committee to the Eighteenth Congress of the Communist Party of the Soviet Union, March 10, 1939, Section I—The Soviet Union and International Affairs," in Stalin, *Leninism: Selected Writings*, 434–79, particularly pp. 434–44; Stalin, Speech of February 9, 1946, "Rech' na predvybornom sobranii izbiratelei Stalinskogo izbiratel'nogo okruga goroda Moskvy," in Robert H. McNeal, ed., *Sochineniia 16 (3)*, pp. 1–22, also in *Bol'shevik*, no. 3, 1946; a general evaluation of the Zhdanov position appears in R. N. Carew Hunt, *The Theory and Practice of Communism*, pp. 245–64.

4. Yves Delbars, *The Real Stalin*, p. 393.

5. H. Montgomery Hyde, *Stalin*, pp. 549, 559. This work is somewhat controversial; however, on the topic of Stalin's health, its assertions are compatible with data from other sources.

6. Delbars, *Real Stalin*, p. 398.

7. Hyde, *Stalin*, p. 559.

8. *Pravda*, November 8, 1946, picture of the parade and accompanying text.

9. Conquest, *Power*, pp. 84, 86, 97, 395–97; Salisbury, *900 Days*, p. 140 fn., Schueller, *Politburo*, p. 19.

10. *New York Times*, December 21, 1980, p. 43, obituary of A. N. Kosygin.

11. Erickson, *Road to Stalingrad*, p. 235; Salisbury, *900 Days*, pp. 303, 569, 588, 604, 666; Talbott, *Khrushchev Remembers*, p. 257.

12. Conquest, pp. 95, 400, 434–35; Salisbury, *900 Days*, p. 143; Talbott, *Khrushchev Remembers*, p. 256. The charge of "Russian nationalism" was by no means unfounded; in the second half of the 1940s, the Zhdanovshchina was to reek of Great Russian chauvinism—moreover, a decade earlier, Zhdanov had been prominently involved in a campaign through which "the writers of history texts received instructions which resulted in a complete revision of attitude toward the Russian past. The nationalist historians were . . . restored to their posts. The new history . . . celebrated Tsarist military victories and territorial expansion." Merle Fainsod, *How Russia is Ruled*, pp. 113, 641 n. 43, with special reference to J. Stalin, A. Zhdanov, and S. Kirov, "Zamechaniia po Povodu Konspekta Uchebnika po 'Istorii SSSR," *Istorik Marksist* 1 (53), (1936), pp. 5–6.

13. Conquest, *Power*, p. 168; Kuznetsov, "Pered voinoi," *Oktiabr'*, 1965, No. 9, pp. 174–82, excerpted in Bialer, *Stalin and His Generals*, pp. 90–98; Salisbury, *900 Days*, pp. 163–66.

14. Salisbury, *900 Days*, p. 666 fn. 8.

15. Abdurakhman Avtorkhanov, *Stalin and the Soviet Communist Party*, p. 253; Conquest, *Power*, pp. 71, 100, 395; "G. M. Popov, Prominent Survivor of the 'Leningrad Affair' Dies," Radio Liberty Research, CRD 37/68.

16. General of the Army A. V. Khrulev, "Stanovlenie strategicheskogo tyla v Velikoi Otechestvennoi voine," *Voennoistoricheskii zhurnal*, 1961, no. 6, pp. 64–80, in Bialer, *Stalin and His Generals*, pp. 368–77; ibid., p. 632; Erickson, *Road to Stalingrad*, p. 235; Salisbury, *900 Days*, p. 561.

17. Patolichev, *Ispytaniye na zrelost'*, pp. 280–84, 3–4, 218–25, 98—T. H. Rigby, "How the Obkom Secretary Was Tempered," pp. 58–61; Conquest, *Power*, pp. 70, 85; Edward Crankshaw, *Khrushchev*, pp. 158–59.

18. B. A. Abramov, "Organizatsionno-partiinaia rabota KPSS v gody chetvertoi piatiletki" (Organizational-Party Work of the C.P.S.U. in the years of the Fourth Five-Year Plan,) *Voprosy Istorii K.P.S.S.*, no. 3, April 1979, p. 61.

19. Salisbury, *900 Days*, p. 634.

20. Ibid., p. 137; Andrew I. Lebed and P. K. Urban, eds., *Who Was Who in the USSR*, p. 210.

21. Conquest, *Power*, pp. 164, 167, 168, 179, 332; Salisbury, *900 Days*, pp. 601, 619, 634, 666 fn. 8.

22. Conquest, *Power*, pp. 164, 206–07, 444.

23. For detailed description of the events in the Soviet occupation zone of Germany, see pp. 90–92.

24. Ambassador Walter Bedell Smith, dispatch to the secretary of state, July 15, 1946, *Foreign Relations of the United States*, vol. 6, pp. 767–68.

25. Roman Kolkowicz, *The Soviet Military and the Communist Party*, pp. 73–75.

26. Boris I. Nicolaevsky, "Malenkov, His Rise and His Policy," *The New Leader*, vol. 36, no. 12, March 23, 1953, pp. 3–4.

27. Kolkowicz, *Soviet Military* p. 72; Clark, *Barbarossa*, p. 514.

28. Alexander Werth, *Russia at War, 1941–1945*, p. 190.

29. Captain F. Belov, Lt. Colonel I. Dmitriev, and Major N. Tushin, "Political Education of the Soviet Troops," in Zbigniew Brzezinski, *Political Controls in the Soviet Army*, Research Program on the USSR, Studies on the USSR, no. 6, 1954, p. 46 fn.; Lebed and Urban, *Who Was Who*, p. 210.

30. Salisbury, *900 Days*, p. 629.

31. Werth, *Russia at War*, p. 307.

32. Lt. General Hoyt S. Vandenburg, Director of Central Intelligence, Memorandum to Fleet Admiral William D. Leahy, U.S.N., Chief of Staff to the Commander-in-Chief, August 27, 1946. Declassified Document No. 75-245-B, Carrollton Press Inc., Declassified Documents Series.

33. S. V. Utechin, *Everyman's Concise Encyclopedia of Russia*, pp. 620–21.

34. "Soviet Anniversary," *The Economist*, vol. 151, no. 5386, November 16, 1946, p. 784.

35. Discussion with Professor Wolfgang Leonhard at Yale University, New Haven, Conn., May 3, 1979.

36. Boris Meissner, *Russland Unter Chruschtschow*, p. 46.

37. Conquest, *Power*, p. 198.

38. Utechin, *Everyman's Encyclopedia*, pp. 80–81; "Soviet Anniversary," *The Economist*, November 16, 1946.

39. Conquest, *Power*, pp. 164, 180, 206, 207. (See also chapter 17)

40. "Soviet Leaders: A Time for Decisions (2)," *Soviet Analyst*, June 29, 1978, Vol. 7, No. 13, p. 5.

41. Conquest, pp. 198, 400; W. W. Kulski, *The Soviet Regime*, p. 700.

42. Erickson, *Road to Stalingrad*, p. 379.

43. Adam Ulam, *Stalin* pp. 544–45 fn.

44. Utechin, *Everyman's Encyclopedia*, p. 492.

45. Earl Browder, "End of the Stalin Era," *The Nation*, vol. 176, no. 11,

March 14, 1953, pp. 221–22.
    46. Phillip J. Jaffe, *The Rise and Fall of American Communism*, p. 78.
    47. A. A. Zhdanov, "29-ya godovshchina velikoi oktiabr'skoi Sotsialisti-cheskoi revolutsii" [On the 29th Anniversary of the Great October Revolution], *Pravda*, November 7, 1946, pp. 1–3. (English text available in United States *Foreign Broadcast Information Service*, European Section Number 222, Thursday, November 7, 1946, pp. R2-R22. See also Drew Middleton, "Soviet 'Unafraid,' Zhdanov Asserts: Stalin Order Urges Prepared-ness," *New York Times*, November 7, 1946, p. 1.
    48. Zhdanov, "29-ya godovshchina."
    49. Ibid.
    50. Ibid.
    51. Ibid.
    52. "Anglo-Amerikanskoe finansovoe soglashenie" [The Anglo-American financial agreement], *Novoe Vremia* (*New Times*), no. 1, January 1, 1946, pp. 5–9.
    53. "Sovetskii narod vstrechaet velikii prazdnik novymi slavnymi trudovymi podvigami—Perevypolnili oktiabr'skii plan" [The Soviet people welcome the great festival with new glorious labor feats—Overfulfillment of the October Plan], *Pravda*, November 6, 1946, p. 1.

Chapter 4

    1. Vladimir Dedijer, *Tito*, p. 291.
    2. Ibid.
    3. Adam Ulam, *Titoism and the Cominform*, pp. 19–22.
    4. Dedijer, *Tito*, p. 113.
    5. Ibid.
    6. Eugenio Reale, *Avec Jacques Duclos au banc des accusés, pp. 16, 38–40.
    7. Dedijer, *Tito*, pp. 114–15.
    8. Conquest, *Great Terror*, p. 582.
    9. Dedijer, *Tito*, pp. 102, 378.
    10. Wolfgang Leonhard, *Child of the Revolution* (shortened English version of *Die Revolution Entlässt Ihre Kinder*), pp. 195–225.
    11. Moša Pijade, *La Fable de l'aide soviétique a l'insurrection nationale Yougoslave*. (Belgrade: Le Livre Yougoslav, 1950), p. 25.
    12. Milovan Djilas, *Conversations with Stalin*, p. 73.
    13. Gordon Wright, *The Ordeal of Total War, 1939–1945*, p. 218.
    14. Vladimir Dedijer, *The Battle Stalin Lost*, p. 59. See also p. 88 n.
    15. Marshal Tito speech in Ljubljana, May 27, 1945, excerpted in Stephen Clissold, ed., *Yugoslavia and the Soviet Union, 1939–1973*, pp. 165–66, discussed pp. 45, 54.
    16. Ulam, *Titoism*, p. 79.
    17. Djilas, *Conversations*, p. 131.
    18. *Soviet-Yugoslav Dispute*, letter of CPSU (from Molotov and Stalin) to C.P.Y. (Tito and Kardelj), May 4, 1948, pp. 35–36.
    19. Dedijer, *Tito*, pp. 313–14.
    20. *Soviet-Yugoslav Dispute*, letter of CPSU to C.P.Y., May 4, 1948, p. 38.

21. Djilas, *Conversations*, p. 143.
22. Ibid.
23. William E. Griffith, *Albania and the Sino-Soviet Rift*, pp. 19–21; Stephen Peters, "Ingredients of the Communist Takeover of Albania," in Hammond, *Anatomy*, pp. 273–92; Anton Logoreci, *The Albanians, Europe's Forgotten Survivors*, pp. 84–103; Peter R. Prifti, *Socialist Albania since 1944*, pp. 196–201.
24. Mehmet Chehou (Shehu), *A propos de l'experience de la guerre de libération nationale et de développement de notre armée nationale*, pp. 99–100.
25. Griffith, *Albania*, passim.
26. "Hoxha Stresses Balkans' Peaceful Role" (May Day message), Tirana, Albanian Home Service, April 30, 1948, 2:00 P.M. EST, FBIS, Balkan Transmissions No. 302, May 3, 1948, pp. EE1–EE2.
27. The Corfu Channel Case, I.C.J. Reports 1949, p. 4; see extended discussion in J. L. Brierly, *The Law of Nations*, pp. 421–30.
28. Logoreci, *Albanians*, pp. 91–92.
29. Djilas, *Conversations*, pp. 181, 182.
30. Ibid., p. 182.
31. Edgar O'Ballance, *The Greek Civil War, 1944–1949*, pp. 14, 115, 212–13.
32. Svetozar Vukmanović(-Tempo), *How and Why the People's Liberation Struggle of Greece Met with Defeat*, p. 69.
33. C. M. Woodhouse, *The Struggle for Greece, 1941–1949*, p. 182; Richard Clogg, "Greece," in Martin McCauley, ed., *Communist Power in Europe, 1944–1949*, p. 195.
34. Woodhouse, *Struggle for Greece*, pp. 99, 142.
35. Vukmanović(-Tempo), *How and Why*, p. 32.
36. Stephen E. Palmer and Robert A. King, *Yugoslav Communism and the Macedonian Question*, p. 129; Woodhouse, *Struggle for Greece*, p. 142.
37. Dedijer, *The Battle Stalin Lost*, p. 78.
38. Woodhouse, *Struggle for Greece*, p. 177; O'Ballance, *Greek Civil War*, pp. 180–81, 212–13.
39. Woodhouse, *Struggle for Greece*, p. 155 fn. 58.
40. Ibid., p. 169.
41. D. George Kazoulas, "The Greek Communists Tried Three Times—and Failed," in Hammond, *Anatomy*, p. 303.
42. Woodhouse, *Struggle for Greece*, pp. 175, 176.
43. O'Ballance, *Greek Civil War*, p. 159.
44. Woodhouse, *Struggle for Greece*, pp. 262–64; O'Ballance, *Greek Civil War*, p. 165.
45. 148th Plenary Meeting, U.N. General Assembly, Speech by Edvard Kardelj, September 29, 1948, Records of the General Assembly, Part I, pp. 318–32.
46. Woodhouse, *Struggle for Greece*, p. 273.
47. Evangelos Averoff-Tossizza, *By Fire and Axe*, p. 319.
48. Ibid., pp. 323–24.
49. Palmer and King, *Yugoslav Communism*, p. 128.
50. Ibid., pp. 53–122.
51. Dedijer, *The Battle Stalin Lost*, p. 78.

52. Vukmanović(-Tempo), *How and Why*, pp. 71–78, 53.
53. Ibid., p. 56.
54. Ibid., p. 76.
55. Ibid., p. 77.
56. Ibid., p. 1.
57. Middleton, *New York Times*, November 7, 1946.
58. Ilya Ehrenburg, *The War: 1941–1945*, p. 176.
59. C. L. Sulzberger, "Balkan Elections to Ignore Allies, Regimes Backed by Reds to Stay," *New York Times*, October 25, 1945, p. 1; Schueller, *Politburo*, p. 40, refers to a Zhdanov visit to the Balkans in 1944, as well as in 1945.
60. Sulzberger, "Balkan Elections."
61. Dedijer, *The Battle Stalin Lost*, pp. 6–7.
62. Djilas, *Conversations*, p. 150.
63. Conquest, *Great Terror*, p. 97.
64. W. W. Kulski, *The Soviet Regime*, pp. 89–91.
65. Ernst Halperin, *The Triumphant Heretic*, p. 84.

Chapter 5

1. Kulski, *Soviet Regime*, pp. 86–91.
2. An analysis of the organizational policies of this period appears in B. A. Abramov, "Organizatsionno-partiinaia rabota KPSS v gody chetvertoi piatiletki" [Party-organizational work of the CPSU in the years of the Fourth Five-Year Plan], *Voprosy Istorii KPSS*, no. 3, April 1979, pp. 55–65.
3. "Ob agitatsionno-propagandistskoi rabote partiinykh organizatsii v sviazi s priniiatiem zakona o piatiletnem plane vosstanovlenia i razvitiia narodnogo khoziaistva SSSR na 1946–50 gg" [On agitation and propaganda work of party organizations in connection with the adoption of the law on the Five-Year Plan for the restoration and development of the national economy of the USSR in the period 1946–50], Central Committee Resolution of March 27, 1946, *Kommunisticheskaia Partiia Sovetskogo Soiuza v rezoliutsiiakh i resheniiakh s'ezdov, konferentsii i plenumov TsK*, Vol. 6, pp. 150–53. (See English text in Robert H. McNeal, ed., *Resolutions and Decisions of the Communist Party of the Soviet Union*, vol. 3, pp. 232–36.)
4. "Postanovlenie TsK VKP(b) o roste partii i o merakh po usileniiu partiino-organizatsionnoi i partiino-politicheskoi raboty s vnov' vstupivshimi v VKP(b)" [On the growth of the party and on measures for strengthening of party organizational and party political work with new members of the CPSU(b)], Resolution of July 26, 1946, ibid., pp. 154–61.
5. "O podgotovke i perepodgotovke rukovodiashchikh partiinykh i sovetskikh rabotnikov" [On the training and retraining of leading party and soviet workers], Central Committee Resolution of August 2, 1946, ibid., pp. 162–72. (English text available in McNeal, *Resolutions and Decisions*, pp. 236–41.
6. It is significant that Zhdanov's close collaborator, A. A. Kuznetsov, asserted with apparent pride that "we can say with assuredness that never in the history of our party has training and retraining of cadres been undertaken on such a large scale." *Pravda*, November 2, 1946, as cited in Abramov, "Organizatsionno-partiinaia rabota," p. 60. Equally significant is the non-

appearance, in this context, of the name of G. M. Malenkov, who had been in charge of cadre affairs in the Central Committee.

7. The chief of the Central Committee's newly established Administration for Inspection of Party Organs was N. S. Patolichev (who, it will be recalled, appeared on the dais during the November 1946 celebration of the anniversary of the October Revolution, an occasion when Zhdanov and his allies almost totally dominated the stage, and who owed his appointment in the Secretariat to Zhdanov and A. A. Kuznetsov.) Ibid., p. 61.

8. Abramov, "Organizatsionno-partiinaia rabota," passim; whichever group could control the appointment of cadres was in an ideal position to emerge successfully from factional struggle, since power derives in good measure from the ability to bestow influence upon (or hand out sinecures to) allies and friends. Of course, the appointment of cadres could serve other (not necessarily unrelated) purposes, such as oppression of "cosmopolitan" Soviet Jews, who suddenly found themselves unable to find work (not to mention being placed in prison camps and even executed) from 1948 onward; see Esther Markish, *The Long Return*, pp. 137–38.

9. G. A. Abramov, pp. 58–59.

10. Alexander Werth, *Russia*, p. 208.

11. Solomon Volkov, *Testimony: The Memoirs of Dmitri Shostakovich*, as related to and edited by Solomon Volkov, pp. 269–70.

12. A. A. Zhdanov, "Doklad t. Zhdanova o zhurnalakh 'Zvezda' i 'Leningrad' " [Report of Comrade Zhdanov regarding the journals *Zvezda* and *Leningrad*], *Bol'shevik*, no. 17–18, September 1946, pp. 4–5.

13. "O zhurnalakh 'Zvezda' i 'Leningrad' " [On the Journals *Zvezda* and *Leningrad*], *Kommunisticheskaia Partiia Sovetskogo Soiuza v rezoliutsiiakh i resheniiakh s'ezdov, konferentsii i plenumov TsK*, pp. 485–88. [Text of Resolution of the Central Committee of the All-Union Communist Party, August 14, 1946.] (See English text in McNeal, *Resolutions and Decisions*, vol. 3, pp. 240–43.)

14. A. A. Zhdanov, "Doklad t. Zhdanova o zhurnalakh 'Zvezda' i 'Leningrad,' " pp. 10–12.

15. Ibid., p. 11.

16. Werth, *Russia*, pp. 349–79.

17. Ibid., pp. 210–11.

18. A. A. Zhdanov, "Vystuplenie na diskussii po knige G. F. Aleksandrova 'Istoriia zapadnoevropeiskoi filosofii,' " *Bol'shevik*, no. 16, August 30, 1947, pp. 7–23; English text in *Political Affairs*, April 1948, Vol. 27, no. 4, pp. 344–66; see also J. Miller and M. Miller, "Andrei Zhdanov's Speech to the Philosophers," *Soviet Studies*, vol. 1, no. 1, June 1949, pp. 46–51; Percy E. Corbett, "The Aleksandrov Story," *World Politics*, vol. I, no. 2, January 1949, pp. 161–74; Kulski, *Soviet Regime*, pp. 23–25; Werth, *Russia*, pp. 213–15.

19. Werth, *Russia*, p. 352 fn.

20. Ellbridge Durbrow, United States Chargé d'Affaires in the Soviet Union, dispatch to the Secretary of State, Moscow, December 2, 1947, *FRUS 1947*, Vol. 4, pp. 628–30; according to Mark Kuchment, although Shcherbakov was an overt antisemite, on a personal level he maintained good relations with Ilya Ehrenburg, who wrote under Shcherbakov's aegis for *Krasnaia Zvezda*. Thus, his antisemitism seems to have been of the "ideological" type, permitting a posture of "*I* decide who is a Jew" (to quote Karl Lueger).

21. Djilas, *Conversations*, p. 170.
22. Charles H. Fairbanks, Jr., "National Cadres as a Force in the Soviet System," in Jeremy Azrael, *Soviet Nationality Policies and Practices*, pp. 151–53. This is an abbreviated text; in the original full manuscript, see pp. 24–29.
23. Israel Emiot, *The Birobidjan Case*, p. 10 (in Yiddish).
24. Interview with Kuchment; see also Markish, *Long Return* (this is a first-hand account by the wife of Peretz Markish, a noted Yiddish and Russian language poet, who was arrested in 1949 and executed in 1952), esp. pp. 140–41; Janet D. Zagoria, ed., *Power and the Soviet Elite, "The Letter of an Old Bolshevik" and other essays by Boris I. Nicolaevsky*, pp. 113–14.
25. Salisbury, "Trofim L. Lysenko Is Dead at 78; Was Science Overlord Under Stalin," *New York Times*, November 24, 1976.
26. Zhores A. Medvedev, *The Rise and Fall of T. D. Lysenko*, pp. 261–62 n; Loren R. Graham, *Science and Philosophy in the Soviet Union*, p. 218; David Joravsky, *The Lysenko Affair*, pp. 137–39, 379–80 n. 138.
27. Graham, *Science and Philosophy*, p. 445; Yurii Zhdanov, "Tovarishu I. V. Stalinu," *Pravda*, August 7, 1948, p. 5; see also *Soviet Studies*, vol. 1, no. 2, October 1949, pp. 175–77.
28. Roy A. Medvedev, *Let History Judge*, p. 484.
29. Graham, *Science and Philosophy*, p. 446.
30. Ibid., p. 444.
31. Ibid., pp. 74, 80, 446–47.
32. Charles P. McVicker, *Titoism*, p. 7.
33. Ibid., pp. 7 8.
34. Brzezinski, *Soviet Bloc*, pp. 37–38.
35. McVicker, *Titoism*, p. 5.
36. Dedijer, *Tito*, p. 268.

Chapter 6

1. E. Varga, *Izmeneniia v ekonomike kapitalizma v itoge vtoroi mirovoi Voiny [Changes in the economy of capitalism as a result of World War II]*; for discussion of this work see "*Diskussiia-po knige E. Varga 'Izmeneniia v ekonomike kapitalizma v itoge vtoroi mirovoi Voiny' 7, 14, 21 Maia, 1947 g.*," *Mirovoe Khoziaistvo i Mirovaia Politika*, no. 11, November 1947. For English text see Leo Gruliow, trans. *Soviet views on the Post-War World Economy—An Official Critique of Eugene Varga's "Changes in the Economy of Capitalism Resulting from the Second World War"*; Frederick C. Barghoorn, "The Varga Discussion and its Significance." *American Slavic and Eastern European Review*, vol. 8, 1948, pp. 214–36; Solomon Schwarz, "The Eclipse of a Soviet Economist," *The New Leader*, February 14, 1948, vol. 31, no. 7, p. 4.
2. Ulam, *Stalin*, p. 707.
3. Schwarz, "Eclipse of a Soviet Economist," p. 4.
4. Ibid.
5. Utechin, *Everyman's Encyclopedia*, p. 599.
6. Barghoorn, "Varga Discussion," pp. 219–21.
7. Ibid.
8. Varga, *Izmeneniia*, p. 291, as cited in "Diskussiia-po knige E. Varga," p. 21 (emphasis added in quotation).

196   Notes to pp. 64–72

9. N. A. Voznesenskii, *Voennaia ekonomika SSSR v period Otechestvennoi Voiny* [The wartime economy of the USSR during the great patriotic war], p. 190. English text in *The Economy of the U.S.S.R. during World War II.*
10. Varga, *Izmeneniia*, p. 33, as cited in Barghoorn, "Varga Discussions," pp. 218–19.
11. "Diskussiia- po knige E. Varga," p. 58.
12. Ibid., p. 21.
13. Ibid., p. 58.
14. Ibid., p. 8.
15. Djilas, *Conversations*, p. 150.
16. "Diskussiia- po knige E. Varga," p. 8.
17. Conquest, *Power*, p. 101.
18. Ibid., p. 95.
19. "Diskussiia- po knige E. Varga," p. 11.
20. Varga, *Izmeneniia*, chapter 11, as cited in ibid., pp. 11–12, and in Barghoorn, "Varga Discussions," p. 223.
21. "Diskussiia- po knige E. Varga," p. 4.
22. Ibid., pp. 59–64; as cited in Barghoorn, "Varga Discussions," pp. 219–20.
23. Varga, *Izmenenia*, pp. 8, 11–12, as cited in Barghoorn, "Varga Discussions," p. 217, and in "Diskussia- po knige E. Varga," p. 20.
24. Voznesenskii, *Voennaia ekonomika*, p. 30.
25. Ibid., p. 31.
26. Ibid., p. 184.
27. Ibid., p. 32.
28. Edvard Kardelj, "Notes on Some Questions of International Development," *Kommunist*, no. 2, 1947; English text in *Political Affairs*, vol. 26, no. 6, June 1947, p. 545.
29. Ibid., p. 531.
30. Voznesenskii, *Voennaia ekonomika*, p. 32.
31. Ibid., pp. 189–90.
32. Marshal Josip Broz Tito, Speech delivered at the Second Congress of the People's Front of Yugoslavia, September 27, 1947; English text available in *Political Affairs*, Vol. 27, No. 1, January 1948, p. 95.
33. Brookings Institution, *Current Developments in United States Foreign Policy*, Vol. 1, No. 5, January 1948, p. 54.
34. Voznesenskii, *Voennaia ekonomika*, p. 190.
35. Kardelj, "Notes..," p. 547.
36. Voznesenskii, *Voennaia ekonomika*, pp. 41–44.
37. Ibid., p. 59.
38. "Diskussiia- po knige E. Varga," p. 31.
39. Ibid., pp. 37–39.
40. Ibid., p. 58.
41. I. Gladkov, "Ob izmeneniakh v ekonomike kapitalizma v resul'tate vtoroi mirovoi Voiny" [Changes in capitalism as a result of the Second World War], *Bol'shevik*, no. 17, September 15, 1947, pp. 57–64; Schwarz, "Eclipse of a Soviet Economist," p. 4.
42. Schwarz, "Eclipse of a Soviet Economist," p. 4.
43. K. V. Ostrovitianov and M. Galaktianov, "Kniga o voennoi ekono-

mike SSSR" [A book on the wartime economy of the USSR], *Pravda*, January 3, 1948, pp. 2–3; English text in *Soviet Press Translations*, Far Eastern Institute, University of Washington, vol. 3, no. 7, April 1, 1948, pp. 216–21.
44. Conquest, *Power*, p. 89.
45. Barghoorn, "Varga Discussions," p. 214.
46. E. Varga, "Infliatsiia i denezhnye reformy v kapitalisticheskikh stranakh" [Inflation and monetary reforms in capitalist countries], *Pravda*, December 24, 1947, p. 4; English text in *Soviet Press Translations*, Far Eastern Institute, University of Washington, vol. 3, no. 4, February 25, 1948, pp. 112–14.
47. Nikita S. Khrushchev, *The Crimes of the Stalin Era*, annotated by Boris I. Nicolaevsky, pp. S21–S22.

Chapter 7

1. Andrija Hebrang, Article in the Yugoslav journal *The Twentieth of October*, May 31, 1946, as cited in François Fejtö, *Histoire des démocraties populaires*, p. 166.
2. E. Varga, "Democratia novogo tipa" [New type of democracy], *Mirovoe Khoziaistvo i Mirovaia Politika*, no. 3, March 1947, pp. 8–9.
3. Stephen Clissold, *Yugoslavia and the Soviet Union, 1939–73*, p. 171.
4. Boris Kidric (Kidrich), *On the Construction of Socialist Economy in the F.P.R.Y.*, Speech delivered to the Fifth Congress of the Communist Party of Yugoslavia, p. 18.
5. Ibid., p. 46.
6. Ibid., p. 49.
7. Dedijer, *Tito*, p. 261.
8. Edward (Edvard) Kardelj, *On People's Democracy in Yugoslavia* (reprint of July 1949 article in *Kommunist*), pp. 7–8, 15, 18–19.
9. Interview with Professor Wolfgang Leonhard, conducted at Yale University, May 3, 1979.
10. *Soviet-Yugoslav Dispute*, Letter from C. C. of the CPSU to C. C. of the C.P.Y., May 4, 1948, pp. 33–34.
11. November 1949 Cominform Resolution, "The CPY in the Power of Murderers and Spies," excerpted in Clissold *Yugoslavia and the Soviet Union*, pp. 225–28; *For a Lasting Peace*, November 29, 1949, p. 2.
12. Ibid.
13. If one is to believe William Stevenson (*A Man Called Intrepid*, pp. 217, 218, 228, illustration pp. 256 ff.), Tito's insurgency in the spring of 1941 was a British "outstanding intelligence coup," which included bringing him to Yugoslavia in 1940, "carrying a British passport issued in Canada" (shown in illustration). Stevenson claims that Tito received "no guidance from Stalin," but, rather, from the West. Regarding the passport, Stevenson adds, "how this came about is still classified information".
14. Secret Dispatch of Ambassador Cannon in Yugoslavia to the U.S. Secretary of State, Belgrade, November 11, 1947, 11:00 A.M. FRUS 1947, vol. 4, pp. 849–50.
15. Jacques Duclos, "Yugoslav Nationalists—Agents of Imperialism," *For a Lasting Peace*, July 1, 1949, p. 2.

Chapter 8

1. Avigdor Dagan, *Moscow and Jerusalem*, pp. 19–20.
2. United Nations Official Records, General Assembly, First Special Session, April 28–May 15, 1947, vol. 1, Gromyko Speech, May 14, 1947, p. 134. See discussion in "The Russians and Palestine," *The Economist*, vol. 152, no. 5413, May 24, 1947, pp. 801–03.
3. United Nations Official Records, General Assembly, Second Session, supp. 11, vols. 1–5.
4. United Nations Special Committee on Palestine, *Report to the General Assembly*, Annexes, Appendices and Maps to the Report of 31 August 1947, pp. 79–102.
5. General Assembly, Second Session, A/P.V. 128, November 29, 1947.
6. Zhdanov, Address to the Cominform meeting, reprinted in *For a Lasting Peace*, November 10, 1947 (first issue printed).
7. Yaacov Ro'i, "Soviet-Israeli Relations, 1947–1954," in Michael Confino and Shimon Shamir, eds., *The U.S.S.R. and the Middle East*, p. 123.
8. Meir Mardor, *Shlichoot Alumah* [Secret mission], pp. 183–294, passim.
9. Leonard Slater, *The Pledge*, p. 234. This work features interviews with several other key participants, who both confirm and supplement Mardor's account.
10. Mardor, *Shlichoot Alumah*, p. 187.
11. According to several accounts, both Slansky and Geminder were affiliated with Beria. See Zagoria, *Power and the Soviet Elite*, p. 173; Conquest, *Power*, p. 170; Fairbanks, "National Cadres," in Azrael, *Soviet Nationality*, pp. 151, 183 fn. 30. This is an abbreviated text. In Fairbanks's original (full) manuscript, see p. 24, 102 fn. 24. These accounts not only help to explain the difference between Czech and Yugoslav policies regarding the Middle East but also perhaps why Czechoslovakia was prepared at first to accept Marshall Plan aid.
12. Mardor, *Shlicoot Alumah*, pp. 189–90; according to the secretary of the Israeli Communist Party, Shmuel Mikunis, in 1949 he was informed by member of the Bulgarian Communist Party that Stalin himself had been behind the pro-Yishuv policy of that period; see Zeev Schiff, *A History of the Israeli Army*, p. 44.
13. Just as Gromyko's U.N. statement was hedged somewhat, so too was Moscow's policy with respect to arms shipments. Mardor's associates discovered that the USSR also was sending weapons to the Syrians (surreptitiously, via Rijeka and Beirut). In April 1948, a vessel called the *Lino* was forced to stop for repairs in Bari, Italy, with a load of hardware destined for Syria. Mardor's colleagues sabotaged the vessel in port, and hijacked most of the weapons for themselves. Mardor's exploit received publicity in 1949, when the Syrians held a "public" trial of some of their compatriots for having been "bribed," allegedly in connection with the "Lino Affair". See Mardor, *Shlichoot Alumah*, pp. 200–44; Associated Press, "Public Trial in Syria Alleges Some Had Been Bribed," March 23, 1949, and *Al-Ayam*, March 24, 1949.
14. Slater, *The Pledge*, p. 315; Mardor, *Shlichoot Alumah*, p. 282.
15. The Soviet policy of selling arms to Middle Eastern states may have

been dictated partly by economic considerations. The Messerschmitts were sold to the Yishuv for about $190,000 per aircraft, including spare parts and ammunition, a fair amount of money at that time for an obsolescent plane. (The cost of the comparable Western plane, the Spitfire, including all equipment, was only $45,000 in 1943; see W. F. Craven and J. L. Cate, *The Army Air Force in World War II, Men and Planes*, p. 360 n. Although inflation might have pushed up the price by 1948, this would have been offset by the increasing obsolescence of the aircraft.) Thus, Czechoslovakia received nearly $5 million for the twenty-five Messerschmitts supplied to the Yishuv, and probably a considerable sum for the other weapons sent to Israel. How much was received from the Syrians is not known. However, given the state of the postwar economies of Eastern Europe, the total of several million dollars in hard currency well may have been a major incentive for such deals.

16. Dagan, *Moscow and Jerusalem*, pp. 36–37; Arie L. Eliav, *Between Hammer and Sickle*, pp. 33–37.

17. Ilya Ehrenburg, *Men, Years—Life*, vol. 6, *Post-War Years, 1945–54*, pp. 125–27.

18. "The Lost Weapons List," *Ma'ariv* (Israeli afternoon daily), January 4–5, 1979, weekly illustrated section, p. 5.

19. Eliav, *Hammer and Sickle*, pp. 33–37; Markish, *Long Return*, pp. 140–70.

20. Dagan, *Moscow and Jerusalem*, p. 42 (emphasis added in quotation).

21. E. Varga, "Protiv reformistskogo napravleniia v rabotakh po imperializmu," [Against reformist tendencies in works on imperialism], *Voprosy Ekonomiki*, no. 3, 1949, p. 86 fn. 5. English text in *Current Digest of the Soviet Press*, vol. 1, no. 19, June 7, 1949, pp. 3–19; and in *Political Affairs*, vol. 28, no. 12, December 1949, pp. 74–86.

22. M. Marinin, "Chto skryvaetsia za krizisom v Palestine?" [What is behind the crisis in Palestine?], *Pravda*, May 4, 1948, p. 4. English text available in *Soviet Press Translations*, vol. 3, no. 11, June 1, 1948, pp. 323–24; M. Melekhov, "Arabskaya liga i nezavisimost' arabskikh stran" [The Arab League and the independence of the Arab states], *Pravda*, March 24, 1948, p. 3. English text available in *Soviet Press Translations*, vol. 3, no. 11, pp. 324–25.

23. "New democracies" subsequently came to be called "popular democracies," a term denoting much closer proximity to "socialism" (that, consequently was endorsed strongly by Tito, who, indeed, has been credited with its authorship, see Borkenau, *European Communism*, p. 484).

Chapter 9

1. *Krasnaia Zvezda*, February 9, 1945, Editorial quoted in Werth, *Russia at War*, p. 966.

2. Werth, *Russia at War*, p. 967; see also Ambassador W. Averell Harriman to the Secretary of State, April 14, 1945, 10:00 P.M. FRUS 1945, vol. 5, pp. 829–31; Ilya Ehrenburg, *Men, Years—Life*, vol. 5, *The War: 1941–1945*, p. 176.

3. Henry Krisch, *German Politics under Soviet Occupation*, p. 26; J. P. Nettl, *The Eastern Zone and Soviet Policy in Germany, 1945–1950*, p. 67.

4. Salisbury, *900 Days*, p. 486.

5. Sulzberger, "Two More Leaders Reported Victims of Purges in Russia," *New York Times*, June 19, 1949.

6. Salisbury, *900 Days*, p. 666 fn.

7. *International Who's Who* (London: Europa Publications Ltd., 1964), pp. 995–96.

8. Boris Meissner, *Russland unter Chruschtschow*, p. 52; Conquest, *Power*, p. 97; Nicolaevsky, "The Abakumov Case," *The New Leader*, vol. 37, no. 2, January 10, 1955, pp. 14–15.

9. Georg Von Rauch and Boris Meissner, *Die Deutsch-Sowjetischen Beziehungen Von 1941 Bis 1967*, p. 21.

10. Erich W. Gniffke, *Jahre mit Ulbricht*, p. 178.

11. Conquest, *Power*, p. 80.

12. Slusser, *Soviet Economic Policy*, p. 167; Rudolf, "The Agencies of Control," in ibid., p. 22.

13. Vladimir Rudolf, "The Execution of Policy," in Slusser, ed., *Soviet Economic Policy*, p. 52.

14. Nikolai Grishin, "The Saxon Uranium Mining Operation ('Vismut')" in ibid., pp. 127–57; interview with Dr. Mark Kuchment, March 5, 1979; Simon Wolin and Robert M. Slusser, eds., *The Soviet Secret Police*, p. 25; Rauch and Meissner, *Die Deutsch-Sowjetischen Beziehungen*, p. 48.

15. Grishin, "Saxon Uranium Mining," pp. 129, 134.

16. Rudolf, "Execution of Policy," pp. 37, 48.

17. Zagoria, *Power and the Soviet Elite*, p. 128; Rudolf Schuster, *Deutschlands Staatliche Existenz im Widerstreit Politischer und Rechtlicher Gesichtspunkte 1945–1963*, pp. 10–11.

18. Grishin, "Saxon Uranium Mining," p. 128.

19. Leonhard, *Die Revolution*, pp. 426–27.

20. Schuster, *Deutschlands Staatliche Existenz*, pp. 10–11.

21. Gniffke, *Jahre*, pp. 250–51.

22. Ibid.

23. Ibid., p. 184.

24. "Letter of October 28, 1948, to the Central Committee of the S.E.D.," Ibid., pp. 364–65.

25. Ibid.

26. Horst Duhnke, *Stalinismus in Deutschland*, pp. 185–86.

27. Gniffke, *Jahre*, p. 185.

28. Ibid.

29. Ibid., pp. 184–85.

30. Leonhard, *Die Revolution*, pp. 361–63; Rudolf, "The Execution of Policy," pp. 56–57.

31. Rudolf, "The Execution of Policy," p. 53.

32. Leonhard, *The Child of the Revolution*, trans. C. M. Woodhouse, (English translation of *Die Revolution entlässt ihre Kinder*), p. 345. References to the English edition are cited under this title.

33. Leonhard, *Die Revolution*, p. 481.

34. Ibid., p. 498.

35. Ibid., p. 497.

36. Ernst Lemmer, *Manches War Doch Anders*, pp. 298–99.

37. Lemmer, *Manches*, pp. 299–300.

38. Alfred Burmeister, *Dissolution and Aftermath of the Comintern*, p. 25; Leonhard, *Die Revolution*, pp. 298–99.

39. Leonhard, *Child of the Revolution*, p. 301.
40. Gniffke, *Jahre*, p. 369.
41. Conquest, *Power*, passim; Schapiro, *Communist Party*, p. 446.
42. Leonhard, *Die Revolution*, p. 473.
43. Ibid., p. 516.
44. Ibid., p. 523.
45. Ibid., pp. 495–96.
46. Colonel S. I. Tiul'panov, "Naissance de la démocratie populaire," *Démocratie nouvelle*, vol. 2, no. 6, June 1948, p. 299.
47. Slusser, *Soviet Economic Policy*, p. 164.
48. Brookings Institution, *Current Developments in United States Foreign Policy*, vol. 2, no. 2, September 1948, p. 23.
49. Jean Edward Smith, ed., *The Papers of General Lucius D. Clay, 1945–49*, vol. 2, *1947–49*, Top secret dispatch from General Clay to the Department of the Army, January 26, 1949, pp. 992–93; "Soviet Tactics in Germany," *Times* (London), January 28, 1949, p. 3; U.S. Political Adviser for Germany Murphy, to the Secretary of State, Berlin, February 3, 1949, 5 P.M., FRUS 1949, vol. 3, p. 505.
50. *SBZ von 1945 bis 1954 — Die Sowjetische Besatzungszone Deutschlands in den Jahren 1945–1954*, Bundesministerium für Gesamtdeutsche Fragen (Bonn: Auslieferung für den Buchhandel, Deutscher Bundes-Verlag, 1956), pp. 98–99; Von Rauch, *History of Soviet Russia*, p. 413.
51. General V. I. Chuikov and General G. S. Lukianshchenko, Order of May 9, 1949, in Guenter Hindrichs and Wolfgang Heidelmeyer, eds., *Documents sur Berlin, 1943–1963*, pp. 105–07.
52. Slusser, *Soviet Economic Policy*, p. 166; Rauch, *History of Soviet Russia*, p. 413.
53. Sergej Ivanovič Tjul'panov (Tiul'panov), "Die Hilfe der Sowjetunion bei der demokratischen Neugestaltung von Wissenschaft und Kultur nach 1945," in Erika Linder, ed., *Deutschland-Sowjetunion — Aus fünf Jahrzehnten Kultureller Zusammenarbeit*, pp. 185–88.
54. Zhdanov, *For a Lasting Peace*, November 10, 1947.

Chapter 10

1. Borkenau, *European Communism*, pp. 227–28.
2. Reale, *Avec Jacques Duclos*, p. 10.
3. Zhdanov, *For a Lasting Peace*, November 10, 1947.
4. G. M. Malenkov, address to the Cominform meeting, reprinted in ibid., November 24, 1947 (second issue printed).
5. Zhdanov, ibid., November 10, 1947.
6. Schapiro, *Communist Party*, pp. 536–37.
7. Jesse D. Clarkson, *A History of Russia*, p. 737.
8. Conquest, *Power*, p. 258.
9. Dedijer, *Tito*, p. 295.
10. Ibid., p. 295.
11. Ibid., p. 296.
12. Delbars, *The Real Stalin*, p. 402.
13. Wan Min, *Polveka KPK i predatel'stvo Mao Tse-duna*, p. 67; English translation: Wang Ming, *Mao's Betrayal*, trans. Vic Schneierson, pp. 63–64.

14. Djilas, *Conversations*, pp. 182–83.

15. Kardelj, "Notes on Some Questions of International Development," *Kommunist* (Belgrade), no. 2, 1947; English text: *Political Affairs*, June 1947, p. 540.

16. Ibid., p. 534.

17. Ibid., pp. 540–41.

18. Ibid., p. 548.

19. Ibid., p. 549.

20. Ibid., p. 543.

21. Zhdanov, *For a Lasting Peace*, November 10, 1947.

22. Ibid.

23. Roger Morgan, *West European Politics since 1945*, pp. 37, 41.

24. Ibid., p. 67.

25. Tim Buck, *Europe's Rebirth*, p. 97.

26. McCagg, *Stalin Embattled*, p. 267; Buck, *Europe's Rebirth*, p. 97.

27. Buck, *Europe's Rebirth*, p. 96.

28. François Fejtö, *The French Communist Party and the Crisis of International Communism*, p. 33 fn. 1.

29. Stephan Mitrovitch, "Remarques Fondamentales Sur la Question de Trieste," *Cahiers de Communisme*, n.s. vol. 23, no. 3, March 1946, pp. 284–306.

30. Brookings Institution, *Current Developments*, vol. 1, no. 7, March 1948, p. 18.

31. Conversation with Professor Stephan Dedijer, of Lund University, Sweden, in Cambridge, Massachusetts, April 24, 1979.

32. Jacques Duclos, "À propos de la dissolution du Parti Communiste Americain," *Cahiers Du Communisme*, n.s. no. 6, April 1945, pp. 21–37.

33. Earl Browder, *Teheran—Our Path in War and Peace*.

34. Jaffe, *Rise and Fall*, pp. 62–63; Joseph R. Starobin, *American Communism in Crisis, 1943–1957*, pp. 74–75.

35. Browder, *Teheran*, pp. 117–20.

36. Starobin, *American Communism*, pp. 81–82; Philip Jaffe, another prominent American Communist of the period, went so far as to suggest that Zhdanov personally directed the composition of the Duclos article; see Jaffe, *Rise and Fall*, p. 78. Jacques Duclos, himself, (*Memoires*, vol. 4, *1945–1952: Sur la Brêche*) is most uninformative on this issue, merely asserting that he had discussed the dissolution of the C.P.U.S.A. with various Western Hemisphere Communist parties.

37. Zhdanov, "29-ya godovshchina," *Pravda*, November 7, 1946, pp. 1–3.

38. Borkenau, *European Communism*, pp. 522–31; Donald L. M. Blackmer, *Unity in Diversity*, pp. 14–17.

39. Ronald Tiersky, *French Communism, 1920–1972*, pp. 166–67.

40. Ibid.; Lilly Marcou, *Le Kominform*, pp. 136–37.

41. Jacques Duclos, "Notre Politique," *Cahiers du Communisme*, vol. 24, no 11, November 1947, pp. 1091–97.

42. *Soviet-Yugoslav Dispute*, letter of V. M. Molotov and I. V. Stalin, C.C. of the CPSU, to Comrade Tito and other members of the C.C. of the C.P.Y., May 22, 1948, pp. 54–57.

Chapter 11

1. John H. Badgley, "The Communist Party of Burma," in Robert A. Scalapino, ed., *The Communist Revolution in Asia*, p. 295.

2. Kardelj, *Problems of International Development: A Marxist Analysis*, cited in Gene D. Overstreet and Marshall Windmiller, *Communism in India*, p. 259.

3. Ibid.

4. Zhdanov, *For a Lasting Peace*, November 10, 1947; J. Brimmell, *Communism in South East Asia*, p. 193; Overstreet and Windmiller, *Communism in India*, pp. 208, 252–54.

5. Brimmel, *Communism in South East Asia*, pp. 255–56.

6. Overstreet and Windmiller, *Communism in India*, p. 268.

7. Ibid., p. 268.

8. "July, 1950 Report on Leftwing Sectarianism," in M. B. Rao, ed., *Documents of the History of the Communist Party of India*, vol. 7, p. 707.

9. Overstreet and Windmiller, *Communism in India*, p. 271.

10. Ibid., p. 562.

11. Ruth T. McVey, "The Southeast Asian Revolts," in Cyril E. Black and Thomas P. Thornton, eds., *Communism and Revolution*, p. 146.

12. Brimmell, *Communism in South East Asia*, pp. 193–94.

13. Dedijer, *The Battle Stalin Lost*, p. 24.

14. Ibid., p. 25.

15. Ibid., pp. 27–29; Fitzroy Maclean, *The Heretic*, p. 315.

16. Dedijer, *The Battle Stalin Lost*, pp. 27–29.

17. Charles Griffin, "Chile Links 2 Ousted Yugoslavs to Comintern Plot on Americans," *New York Times*, October 10, 1947, p. 1; "Conflict of the Antipodes," *East Europe* (London), October 16, 1947, vol. 3, no. 152, pp. 1–2.

18. "Yugoslavs Cut Chilean Ties; Hint Santiago is U.S. Puppet," *New York Times*, October 12, 1947, p. 1.

19. "Communism in Chile," editorial, *New York Times*, October 11, 1947, p. 16.

20. Edward Taborsky, *Communism in Czechoslovakia 1948–1960*, p. 20.

21. Ibid., pp. 101–06.

22. Zhdanov, *For a Lasting Peace*, November 10, 1947.

Chapter 12

1. I. V. Stalin, "Rech'na predvybornon sobranii izbiratelei Stalinskogo izbiratel'nogo okruga goroda Moskvy," February 9, 1946, *Sochineniia*, vol. 16 (McNeal edition, vol. 3), pp. 2–3; *Bol'shevik*, no. 3, 1946.

2. Stalin, Otvet Korrespondent, "Pravdy," *Sochineniia*, 16, p. 43; *Pravda*, March 14, 1946.

3. Stalin, "Otvet t-shchu Razinu," letter to Comrade [Professor Colonel] Razin, *Bol'shevik*, no. 3, February 1947, pp. 6–8; *Sochineniia*, vol. 16, pp. 29–34; complete English text available in *Political Affairs*, May 1947, vol. 26, no. 5, pp. 415–17.

4. McCagg, *Stalin Embattled*, pp. 233–35.

5. Stalin, "Otvet t-shchu Razinu," *Sochineniia*, pp. 30–31.

6. Ibid., p. 33.

7. Ibid., p. 32.

8. Mark Vishniak, "The Red Terror," *New Leader*, vol. 32, no. 22, May 28, 1949, p. 10.

9. Associated Press, "Russia 'Scoops' Reporter Who Questioned Premier," *New York Times*, September 25, 1946, p. 3.

10. "Otvety na voprosy zadannye Moskovskim korrespondentom 'Sunday Times' g-nom A. Werth poluchennye 17-go sentiabria 1946 g" [Replies to questions posed by *Sunday Times* correspondent Mr. A. Werth on September 17, 1946], *Sochineniia*, vol. 16, p. 54; *Izvestia*, September 24, 1946; complete English text in *New York Times*, September 25, 1946, p. 3.

11. Ibid., *Sochineniia*, vol. 16, p. 55.

12. Ibid., p. 56.

13. Ibid.

14. Werth, *Russia*, pp. 301–2; Thomas Wolfe, *Soviet Power and Europe, 1945–70*, p. 25.

15. McCagg, *Stalin Embattled*, pp. 273–74.

16. Stalin, "Privetstvie Moskve" [Salute to Moscow], *Sochineniia*, vol. 16, p. 95; *Pravda*, September 7, 1947.

17. Zhdanov, *For a Lasting Peace*, November 10, 1947, p. 2.

18. McCagg, *Stalin Embattled*, pp. 281, 336 fn. 59.

19. "Ekonomicheskie problemy sotsializma v SSSR" [Economic problems of socialism] (written February 1–September 28, 1952), *Sochineniia*, vol. 16, p. 226; *Pravda*, October 3 and 4, 1952; English text in Bruce Franklin, ed., *The Essential Stalin*, pp. 445–71.

20. "Ekonomicheskie problemy," p. 227.

21. Ibid., p. 231.

22. Ibid., p. 230.

23. Ibid., pp. 227–31.

24. "Transcript of Interview Between Stalin and Stassen on World Cooperation," *New York Times*, May 4, 1947, p. 50. By contrast, see English text released by Soviet Embassy in London, *Soviet News*, May 9, 1947; Russian text, "Interviu s g-nom Stassenom, 9 aprelia 1947 g.", *Sochineniia*, vol. 16, pp. 75–92; *Pravda*, May 8, 1947.

25. Ambassador Walter Bedell Smith, dispatch to the Secretary of State, Moscow, April 14, 1947, 2 P.M., FRUS 1947, vol. 4, pp. 552–53.

26. Ibid., p. 552 fn.

27. "Interview Between Stalin and Stassen," *New York Times*, May 4, 1947, p. 50.

28. Varga, *Izmeneniia*, chapter 15; also "Priblizhenie...," *Pravda*, Nov. 27, 1946.

29. "Zapis' besedy tov. I. V. Stalina s deiatelem respublikanskoi partii S.SH.A. Garol'dom Stassenom 9 aprelia 1947 goda," *Pravda*, May 8, 1947, pp. 1–2; *Sochineniia*, vol. 16, pp. 75–92.

30. "Soviet Calls Text of Stassen Wrong," Associated Press, *New York Times*, May 9, 1947, p. 3; "The Stalin-Stassen Interview—Puzzling Accusation by Moscow," *The Times* (London), May 9, 1947, p. 3.

31. *Vie soviétique*, "Supplément," Mai 1947, Paris: See also Joseph Staline, *Aprés la victoire, pour une paix durable*, Éditions Sociales (a collection of most of Stalin's works between 1945 and 1949), pp. 79–93.

32. "Stassen Praises Press," Associated Press, *New York Times*, May 9, 1947, p. 3.
33. Leonhard, *Die Revolution*, p. 126.
34. Nicholas V. Riasanovsky, *A History of Russia*, p. 271.
35. Thomas W. Wolfe, *Soviet Power and Europe*, p. 25.
36. G. M. Malenkov, "Tovarishch Stalin—Vozhd' progressivnogo chelovechestva" [Comrade Stalin—The leader of progressive mankind], *Pravda*, December 21, 1949, p. 2.
37. V. M. Molotov, Speech on the Occasion of the Thirtieth Anniversary of the October Revolution, November 6, 1947, *Problems of Foreign Policy*, pp. 478–79, 494.
38. Ibid., pp. 485–91.
39. Ibid., p. 483.
40. Ibid., p. 491.
41. Molotov, "Statement on the American Draft Treaty on the Disarmament and Demilitarization of Germany," at meeting of Council of Foreign Ministers, July 9, 1946, *Problems of Foreign Policy*, p. 62; Molotov, "Germany and Reparations," statement at meeting of Council of Foreign Ministers, March 17, 1947, ibid., p. 367.
42. Molotov, "Germany and Reparations," pp. 364–70.
43. Molotov, "Provisional Political Organization of Germany," statement at meeting of Council of Foreign Ministers, March 22, 1947, *Problems of Foreign Policy*, p. 397; Molotov, "The State Structure of Germany," statement at meeting of Council of Foreign Ministers, April 2, 1947, *Problems of Foreign Policy*, p. 410; Molotov, "Tasks of the Conference," statement at Conference of Foreign Ministers, June 28, 1947, *Problems of Foreign Policy*, p. 469.

Chapter 13

1. Sulzberger, C. L., "Malenkov's Rise to Power is Key Soviet Development," *New York Times*, June 23, 1949, p. 3.
2. Y. Leino, *Kommunisti Sisäministerinä* (Helsinki, 1958), pp. 98–105, as referred to in A. F. Upton, *Communism in Scandinavia and Finland*, pp. 256–57.
3. Upton, *Communism in Scandinavia and Finland*; pp. 249–50.
4. Delbars, *The Real Stalin*, pp. 248–49.
5. *Soviet Yugoslav Dispute*, letter of C.C. of CPSU to C.C. of C.P.Y., May 4, 1948, passim.
6. Letter of Mr. Hamilton to the Secretary of State, March 15, 1945, 3 P.M., FRUS 1945, vol. 4, p. 607.
7. Werth, *Russia at War*, p. 307.
8. Delbars, *The Real Stalin*, p. 400.
9. Khrushchev, *Crimes*, pp. S21–S22.

Chapter 14

1. Dedijer, *Tito*, p. 277.
2. Ibid., p. 325.
3. Ibid.
4. Ibid., pp. 333–34.

5. Conquest, *Power*, pp. 92–93.
6. Alliyueva, *Only One Year*, p. 384.
7. Ibid., p. 385.
8. Djilas, *Conversations*, p. 171.
9. Dedijer, *Tito*, p. 315.
10. Djilas, *Conversations*, p. 172.
11. Ibid., p. 181.
12. Ibid., p. 179.
13. Ibid., pp. 179–80.
14. Ibid., p. 179.
15. Ibid., p. 185.
16. See *Tanjug* (in English), January 30, 1980; *Nedeljne Novosti* (Belgrade), January 27, 1980; and *Vjesnik* (Zagreb), January 23, 1980, all cited in Zdenko Antic, "Kardelj Describes Clashes with Stalin over Federation with Bulgaria," RFE-RL, RAD Background Report/28 (Yugoslavia), February 7, 1980.
17. There is a vast amount of literature on this topic, of which one particularly useful contribution is the work by Stephen E. Palmer, Jr., and Robert R. King, *Yugoslav Communism and the Macedonian Question*; see Chapter 7, "Continuing Interest in Aegean and Pirin Macedonia," pp. 117–30.
18. Djilas, *Conversations*, p. 181.
19. Ibid., p. 177.
20. Ibid., pp. 88–89.
21. *Borba*, August 7, 1949 (see Clissold, p. 165).
22. Leonhard, *Die Revolution*, p. 483.
23. Craig R. Whitney, "Lev Kopolev, A Soviet Dissident Who Does Not Want to Emigrate, Speaks Out," *New York Times*, July 29, 1979, p. 2.
24. Djilas, *Conversations*, pp. 168–69.
25. Dedijer, *Tito*, pp. 312–13.
26. *Soviet Yugoslav Dispute*, letter from C.C. of CPSU to C.C. of C.P.Y., May 4, 1948, pp. 40–41.
27. Halperin, *Triumphant Heretic*, p. 77.
28. *Soviet Yugoslav Dispute*, letter from J. B. Tito and E. Kardelj to J. V. Stalin and V. M. Molotov, May 17, 1948, p. 53.
29. Ibid., letter from V. M. Molotov and J. V. Stalin, C.C. of CPSU, to Comrade Tito and other members of the C.C. of C.P.Y., May 22, 1948, pp. 54–57.
30. Halperin, *Triumphant Heretic*, p. 73.
31. G. M. Dimitrov, "How to Avert a New Munich," statement before a *Rude Pravo* correspondent (organ of the C.P. of Czechoslovakia), *Rabotnichesko Delo*, no. 238, October 12, 1947, in G. M. Dimitrov, *Works*, vol. 13 (Sofia: Bulgarian Communist Party, 1955), pp. 247–52; and *Selected Works*, vol. 3, pp. 91–92.
32. G. M. Dimitrov, "A New World War Today is Neither Inevitable Nor Imminent," Speech at a Mass Meeting in Prague, April 23, 1948, *Rabotnichesko Delo*, no. 97, April 25, 1948, in *Works*, vol. 14, pp. 68–77; *Selected Works*, vol. 3, p. 230.
33. Ibid., *Selected Works*, vol. 3, p. 232.
34. Djilas, *Conversations*, p. 180.

35. *Borba*, December 12, 1949, as cited in Ulam, *Titoism*, p. 210; Dedijer, *Tito*, p. 350.

36. G. M. Dimitrov, Speech at Vassil Levski Military School on April 30, 1948, *Rabotnichesko Delo*, no. 103, May 4, 1948, in *Works*, vol. 14, pp. 90–96; *Selected Works*, vol. 3, p. 242.

37. *For a Lasting Peace*, July 1, 1948, p. 1.

38. Dedijer, *Tito*, p. 359.

39. Associated Press, "Bulgaria Stands by Yugoslav Ties," *New York Times*, July 1, 1948, p. 8.

40. Fejtö, *Histoire des démocraties populaires*, p. 240.

41. Resolution of the Central Committee of the Bulgarian Workers Party, June 12, 1948, *Rabotnichesko Delo*, no. 166, July 16, 1948, as quoted in *Works*, vol. 14, and in "Reds in Bulgaria Decree Self-Purge," *New York Times*, July 10, 1948, p. 15.

42. Report of G. M. Dimitrov at Fifth Congress of the Bulgarian Workers Party, *Pravda*, December 21, 1948, pp. 3–4; *For a Lasting Peace*, January 1, 1949, p. 2.

43. In 1972 Suslov wrote about his participation at that meeting, but, not surprisingly (given the delicate nature of relations between Belgrade and Moscow in the 1970s), in referring to Dimitrov's speech, Suslov ignored all references to Belgrade. Mikhail Suslov, "Georgi Dimitrov—Founder of Socialist Bulgaria, Symbol of Eternal Bulgarian-Soviet Fraternity," in Petrin Michev and Petra Radinkov, eds., *Memories of Georgi Dimitrov*, pp. 274–75.

44. "Communist Party of Yugoslavia in the Power of Murderers and Spies," resolution of the Information Bureau, *For a Lasting Peace*, November 29, 1949, p. 2.

45. Tsola Dragoycheva, "On the Class and Internationalist Positions," *Septemvri*, no. 1, January, 1979, as cited in Patrick Moore, with G. S., "The Macedonian Polemic Rides Again: Tsola Dragoycheva's Memoirs," *Radio Free Europe Research*, RAD Background Report/26 (Bulgaria), January 31, 1979.

46. Letter of Georgi Dimitrov to Traicho Kostov, January 13, 1945, according to Dragoycheva; see "On the Class and International Positions," p. 75, in Moore, "Macedonian Polemic," p. 6.

47. Dragoycheva, "On the Class and Internationalist Positions," pp. 74–5; cited in Moore, "Macedonian Polemic," p. 7. Dragoycheva claims that the first sentence is quoted from an entry in Georgi Cimitrov's personal diary, August 1, 1947.

48. Ibid.; see Dimitrov, *For a Lasting Peace*, January 1, 1949, p. 2.

49. See Robert R. King, *Minorities under Communism*, pp. 187–219; Palmer and King, *Yugoslav Communism*; Gavriel D. Ra'anan, *Yugoslavia after Tito*, pp. 9–16.

50. *Borba*, December 12, 1949, as cited in Ulam, *Titoism* p. 210.

51. Ulam, *Titoism*, pp. 210–11.

52. *Borba*, December 12, 1949, as cited in Ulam, *Titoism*, p. 210.

53. Conquest, *Great Purge*, p. 498.

54. Antonov-Ovseyenko, *Time of Stalin*, p. 285.

55. Conquest, *Power*, pp. 164–65.

56. Ibid., p. 163. The fact that the doctors were innocent of "anti-Soviet

plots" does not prove that Stalin was innocent of having the victims murdered.

57. Associated Press, "Finnish Newspapers Accused," *New York Times*, September 9, 1948.

58. James H. Billington, "Finland," in Black and Thornton, *Communism and Revolution*, p. 127.

59. Associated Press, "Finnish Reds Admit Blunders," *New York Times*, September 9, 1948.

60. Upton, *Communism in Scandinavia and Finland*, p. 299.

61. Associated Press, "Yugoslav Reds Mourn," *New York Times*, September 2, 1948.

62. Associated Press, "End to Split Held Possible," *New York Times*, September 2, 1948.

63. Conquest, *Power*, p. 93.

64. Graham, *Science and Philosophy*, pp. 445–46.

65. Conquest, *Power*, p. 97; Sulzberger, "Two More Leaders Reported Victims of Purge in Russia," *New York Times*, June 19, 1949.

66. Antonov-Ovseyenko, *Time of Stalin*, pp. 298–99, 282.

67. Talbott, *Khrushchev Remembers*, p. 257.

68. A. Kosygin, "Nashimi uspekhami my obiazany velikomy Stalinu" [We are obliged to the great Stalin for our successes], *Pravda*, December 21, 1949, p. 10; condensed English text in *Current Digest*, vol. 1, no. 52, January 24, 1950, pp. 31–32.

69. N. Khrushchev, "Stalinskaia druzhba narodov zalog nepobedimosti nashei Rodiny" (Stalinist friendship of peoples—Guarantee of our motherland's invincibility), *Pravda*, December 21, 1949, p. 9; condensed English text in *Current Digest*, vol. 1, no. 2, pp. 30–31. L. Beria, "Velikii vdokhnovitel' i organizator pobedy kommunizma" (Great inspirer and organizer of communism's victories), *Pravda*, December 21, 1949, p. 4; complete English text in *Current Digest*, pp. 11–16.

70. G. Malenkov, "Tovarishch Stalin—Vozhd' progressivnovo chelovechestva," (Comrade Stalin-The leader of progressive mankind), *Pravda*, December 21, 1949, p. 2; complete English text in *Current Digest*, pp. 3–6.

71. V. Molotov, "Stalin i stalinskoe rukovodstvo" (Stalin and Stalinist leadership), *Pravda*, December 21, 1949, p. 3; complete English text in *Current Digest*, pp. 6–11.

72. A. Mikoyan, "Velikii zodchii kommunizma" (Great architect of communism), *Pravda*, December 21, 1949, p. 6; complete English text in *Current Digest*, pp. 19–24.

73. Interview with Professor Wolfgang Leonhard at Yale University, conducted May 3, 1979.

74. Christian Duevel, "M. A. Suslov's Role in Postwar Soviet Politics," *Radio Liberation*, Munich, August 4, 1958, p. 3. Duevel cites an article by Boris Souvarine, "Confidences d'un diplomate communiste," *Est & Ouest*, no. 190, March 1–15, 1958.

75. Slobodan Stankovic, "Memoirs of Yugoslavia's Former Ambassador in Moscow, Part II," *Radio Free Europe-Radio Liberty*, RAD Background Report/9 (Yugoslavia), January 20, 1978, p. 11, citing and quoting Veljko Micunović's Memoirs, pp. 317–18. See also Talbott, *Khrushchev Remembers*, pp. 256–57. (Khrushchev publicly attacked Malenkov for his

part in the Leningrad Affair during the Twenty-second CPSU Congress in 1961.)

Chapter 15

1. Edvard Kardelj, "Yugoslavia's Foreign Policy," Address in the Federal Assembly on December 29, 1948, pp. 7–9.

2. Ibid., p. 60.

3. Josip Broz Tito, *Political Report of the Central Committee of the Communist Party of Yugoslavia*, Report delivered at the Fifth Congress of the C.P.Y., p. 128.

4. Milovan Djilas, *Report on Agitation-Propaganda Work of the Central Committee of the Communist Party of Yugoslavia*, Report delivered at the Fifth Congress of the C.P.Y., pp. 58–59.

5. Conquest, *Power*, p. 95.

6. "O nedostatkakh i zadachakh nauchno-issledovatel'skoi raboty v oblasti ekonomiki" [Concerning shortcomings and tasks of research work in the field of economics], *Voprosy Ekonomiki*, no. 8, 1948, pp. 66–110; no. 9, 1948, pp. 53–116.

7. Dr. Aron Katsenelinboigen, *Soviet Economic Thought and Political Power in the U.S.S.R.*, excerpts from which, while still in manuscript, were sent by Dr. Katsenelinboigen to the author of this study; Conquest, *Power*, p. 89.

8. Conquest, *Power*, p. 95.

9. "O nedostatkakh," p. 96; condensed English text in CDSP, vol. I, no. 30, April 19, 1949, pp. 3–30.

10. Varga, "Pis'mo v redaktsiiu," letter to the editor, *Pravda*, March 15, 1949, p. 6.

11. Varga, "Protiv reformistskogo napravleniia v rabotakh po imperializmu" [Against reformist tendencies in works on imperialism], *Voprosy Ekonomiki*, no. 3, 1949, p. 83; complete English text in *Current Digest*, June 7, 1949, vol. 1, no. 19, pp. 3–19.

12. Varga, "Protiv reformistskogo napravleniia," p. 86.

13. Ibid., p. 85.

14. Ibid., p. 87.

15. Varga, "Upadok Angliiskogo imperializma," *Voprosy Ekonomiki*, no. 4, 1950, pp. 68–69; condensed English text in *Current Digest*, vol. 2, no. 32, September 23, 1950, pp. 3–10.

16. Varga, "Upadok Angiliiskogo imperializma," p. 69.

17. Ibid.

18. Alexander C. Kirk, Allied Force Headquarters, dispatch to the Secretary of State, Caserta, February 5, 1945, 3 P.M., FRUS 1945, vol. 5, pp. 1209–10.

19. Talbott, *Khrushchev Remembers*, p. 250.

20. J. Miller and M. Miller, "Voprosy Filosofii (Problems of Philosophy)," *Soviet Studies*, vol. 1, no. 2, October 1949, pp. 210–30.

21. Miller and Miller, "Voprosy Filosofii," p. 213.

22. Crankshaw, *Khrushchev*, p. 219.

23. Ibid., p. 200; Carl A. Linden, *Khrushchev and the Soviet Leadership, 1957–1964*, pp. 28–29, 49.

24. Deutscher, *Stalin*, pp. 300–2.

Chapter 16

1. Djilas, *Conversations*, p. 180.

Chapter 17

1. Conquest, *Power*, p. 109.
2. Ibid.
3. Ibid., p. 103–4.
4. M. Iovchuk, "Vydaiushchiisia deitel' Kommunisticheskoi Partii" [An outstanding figure of the Communist Party], *Kommunist*, no. 3, 1976, pp. 80–86.
5. M. A. Suslov, "Po povudu statei P. Fedoseeva (*Izvestia* za 12 i 21 dekabria)" [Concerning the articles by P. Fedoseen (in *Izvestia* of December 12, and 21)], *Pravda*, December 24, 1952, p. 2; and *Izvestia*, December 25, p. 2. Complete English text available in *Current Digest*, vol. 4, no. 50, January 24, 1953, pp. 14–15.
6. P. N. Fedoseev, "Pis'mo v redaktsiiu," letter to the editor, *Pravda*, January 2, 1953, p. 4; complete English text in *Current Digest*, vol. 4, no. 50, January 24, 1953, pp. 15–16.
7. N. Kurbatov, "O knigakh I. Gladkova po voprosam planirovaniia sovetskogo khoziaistva" [Concerning I. Gladkov's books on problems of planning Soviet economy], *Kommunist*, no. 1, January 1953, pp. 100–16; complete English text in *Current Digest*, vol. 5, no. 17, June 6, 1953, pp. 13–14; A. Sobolev, "Do kontsa preodolet' sub'ektivistskie oshibki v ekonomicheskoi nauke" [Completely overcome subjectivist errors in economics], *Pravda*, January 12, 1953, p. 2; complete English text available in *Current Digest*, vol. 4, no. 52, February 7, 1953, pp. 9–10.
8. "V sobranie Akademii nauk SSSR" (In a meeting of the U.S.S.R. Academy of Sciences], *Pravda*, January 8, 1953, p. 2; complete English text in *Current Digest*, vol. 4, no. 52, February 7, 1953, pp. 10–11.
9. "Obshchee sobranie Akademii nauk SSSR" [General Meeting of the U.S.S.R. Academy of Sciences], *Izvestia*, February 3, 1953, p. 1; complete English text available in *Current Digest*, vol. 5, no 3, February 23, 1953, pp. 1, 46.
10. *For a Lasting Peace*, November 29, 1949, p. 1.
11. Conquest, *Power*, pp. 163–67.
12. Ibid., p. 188.
13. Ibid., p. 189.
14. Antonov-Ovseyenko, *Time of Stalin*, pp. 295, 301.
15. Talbott, *Khrushchev Remembers*, p. 282.
16. Antonov-Ovseyenko, *Time of Stalin*, p. 303.
17. Conquest, *Power*, p. 180.
18. Ibid., p. 123.
19. Yurii A. Zhdanov, "Protiv sub'ektivistskikh izvrashchenii v estestvoznanii" [Against subjectivist distortions in the natural sciences], *Pravda*, January 16, 1953, p. 3; complete English text in *Current Digest*, vol. 4, no. 52, January 16, 1953, pp. 12–13, 22.
20. Yurii A. Zhdanov, Ibid.
21. Conquest, *Power*, pp. 176–213, esp. p. 182.

Appendix A

1. *Pravda*, September 25, 1936; see Wolin and Slusser, *Soviet Secret Police*, p. 50 fn. 88; Alexandre Ouralov, *Staline au pouvoir*, pp. 20–25; Conquest, *Great Terror*, p. 218.
2. "20-Letiiu VChK-OGPU-NKVD" [20 years Cheka-OGPU-NKVD], *Pravda*, December 21, 1937, p. 1; Konstantin Shteppa, "Feliks Dzerzhinski," in Wolin and Slusser, *Soviet Secret Police*, p. 95 fn. 23.
3. Zagoria, *Power and the Soviet Elite*, pp. 93–95.
4. Conquest, *Great Terror*, p. 329.
5. Ibid., p. 635.
6. Zagoria, *Power and the Soviet Elite*, p. 97.
7. Conquest, *Great Terror*, p. 327.

Appendix B

1. Based on interviews with Dr. Mark Kuchment on March 5 and April 17, 1979. Dr. Kuchment wrote his dissertation at the Institute of the History of Science and Technology of the Academy of Sciences, in Moscow, at the time when Aleksandrov was in charge of that institute (during the late 1940s and early 1950s). Subsequently, Dr. Kuchment served as associate professor and assistant dean of the Faculty of Sciences of the Machine Tools Institute in Moscow. He knew several members of the Ehrenburg family and, because of his acquaintance with both parties, he was able to provide insights into Aleksandrov's attack upon Ilya Ehrenburg in 1945.
2. For a brief biographical article concerning Aleksandrov, see Percy E. Corbett, "The Aleksandrov Story," *World Politics*, vol. 1, no. 2, January 1949, pp. 161–74.
3. Ilya Ehrenburg, *Liudi, gody, zhizn'* [Men, years—life], vol. 5, *The War: 1941–45* (in English), pp. 175–77.
4. Discussion with Dr. Alexander M. Nekrich (former Senior Scholar of the Institute of World History of the USSR Academy of Sciences), February 6, 1979, at the Russian Research Center of Harvard University.
5. Conquest, *Power*, p. 400.
6. G. F. Aleksandrov, "Pod velikim znamenem Lenina-Stalina." Doklad tov. G. F. Aleksandrova 21 ianvaria 1946 goda na torzhestvenno-traurnom zasedanii, posviashchennom XXII godovshchine so dnia smerti V. I. Lenina [Under the banner of Lenin-Stalin. Report of Comrade G. F. Aleksandrov, January 21, 1946, on the occasion of the twenty-second anniversary of the death of V. I. Lenin], *Bol'shevik*, no. 1, January 1946, pp. 1–12.
7. Fairbanks, "National Cadres," pp. 184–86.
8. Corbett, "Aleksandrov Story," p. 163; Lebed and Urban, *Who Was Who*, p. 11.
9. G. F. Aleksandrov, *O sovetskoi demokratii* [Concerning Soviet democracy] p. 4. The English translation of this report is available under the title *The Pattern of Soviet Democracy*, translated by Leo Gruliow.
10. Ibid., p. 6.
11. Ibid., p. 14
12. Ibid., p. 20.
13. Ibid., pp. 25, 30–31, 33–37.

14. M. Suslov, *Pravda*, December 24, 1952, p. 2
15. Utechin, *Everyman's Encyclopedia*, pp. 14, 335; Conquest, *Power*, p. 248.
16. Interviews with Dr. Kuchment.
17. Conquest, ibid. p. 258.

Appendix C

1. Conquest, *Great Terror*, pp. 136, 195, 220, 623; *Power*, pp. 233, 272, 443.
2. Roy A. Medvedev, *Let History Judge*, pp. 242, 246–47.
3. According to Dr. Mark Kuchment, who knew B. M. Kedrov personally, his political downfall was due to his family's peculiar history (i.e., its connections with the Yezhovshchina); in addition, he had the "liability," in the antisemitic period, of being married to a Jewish woman.
4. *Pravda*, December 17, 1953, p. 2. Text available in Conquest, *Power*, pp. 440–44.
5. Discussion with Dr. Mark Kuchment, April 21, 1979; United States Central Intelligence Agency, *Membership, USSR Academy of Sciences*, March 1977 (cr 77-11360), p. 14; A. I. Lebed et al., *Who's Who in the USSR, 1965–66*, p. 363.
6. Khrushchev, *Crimes*, S51–S63.
7. Conquest, *Great Terror*, p. 195, remarks that it was strange for Khrushchev to choose Kedrov, in view of the fact that "Kedrov himself had behaved with the most notorious cruelty as representative of the Cheka in the Archangel area during the Civil War and his son (who shared his fate) had been one of the N.K.V.D.'s most brutal interrogators in extracting false confessions in the Zinoviev and Pyatakov cases."

Appendix D

1. Robert H. McNeal's volume *Stalin's Works* contains all of Stalin's works during this period, with the exception of a few military orders, which included Stalin's name for formalistic reasons only, and a few "trivial" greetings to various persons (see McNeal edition, pp. 154–55, esp. fns. 10, 11); McNeal does not reprint those, nor am I counting them in the above totals.
2. Crankshaw, *Khrushchev*, p. 286.

Appendix E

1. "O nedostatkakh i zadachakh nauchno-issledovatel'skoi raboty v oblasti ekonomiki," Rasshirennaia sessiia Uchenogo soveta Instituta ekonomiki Akademii nauk SSSR [Concerning shortcomings and tasks of research work in the field of economics, Augmented session of the Learned Council of the Economic Institute of the Academy of Sciences of the USSR], *Voprosy Ekonomiki*, no. 8, 1948, pp. 66–110; no. 9, 1948, pp. 52–116; see no. 9, p. 57. Condensed English text in *Current Digest*, vol. 1, no. 6, March 8, 1949, pp. 2–11; vol. 1, no. 12, April 12, 1949; vol. 1, no. 30, April 19, 1949, pp. 3–30.
2. Ibid., *Voprosy Ekonomiki*, no. 9, p. 57.
3. Ibid.

4. Ibid.

5. Varga, "Pis'mo v redaktsiiu," letter to the Editor, *Pravda*, March 15, 1949, p. 6; complete English text in *Current Digest*, vol. 1, no. 10, April 15, 1949, p. 45.

6. Conquest, *Power*, p. 91.

7. Varga, "Protiv reformistskogo napravlenniia," p. 79; complete English text in *Current Digest*, vol. 1, no. 19, June 7, 1949, pp. 3–9.

8. Varga, "Protiv reformistskogo napravleniia," p. 88.

9. Ibid.

10. Conquest, *Power*, p. 90.

11. Varga, "Rost bezrabotitsy v stranakh kapitalizma" [Growth of unemployment in capitalist countries], *Pravda*, March 19, 1950, pp. 2–3; "Ekonomika kapitalisticheskikh stran pod udarami monopolii S.Sh.A." [The economy of the capitalist countries under the blows of U.S. monopolies], *Pravda*, May 10, 1950, pp. 2–3; "Upadok Angliiskogo imperializma" [The decline of British imperialism], *Voprosy Ekonomiki*, no. 4, 1950, pp. 48–71; "Anglo-Amerikanskaia bor'ba za neft' na blizhnem vostoke" [Anglo-American struggle for oil in the Middle East], *Pravda*, October 22, 1951, p. 2.

12. Varga, "Ekonomika Anglii v tiskakh Amerikanskoi 'druzhby' " [Britain's economy in the grip of American "friendship"], *Pravda*, November 25, 1952, p. 3; complete English text in *Current Digest*, vol. 4, no. 47, January 3, 1952, pp. 23–24, 46.

Bibliography

Oral History, Personal Interviews, Discussions, Correspondence
Prof. Frederick C. Barghoorn, Yale University, discussion, May 3, 1979, regarding the Varga Affair. Professor Barghoorn was Press Attaché, the U.S. Embassy, Moscow, 1943–47.
Earl Browder, memoirs. Columbia University Oral History Project, Butler Library.
Prof. Stephan Dedijer, Lund University, Sweden, discussion, April 24, 1979. Professor Dedijer is the brother of Vladimir Dedijer, Tito's former associate and biographer.
Prof. Herman Field, Tufts University, discussion, February 27, 1979. Professor Field, like his brother Noel, was arrested in Eastern Europe in 1949, a development related to the purges of Rajk and Slansky.
Prof. Aron Katsenelinboigen, University of Pennsylvania, correspondence, summer 1979. Professor Katsenelinboigen was a member of the USSR Academy of Sciences and an acquaintance of K. V. Ostrovitianov.
Dr. Miroslav Kerner, discussion, September 10, 1979. Dr Kerner was the head of the Czechoslovak Ministry of Food, Division of Exports and Imports, during the immediate postwar period and was well acquainted with key members (Communist and non-Communist) of the postwar Beneš government. He was also Director-General of the U.N.R.R.A. for Czechoslovakia.
Dr. Mark Kuchment, the Russian Research Center, Harvard University, discussions, March 5, and April 17, 1979. Dr. Kuchment was Associate Professor and Assistant Dean of the Faculty of Sciences of the Machine Tools Institute in Moscow. He wrote his doctoral dissertation for the Institute of History of Sciences and Technology of the USSR Academy of Sciences, then headed by G. F. Aleksandrov, and was an acquaintance of (and is an expert on) Ilya Ehrenburg and of the Kedrov family.
Prof. Wolfgang Leonhard, Yale University, discussion, May 3, 1979. Professor Leonhard was a student at the Comintern School and a member of the National Committee for a Free Germany in Mos-

215

cow during World War II. Subsequently, in Berlin, he worked with the Soviet Military Administration in Germany as the Deputy Chief Press Officer of the Central Committee of the K.P.D., as a member of the Central Secretariat of the S.E.D., and a member of the faculty of the Karl Marx Party Academy. In March, 1949, Professor Leonhard took refuge in Yugoslavia, where he spent the next year and a half.

Dr. Alexander M. Nekrich, the Russian Research Center, Harvard University, discussions, February 6 and March 9, 1979. Dr. Nekrich was a Senior Scholar of the Institute of World History of the USSR Academy of Sciences and was author of the highly controversial book, *June 22, 1941*, published in the USSR, which blamed Stalin for the major setbacks suffered by the Soviet Union during the initial stages of Operation Barbarossa. He obtained knowledge of Stalin's manipulation of factional conflict.

Mr. Harold E. Stassen, and Mr. Robert Matteson, his associate, discussions (by telephone), July 10, 1980, concerning their meeting with Stalin, April 9, 1947, and its aftermath. Following these conversations, the author of this study was able to obtain the transcript of the 1947 meeting.

Other Memoirs and Firsthand Accounts

Alliluyeva, Svetlana. *Twenty Letters to a Friend*. New York: Harper & Row, 1967.

_____. *Only One Year*. New York: Harper & Row, 1969.

Avtorkhanov, Abdurakhman. *Stalin and the Soviet Communist Party*. New York: Frederick A. Praeger Press, 1959.

Bialer, Seweryn, ed. *Stalin and His Generals — Soviet Military Memoirs of World War II*. New York: Pegasus, 1966.

Browder, Earl. *Teheran*. New York: International Publishers, 1944.

Brzezinski, Zbigniew K., ed. *Political Controls in the Soviet Army*. New York: Research Program on the USSR, Studies on the USSR No. 6, 1954. (Collected first-hand accounts.)

Buck, Tim. *Europe's Rebirth*. Toronto: Progress Books, 1947.

_____. *Canada: The Communist View*. Toronto: Progress Books, 1948. (Account of a Canadian Communist leader.)

Burmeister, Alfred. *Dissolution and Aftermath of the Comintern: Experiences and Observations 1937–1947*. New York: Research Program on the USSR, Mimeographed Series No. 11, 1955.

Castro Delgado, Enrique. *Mi Fe Se Perdió En Moscu*. Mexico: Editorial Horizontes, 1951. (Account of a Spanish Communist.)

Duclos, Jacques. *Mémoires, vol. 4, 1945—1952: Sur la Brèche*. Paris: Librairie Arthème Fayard, 1971.

Emiot, Israel. *The Birobidjan Case*. Rochester, New York: Sol Bogorod, 1960. (Account of a former associate of the Jewish Anti-Fascist Committee; in Yiddish.)

Foster, William Z. *The New Europe*. New York: International Publishers, 1947.

_____. *History of the Communist Party of the USA*. New York: Greenwood Press, 1968.

Gniffke, Erich W. *Jahre mit Ulbricht*. Cologne: Verlag Wissenschaft und Politik, 1966. (Account of a former official in the Soviet occupation zone of Germany.)

Jaffe, Philip J. *The Rise and Fall of American Communism*. New York: Horizon Press, 1975. ("Browderite" account of developments in C.P.U.S.A.)

Katsenelinboigen, Aron. *Soviet Economic Thought and Political Power in the U.S.S.R.* New York: Pergamon Press, 1979. (Account by a former member of the Soviet Academy of Sciences and acquaintance of K. V. Ostrovitianov.) Professor Katsenelinboigen kindly provided the author of this study with relevant excerpts of his manuscript while still in draft form.

Lemmer, Ernst. *Manches War Doch Anders*. Frankfurt am Main: Verlag Heinrich Scheffler, 1968. (Account of a former official in the Soviet occupation zone of Germany.)

Leonhard, Wolfgang. *Die Revolution Entlässt Ihre Kinder*. Cologne-Berlin: Kiepenheuer und Witsch, 1955. (A significantly shortened English version is available under the title *Child of the Revolution*. Chicago: Henry Regnery Co., 1958.)

Linder, Dr. Erika, ed. *Deutschland-Sowjetunion—Aus fünf Jahrzehnten Kultureller Zusammenarbeit*. Lomonosov University, Moscow; and Humboldt University, Berlin, 1966.

Mardor, Meir. *Schlichoot Alumah*. Israel: Marachot, Israel Defense Forces, 1957. (Yishuv operative in Eastern Europe, 1947–48; in Hebrew.)

Markish, Esther. *The Long Return*. New York: Ballantine Books, 1978. (Account by wife of Peretz Markish, poet and victim of the "anticosmopolitan" purge.)

Medvedev, Roy A. *Let History Judge*. New York: Alfred A. Knopf, 1972.

Medvedev, Zhores A. *The Rise and Fall of T. D. Lysenko*. New York: Columbia University Press, 1969.

Ouralov, Alexandre. *Staline au pouvoir*. Translated by Jacques

Fondeur. Paris: Les Isles D'Or, 1951. English edition: Alexander Uralov, *The Reign of Stalin*. Westport, Conn.: Hyperion Press Inc., 1975.

Rao, M. B., ed. *Documents of the History of the Communist Party of India, 1948–1950*, vol. 7. New Delhi: People's Publishing House, 1976.

Reale, Eugenio. *Avec Jacques Duclos au banc des accusés*. Paris: Librairie Plon, 1958.

Slusser, Robert E., ed. *Soviet Economic Policy in Postwar Germany*. New York: Research Program on the USSR, Studies on the USSR No. 3, 1953. (Firsthand accounts by former Soviet officials in the Soviet occupation zone of Germany.)

Smith, Jean Edward, ed. *The Papers of Lucius D. Clay*. 2 vols. Bloomington: Indiana University Press, 1974.

Starobin, Joseph R. *American Communism in Crisis, 1943–57*. Cambridge: Harvard University Press, 1972.

Stassen, Harold E., and Matteson, Robert. "Transcript of Conference between Generalissimo Stalin and Harold E. Stassen, at the Kremlin in Moscow, on April 9, 1947." 032/5-247, United States of America, General Services Administration, National Archives and Records Series.

Taborsky, Edward. *Communism in Czechoslovakia, 1948–1960*. Princeton, N.J.: Princeton University Press, 1961.

Soviet Sources: Books and Monographs

Aleksandrov, G. F. *O Sovetskoi Demokratii*. Stenograma Doklada, prochitanogo 4 dekabria 1946 goda, na sessii Akademii Nauk SSSR. Moscow: Isdatel'stvo "Pravda," 1947. English edition: *The Pattern of Soviet Democracy*. Translated by Leo Gruliow. Russian Translation Program of the American Council of Learned Societies, Public Affairs Press, Washington, D.C., 1948.

Antonov-Ovseyenko, Anton. *The Time of Stalin: Portrait of a Tyranny*. Translated by George Saunders. New York: Harper & Row, 1981.

Ehrenburg, Ilya. *European Crossroad*. New York: Alfred A. Knopf, 1947.

———. *Liudi, gody, zhizn'* [Men, years–life]. Vols. 5 and 6. Moscow: Izdatel'stvo Khudozhestvennaia Literatura, 1967. English edition: Volume 5: *The War: 1941–45*. Cleveland and New York: The World Publishing Co., 1964. Volume 6: *Post-war Years: 1945–54*. London: MacGibbon & Kee, 1966.

Fedoseev, P. N., and Chernenko, K. U., eds. Kommunisticheskaia

Partiia Sovetskogo Soiuza v resoliutsiiakh i resheniiahk s'ezdov, konferentsii i plenumov TsK. Tom Shestoi. Moscow: Izdatel'stvo Politicheskoi Literatury, 1971. (For English language work on this matter, refer to Robert H. McNeal, ed., *Resolutions and Decisions of the Communist Party of the Soviet Union*, vol. 3, *The Stalin Years: 1929–1953*. Toronto: University of Toronto Press, 1974; and idem, *Guide to the Decisions of the Communist Party of the Soviet Union, 1917–1967*. Toronto: University of Toronto Press, 1972.)

Goliakov, S., and Ponizovsky, P. *Le Vrai Sorge*. Translated by M. Matignon. Moscow and Paris: Novosti and Opera Mundi et Librairie Arthème Fayard, 1967.

Khrushchev, Nikita S. *The Crimes of the Stalin Era*. Text of address to the Twentieth Congress of the C.P.S.U. Annotated by Boris I. Nicolaevsky. Booklet. New York: *The New Leader*, 1962.

_____. *Khrushchev Remembers*. Edited and translated by Strobe Talbott. Boston: Little Brown and Company, 1970.

Molotov, V. M. *Problems of Foreign Policy*. Speeches and Statements, April 1945–November 1948. Moscow: Foreign Languages Publishing House, 1949.

Nekrich, A. M. *1941 22 iyunia*. Moscow: Izdatel'stvo "Nauka," 1965. English edition: *June 22, 1941*. Edited by Vladimir Petrov. University of South Carolina Press, 1968. This volume includes the subsequent, February 16, 1966, conference "discussing" Nekrich's work, as well as the text of an article from the September 1967 *Voprosy Istorii KPSS*, by G. A. Deborin and B. S. Telpukhovskii (under the title of "In the Ideological Captivity of the Falsifiers of History"), strongly attacking Nekrich.

Patolichev, N. S. *Ispytaniye na zrelost'* [Test of maturity]. Moscow: Izdatel'stvo Politicheskoy Literatury, 1977. See Rigby, T. H.

Pospelov, P. N., et al., eds. *The Great Patriotic War of the Soviet Union*. Moscow: Progress Publishers, 1970.

Prokharov, A. M. *Bol'shaia Sovetskaia Entsiklopedia*. Moskva, 1974.

Shostakovich, Dmitri. *Memoirs*. See Volkov, Solomon.

Stalin, I. V. *Sochineniia* [Works]. Tom 3 (16), *1946–1953*. Edited by Robert H. McNeal. Stanford, Cal: The Hoover Institution on War, Revolution and Peace, 1967. (See also McNeal, ed., *Stalin's Works, An Annotated Bibliography*. Stanford, Calif.: The Hoover Institution on War, Revolution and Peace, 1967.)

Talbott, Strobe. See Nikita S. Khrushchev.

Varga, Evgenii. *Izmeneniia v ekonomike kapitalizma v itoge vtoroi mirovoi Voiny* [Changes in the economy of capitalism as a result of the Second World War]. Moscow: OGIZ-Gosudarstvennoe Isdatel'stvo Politicheskoi Literatury, 1946.

Volkov, Solomon. *Testimony: The Memoirs of Dmitri Shostakovich.* (As related to and edited by Solomon Volkov; translated from the Russian by Antonina W. Bouis.) New York: Harper & Row, 1979.

Voznesenskii, N. A. *Piatiletnii plan vosstanovleniia i razvitiia narodnogo khoziaistva SSSR na 1946–1950 gg.* Doklad i zakliuchitel'noe slovo na pervoi sessii Verkhovnogo Soveta SSSR 15-18 marta 1946 g. Moscow: OGIZ-Gosudarstvennoe Izdatel'stvo Politicheskoi Literatury, 1946. English edition: *Five-Year Plan for the Restoration and Development of the National Economy of the U.S.S.R. for 1946–1950.* Washington, D.C.: Information Bulletin of the Embassy of the Union of Soviet Socialist Republics, April 1946.

————. *Voennaia ekonomika SSSR v period Otechestvennoi Voiny* [The wartime economy of the U.S.S.R. during the Great Patriotic War]. Moscow: OGIZ-Gosudarstvennoe Izdatel'stvo Politicheskoi Literatury, 1948. English edition: *The Economy of the U.S.S.R. during World War II.* Washington, D.C.: Public Affairs Press, in cooperation with the Translation Program of the American Council of Learned Sciences, 1948.

Wan Min. *Polveka KPK i predatel'stvo Mao Tse-duna.* Moscow: Izdatel'stvo Politicheskoi Literatury, 1975. English edition: Wang Ming. *Mao's Betrayal.* Translated by Vic Schneierson. Moscow: Progress Publishers, 1979.

Zhukov, G. K. *Vospominaniia i razmyshleniia* [Reminiscences and reflections]. Moscow: Izdatel'stvo Agenstva Pechati Novosti, 1969. English edition: *The Memoirs of Marshal Zhukov.* London: Jonathan Cape, Ltd., 1971.

*Soviet Sources: Articles**

Abramov, B. A. "Organizatsionno-partiniaia rabota KPSS v gody chetvertoi piatiletki." *Voprosy Istorii KPSS,* no. 3, April 1979, pp. 55–65.

Aleksandrov, G. F. "Ob istorii uchenii o razvitii obshchestva." *Bol'shevik,* nos. 23–24, December 1945, pp. 25–52.

————. "Pod velikim znamenem Lenina-Stalina." *Bol'shevik,* no. 1, January 1946, pp. 1–12.

Beria, L. P. "Velikii vdokhnovitel' i organizator pobedy kommunizma."

---

*Translations of individual articles from Soviet sources, wherever available, are cited in the appropriate notes to the text.

Pravda, December 21, 1949, p. 4.

Fedoseev, P. N. "Pismo v redaktsiiu." *Pravda*, January 2, 1953, p. 4.

Galaktianov, M. "Chto kroetsia za planami oborony Britanskoi Imperii?" *Novoe Vremia*, no. 22, November 15, 1946, pp. 3–6.

_____. "Kto zatevaet novuiu gonku vooruzhenii." *Novoe Vremia*, no. 17, April 25, 1947, pp. 3–6.

Gladkov, I. "Ob izmeneniiakh v ekonomike kapitalizma v rezul'tate vtoroi mirovoi Voiny." *Bol'shevik*, no. 17, September 15, 1947, pp. 57–64.

Iovchuk, M. "Vydaiushchiisia deiatel' kommunisticheskoi partii." *Kommunist*, no. 3, February 1976, pp. 80–86.

Khrushchev, N. S. "Stalinskaia druzhba naradov-zalog nepobedimosti nashei rodiny." *Pravda*, December 21, 1949, p. 9.

Kosygin, A. N. "Nashimi uspekhami my obiazany velikomy Stalinu." *Pravda*, December 21, 1949, p. 10.

Kurbatov, N. "O knigakh I. Gladkova po voprosam planirovaniia sovetskogo khozhiaistva." *Kommunist*, no. 1, January 1953, pp. 110–16.

Malenkov, G. M. "Tovarishch Stalin—Vozhd' progressivnogo chelovechestva." *Pravda*, December 21, 1949, p. 2.

Marinin, M. "Chto skryvaetsia za krizisom v Palestine?" *Pravda*, May 4, 1948, p. 4.

Melekhov, M. "Arabskaia liga i nezavisimost' arabskikh stran." *Pravda*, March 24, 1948, p. 3.

Mikoyan, A. I. "Velikii zodchii kommunizma." *Pravda*, December 21, 1949, p. 6.

Molotov, V. M. "Stalin i Stalinskoe rukovodstvo." *Pravda*, December 21, 1949, p. 3.

Ostrovitianov, K. V., and Galaktianov, M. "Kniga o voennoi ekonomike SSSR." *Pravda*, January 3, 1948, pp. 2–3.

Rodinov, P. "Plamennyi borets za kommunizm." *Pravda*, March 10, 1976, p. 6.

Sobolev, A. "Do kontsa preodolet' sub'ektivistskie oshibki v ekonomicheskoi nauke." *Pravda*, January 12, 1953, p. 2.

Suslov, M. A. "Po povodu statei P. Fedoseeva." *Pravda*, December 24, 1952, p. 2.

_____. "Georgi Dimitrov—Founder of Socialist Bulgaria, Symbol of Eternal Bulgarian-Soviet Fraternity." In *Memories of Georgi Dimitrov*, edited by Petrin Michev and Petra Radinkova, pp. 271–76. Sophia, Bulgaria: Sophia Press, 1972.

Tiul'panov, S. I. "Naissance de la démocratie populaire." *Démocratie nouvelle*, vol. 2, no. 6, June 1948, pp. 296–300.

_____. *"Die Hilfe der Sowjetunion bei der demokratischen Neugestaltung von Wissenschaft und Kultur nach 1945."* In *Deutschland-Sowjetunion—Aus fünf Jahrzehnten Kultureller Zusammenarbeit,* edited by Dr. Erika Linger, pp. 185–88. Lomonosov University, Moscow, and Humboldt University, Berlin, 1966.

Varga, E. "Anglo-Amerikanskoe finansovoe soglashenie." *Novoe Vremia,* no. 1, January 1946, pp. 5–9.

_____. "Priblizhenie ekonomicheskogo krizisa v kapitalisticheskom mire." *Pravda,* November 27, 1946, p. 3.

_____. "Demokratiia novogo tipa." *Mirovoe Khoziaistvo i Mirovaia Politika,* no. 3, March 1947, pp. 3–14.

_____. "Infliatsiia i denezhnye reformy v kapitalisticheskikh stranakh." *Pravda,* December 24, 1947, p. 4.

_____. "Protiv reformistskogo napravleniia v rabotakh po imperializmu." *Voprosy Ekonomiki,* no. 3, 1949, pp. 79–88.

_____. "Pis'mo v redaktsiiu." *Pravda,* March 15, 1949, p. 6.

_____. "Rost bezrabotitsy v stranakh kapitalizma." *Pravda,* March 19, 1950, pp. 2–3.

_____. "Ekonomika kapitalisticheskikh stran pod udarami monopolii S.Sh.A." *Pravda,* May 10, 1950. pp. 2–3.

_____. "Upadok Angliiskogo imperializma." *Voprosy Ekonomiki,* no. 4, 1950, pp. 48–71.

_____. "Anglo-Amerikanskaia bor'ba za neft' na blizhnem vostoke." *Pravda,* October 22, 1951, p. 2.

_____. "Ekonomika Anglii v tiskakh Amerikanskoi 'druzhby.'" *Pravda,* November 25, 1952, p. 3.

_____. "Political Testament." *New Left Review,* no. 62, July/August 1970, pp. 31–44. (Samizdat tract.)

Zhdanov, A. A. "Doklad t. Zhdanova o zhurnalakh 'Zvezda' i 'Leningrad.' " *Bol'shevik,* no. 17, September 1946, pp. 4–19.

_____. "29-ya godovshchina velikoi oktiabr'skoi Sots'ialisticheskoi revolutsii." *Pravda,* November 7, 1946, pp. 1–3.

_____. "Vystuplenie na diskussii po knige G. F. Aleksandrov 'Istoriia zapadnoevropeiskoi filosofii.' " *Bol'shevik,* no. 16, August 30, 1947, pp. 7–23.

Zhdanov, Yurii. "Tovarishu I. V. Stalinu." *Pravda,* August 7, 1948, p. 5.

_____. "Protiv sub'ektivistskikh izvrashchenii v estestvoznanii." *Pravda,* January 16, 1953.

Soviet Sources: Documents without Specified Authors

"20-Letiiu VChK-OGPU-NKVD." *Pravda,* December 21, 1937, p. 1.

(photograph)

Ukaz. *Pravda*, September 7, 1940, p. 1.

―――. *Pravda*, September 7, 1940, p. 3.

―――. *Pravda*, May 7, 1941, p. 1.

"Sovetskii narod vstrechaet velikii prazdnik novymi slavnymi trudovymi podvigami." *Pravda*, November 6, 1946. p. 1.

"Diskussiia-po knige E. Varga 'Izmeneniia v ekonomike kapitalizma v itoge vtoroi mirovoi voiny', 7, 14, 21 Maia 1947 g." *Mirovoe Khoziaistvo i Mirovaia Politika*, no. 11, November 1947 (prilozhenie k zhurnalu).

"O nedostatkakh i zadachakh nauchno-issledovatel'skoi raboty v oblasti ekonomiki." Rasshirennaia sessiia Uchenogo soveta Instituta ekonomiki Akademii nauk SSSR. *Voprosy Ekonomiki*, no. 8, 1948, pp. 66–110; no. 9, 1948, pp. 53–116.

"Obshchee sobranie Akademii nauk SSSR." *Izvestia*, February 3, 1953, p. 1.

"V sobranie Akademii nauk SSSR." *Pravda*, January 8, 1953, p. 2.

Pravda, photographs of the parade rostrum for May Day and October Revolution parades, May 2, 1945; November 8, 1946; May 2, 1947; November 8, 1947; May 2, 1948.

For a Lasting Peace, For a People's Democracy, editions from 1947 to 1949.

Yugoslav Sources

Dedijer, Vladimir. *Tito*. New York: Simon & Schuster, 1953.

―――. *The Battle Stalin Lost*. New York: Grosset and Dunlap, 1970.

Djilas, Milovan. *Report on Agitation-Propaganda Work of the Central Committee of the Communist Party of Yugoslavia*. Report delivered at the Fifth Congress of the C.P.Y. Belgrade: Office of Information of the FPRY, 1948.

―――. *Conversations with Stalin*. Translated by Michael B. Petrovich. New York: Harcourt, Brace & World, 1962.

Kardelj, Edvard. *After Five Years*. Reprint of an article in *Borba*, June 28, 1953. New York: Yugoslav Information Center, July 1953.

―――. "Notes on Some Questions of International Development." *Kommunist* (Belgrade), no. 2, January 1947. English text: *Political Affairs*, vol. 26, no. 6, June 1947, pp. 531–54.

―――. *On People's Democracy in Yugoslavia*. Reprint of an article in Belgrade *Kommunist*, July 1949, which constituted an extended version of a May 1949 speech. New York: Yugoslav Information Center, 1949.

_____. *Le Parti communiste de Yougoslavie dans sa lutte pour la Yougoslavie nouvelle et le socialisme*. Report delivered at the Fifth Congress of the C.P.Y. Paris: Le Livre Yougoslave, 1949.

_____. Speech of September 29, 1948, United Nations, Official Records of the Third Session of the General Assembly. Part I. Plenary Meetings of the General Assembly, September 21–December 12, 1948, Pallais de Chaillot, Paris, 1948.

_____. *Yugoslavia's Foreign Policy*. Address to Yugoslav Federal Assembly, December 29, 1948. Belgrade: Yugoslav Information Center, 1949.

Kidrič, Boris. *On the Construction of Socialist Economy in the F.P.R.Y.* Speech delivered at the Fifth Congress of the C.P.Y. Belgrade: Office of Information of the F.P.R.Y., 1948.

Pijade, Moša. *La Fable de l'aide soviétique à l'insurrection nationale Yougoslave*. Paris: Le Livre Yougoslave, 1950.

Tito, Josip Broz. "The People's Front and the New Yugoslavia." Address delivered at the Second Congress of the People's Front of Yugoslavia, September 27, 1947. English text: *Political Affairs*, vol, 28, no. 1, January 1948, pp. 76–96.

_____. *Political Report to the Central Committee of the Communist Party of Yugoslavia*. Report delivered at the Fifth Congress of the C.P.Y. Belgrade: Office of Information of the F.P.R.Y., 1948.

Vukmanović(-Tempo), Svetozar. *How and Why the People's Liberation Struggle of Greece Met With Defeat*. London: Merrit and Hatcher Ltd., 1950.

Bulgarian Sources

Dimitrov, Georgi M. *Works*. Vols. 13 and 14. Sofia: Bulgarian Communist Party, 1955.

Dimitrov, Georgi. *Selected Works*. Vols. 2 and 3. Sofia: Sofia Press, 1972.

Michev, Petrin, and Radinkova, Petra, eds. *Memories of Georgi Dimitrov*. Sofia: Sofia Press, 1972.

Albanian Sources

Hoxha, Enver. May Day Speech, April 30, 1948. *Foreign Broadcast Information Service-Balkan Transmissions*, May 3, 1948, EE1-EE3.

Shehu (Chehou), Mehmet. *A propos de l'expérience de la guerre de libération nationale et de developpement de notre armée nationale*. Paris: Editions Git-le-Coeur. (Translation of Shehu

Speech of April 18, 1947 from the Albanian. No publication date is given in the French edition; however, a January 1962 introduction is included.)

Other Communist Sources

Browder, Earl. "End of the Stalin Era." *The Nation*, vol. 176, no. 11, March 14, 1953, pp. 221–22.

Casanova, Laurent. "Jdanov et le mouvement ouvrier international." *Cahiers du Communisme*, vol. 25, no. 2, October 1948, pp. 1081–92.

Communist Party of the U.S.A. "Present Situation and the Next Tasks." Resolution of July 28, 1945. *Political Affairs*, vol. 24, no. 9, September 1945, pp. 816–32.

Duclos, Jacques. "A propos de la dissolution du Parti Communiste Americain." *Cahiers du Communisme*, n.s. no. 6, April 1945, pp. 21–38.

———. "Notre Politique." *Cahiers du Communisme*, vol. 24, no. 11, pp. 1091–97.

———. "Yugoslav Nationalists: Agents for Imperialism." *For a Lasting Peace, For a People's Democracy*, July 1, 1949, p. 2.

Foster, William Z. "The Danger of American Imperialism in the Postwar Period." *Political Affairs*, vol. 24, no. 6, June 1945, pp. 493–500.

———. "Letter to the National Committee, C.P.S.U.," submitted January 20, 1944. *Political Affairs*, vol. 24, no. 7, July 1945, pp. 640–55.

———. "American Imperialism and the War Danger." *Political Affairs*, vol. 16, no. 8, August 1947, pp. 672–87.

Mitrovitch, Stephan. "Remarques fondamentales sur la question de Trieste." *Cahiers du Communisme*, n.s. vol. 23, no. 3, March 1946, pp. 284–306.

Vie Soviétique. "Supplément." Mai 1947, Paris.

Western Sources: Books and Monographs

Adams, Arthur E. *Stalin and His Times*. New York: Holt, Rinehart & Winston, Inc., 1972.

Armstrong, Hamilton Fish. *Tito and Goliath*. New York: The Macmillan Co., 1951.

Auriol, Vincent. *Journal du Septennat, 1947–1954*. Vol. 2, *1948*. Paris: Librairie Armand Colin, 1974.

Auty, Phyllis. *Yugoslavia*. New York: Walker & Co., 1965.

Averoff Tossizza, Evangelos. *By Fire and Axe*. New Rochelle, New York: Caratzas Brothers Publishers, 1978.

Azrael, Jeremy R. *Soviet Nationality Policies and Practices*. New York: Praeger Publishers, 1978. (See especially Charles O. Fairbanks, Jr., "National Cadres as a Force in the Soviet System: The Evidence of Beria's Career, 1949–1953.")

Barghoorn, Frederick C. *Politics in the USSR*. Boston and Toronto: Little Brown & Co., 1966.

Black, Cyril E., and Thornton, Thomas P. *Communism and Revolution*. Princeton, N.J.: Princeton University Press, 1964.

Blackmer, Donald L. M. *Unity in Diversity*. Cambridge: M.I.T. Press, 1968.

Borkenau, Franz. *European Communism*. London: Faber & Faber, 1953.

Brierly, J. L. *The Law of Nations*. New York and Oxford: Oxford University Press, 1963.

Brimmell, J. *Communism in South East Asia: A Political Analysis*. London: Royal Institute of International Affairs, Oxford University Press, 1959.

Brookings Institution, The. *Current Developments in United States Foreign Policy*. Vols. 1 and 2. 1948.

Brzezinski, Zbigniew K. *The Permanent Purge*. Cambridge: Harvard University Press, 1956.

————. *The Soviet Bloc: Unity and Conflict*. New York: Frederick A. Praeger, 1961.

Bundesministerium Für Gesamtdeutsche Fragen. *SBZ von 1945 bis 1954*. Bonn: Deutscher Bundesverlag, 1956.

Carew Hunt, R. N. *The Theory and Practice of Communism*. Great Britain: Penguin Books, 1971.

Cattell, David T. *Communism and the Spanish Civil War*. Berkeley and Los Angeles, 1955.

Clark, Alan. *Barbarossa: The Russian-German Conflict, 1941–1945*. New York: Signet Books, 1966.

Clarkson, Jesse D. *A History of Russia*. New York: Random House, 1962.

Clissold, Stephen, ed. *A Short History of Yugoslavia from Early Times to 1966*. Cambridge: Cambridge University Press, 1966.

————. *Yugoslavia and the Soviet Union, 1939–1973*. London: Oxford University Press, 1975.

Colton, Joel. *Leon Blum: Humanist in Politics*. Cambridge, Mass., and London: M.I.T. Press, 1966.

Colton, Timothy J. *Commissars, Commanders and Civilian*

Authority: The Structure of Soviet Military Politics. Cambridge: Harvard University Press, 1979.

Confino, Michael, and Shamir, Shimon, eds. *The USSR and the Middle East.* New York and Toronto: A Halstead Press Book, John Wiley & Sons, 1973.

Conquest, Robert. *Power and Policy in the USSR.* New York: Harper Torch Books, 1967.

_____. *The Great Terror.* Harmondsworth, Great Britain: Pelican Books, 1971.

Crankshaw, Edward. *Cracks in the Kremlin Wall.* New York: Viking Press, 1952.

_____. *Khrushchev: A Career.* New York: Viking Press, 1966.

Craven, W. F., and Cate, J. L. *The Army Air Force in World War II: Men and Planes.* Chicago: University of Chicago Press, 1957.

Crozier, Brian. *DeGaulle.* New York: Charles Scribner's Sons, 1973.

Dagan, Avigdor. *Moscow and Jerusalem.* London: Abelard-Schuman, 1970.

Daniels, Robert V. *A Documentary History of Communism.* New York: Random House, 1960.

Deakin, F. W., and Storry, G. R. *The Case of Richard Sorge.* Great Britain: Trinity Press, 1966.

Degras, Jane. *Soviet Documents on Foreign Policy.* Vol. 3. London: Oxford University Press, 1953.

Delbars, Yves. *The Real Stalin.* London: Allen & Unwin, 1953.

Deuerlein, Ernst, ed. *DDR 1945—1970, Geschichte und Bestandsaufnahme.* Munich: Deutscher Taschen Buch Verlag, 1971.

Deutscher, Isaac. *Stalin: A Political Biography.* New York: Oxford University Press, 1967.

Donaldson, Robert H. *Soviet Policy toward India: Ideology and Strategy.* Cambridge: Harvard University Press, 1974.

Duhnke, Horst. *Stalinismus in Deutschland.* Federal Republic of Germany: Verlag für Politik und Wirtschaft, 1955.

Ebon, Martin. *Malenkov: Stalin's Successor.* New York: McGraw Hill Book Co., 1953.

Elgey, Georgette. *Histoire de la IVe République.* Paris: Librairie Arthème Fayard, 1965.

_____. *La République des illusions, 1945—51.* Paris: Librairie Arthème Fayard, 1965.

Eliav, Arie L. *Between Hammer and Sickle.* New York: Signet Book, New America Library, 1969.

Erickson, John. *The Soviet High Command.* New York: St. Martin's

Press, 1962.

———. *The Road to Stalingrad.* Vol. 1. London: Weidenfeld & Nicolson, 1975.

Erlich, Alexander. *Soviet Views on Soviet Economic Development.* Cambridge: Harvard University Press, 1955.

Fainsod, Merle. *How Russia is Ruled.* Cambridge: Harvard University Press, 1953.

Fejtö, François. *Histoires des démocraties populaires.* Paris: Éditions du Seuil, 1952.

———. *The French Communist Party and the Crisis of International Communism.* Cambridge: M.I.T. Press, 1967.

Franklin, Bruce, ed. *The Essential Stalin.* Garden City, N.J.: Anchor Books, 1972.

Gluckstein, Ygael. *Stalin's Satellites in Europe.* London: Allen & Unwin, 1952.

Graham, Loren R. *Science and Philosophy in the Soviet Union.* New York: Alfred A. Knopf, 1972.

Griffith, William E. *Albania and the Sino-Soviet Rift.* Cambridge: M.I.T. Press, 1963.

Halperin, Ernst. *The Triumphant Heretic.* London: William Heineman, Ltd., 1958.

Hammond, Thomas T., ed. *The Anatomy of Communist Takeovers.* New Haven and London: Yale University Press, 1975.

Harper, Samuel N., and Thompson, Ronald. *The Government of the Soviet Union.* New York: D. Van Nostrand Co., Inc., 1950.

Hindrichs, Gunter, and Heidelmeyer, Wolfgang, eds. *Documents sur Berlin 1943–1963.* Munich: R. Oldenbourg Verlag, 1964.

Hingley, Ronald. *The Russian Secret Police.* New York: Simon & Schuster, 1970.

Horelick, Arnold L.; Johnson, A. Ross; and Steinbruner, John D. *The Study of Soviet Foreign Policy: A Review of Decision-Theory-Related Approaches.* Santa Monica, Calif.: The Rand Corporation (R-1334), December 1973.

Hyde, R. Montgomery. *Stalin.* London: Hart-Davis, 1971.

Irving, David. *Hitler's War.* New York: Viking Press, 1977.

Johnson, A. Ross. *The Transformation of Communist Ideology: The Yugoslav Case, 1945–53.* Cambridge: M.I.T. Press, 1972.

Johnson, Chalmers A. *Peasant Nationalism and Communist Power.* Stanford, Cal.: Stanford University Press, 1962.

Joravsky, David. *The Lysenko Affair.* Cambridge: Harvard University Press, 1970.

Jukes, Geoffrey. *The Soviet Union in Asia.* Berkeley and Los Angeles:

University of California Press, 1973.

Kagan, Benjamin. *The Secret Battle for Israel*. Cleveland and New York: The World Publishing Company, 1966.

Kautsky, John H. *Moscow and the Communist Party of India*. New York: John Wiley & Sons, 1956.

Kennan, George E. *Memoirs, 1925–50*. New York: Bantam Books, 1969.

King, Robert R. *Minorities under Communism*. Cambridge: Harvard University Press, 1973.

Kolkowicz, Roman. *The Soviet Military and the Communist Party*. Princeton, N.J.: Princeton University Press, 1967.

Krisch, Henry. *German Politics under Soviet Occupation*. New York and London: Columbia University Press, 1974.

Kulski, W. W. *The Soviet Regime*. Syracuse, New York: Syracuse University Press, 1954.

Lazitch, Bronko, and Drachkovitch, Milorad M. *Biographical Directory of the Comintern*. Stanford, Calif.: The Hoover Institute Press, Stanford University, 1973.

Leach, Barry A. *German Strategy Against Russia, 1939–1941*. Oxford: Clarendon Press, 1973.

Lebed, Andrew I., et al., eds. *Who's Who in the USSR 1065–1966*. 2nd ed. New York and London: Scarecrow Press, Inc., 1966.

Lebed, Andrew I., and Urban, P. K., eds. *Who Was Who in the USSR*. Metuchen, N.J.: Scarecrow Press, Inc., 1972.

Linden, Carl A. *Khrushchev and the Soviet Leadership, 1957–64*. Baltimore: Johns Hopkins Press, 1966.

Logorecci, Anton. *The Albanians: Europe's Forgotten Survivors*. Boulder, Colorado: Westview Press, 1977.

McCagg, William O., Jr. *Stalin Embattled, 1943–48*. Detroit: Wayne State University Press, 1978.

McCauly, Martin, ed. *Communist Power in Europe, 1944–49*. New York: Barnes and Noble Books, Harper and Row, 1977.

McLane, Charles B. *Soviet Strategies in Southeast Asia*. Princeton: Princeton University Press, 1966.

Maclean, Fitzroy. *The Heretic*. New York: Harper & Row, 1957.

McVey, Ruth T. *The Calcutta Conference and the Southeast Asian Uprisings*. Ithaca, New York: Cornell University Interim Report Series, 1958.

McVicker, Charles P. *Titoism*. New York: Alfred A. Knopf, 1972.

Marcou, Lilly. *Le Kominform*. Presses de la Fondation Nationale des Sciences Politiques, 1977.

Marie, Jean-Jacques. *Staline*. Paris: Editions du Seuil, 1967.

Mastny, Vojtech. *Russia's Road to Cold War.* New York, 1979.
Meissner, Boris. *Russland im Umbruch.* Frankfurt am Main: Verlag für Geschichte und Politik, 1951.
_____. *Russland unter Chruschtschow.* Munich: R. Oldenbourg Verlag, 1960.
Morgan, Roger. *West European Politics since 1945.* New York: Capricorn Books, 1973.
Nettl, J. P. *The Eastern Zone and Soviet Policy in Germany, 1945–50.* London, New York, Toronto: Oxford University Press, 1951.
O'Ballance, Edgar. *The Greek Civil War, 1944–1949.* New York: Frederick A. Praeger Press, 1969.
Overstreet, Gene D., and Windmiller, Marshall. *Communism in India.* Berkeley and Los Angeles: University of California Press, 1959.
Palmer, Stephen E., Jr., and King, Robert R. *Yugoslav Communism and the Macedonian Question.* Hamden, Conn.: Archon Books, 1971.
Payne, Robert. *The Rise and Fall of Stalin.* New York: Simon & Schuster, 1965.
Prifti, Peter R. *Socialist Albania since 1944: Domestic and Foreign Policy Developments.* Cambridge: M.I.T. Press, 1978.
Ra'anan, Uri. "Some Political Perspectives concerning the U.S.-Soviet Strategic Balance." In *The Superpowers in a Multi-Nuclear World*, edited by Geoffrey Kemp, Robert L. Pfaltzgraff, Jr., and Uri Ra'anan, pp. 15–26. Lexington, Mass.: D. C. Heath, 1974.
Rauch, Georg Von. *A History of Soviet Russia.* New York: Frederick A. Praeger Press, 1957.
Rauch, Georg Von, and Meissner, Boris. *Die deutsch-sowjetischen Beziehungen von 1941 bis 1967.* Würzburg: Hans Otto Holzner Verlag, 1967.
Remnek, Richard B. *Soviet Scholars and Soviet Foreign Policy.* Durham, N.C.: Carolina Academic Press, 1975.
Riasanovsky, Nicholas V. *A History of Russia.* 3rd ed. New York: Oxford University Press, 1977.
Rigby, T. H., ed. *The Stalin Dictatorship.* Sydney, Australia: Sydney University Press, 1968.
Rieber, Alfred J. *Stalin and the French Communist Party, 1941–47.* New York and London: Columbia University Press, 1962.
Salisbury, Harrison E. *Moscow Journal.* Chicago: The University of Chicago Press, 1961.
_____. *900 Days: The Siege of Leningrad.* New York: Avon Books, 1970.
Scalapino, Robert A., ed. *The Communist Revolution in Asia.*

Englewood Cliffs, N.J.: Prentice-Hall, 1975.

Schapiro, Leonard. *The Communist Party of the Soviet Union.* New York: Vintage Books, 1971.

Schiff, Zeev, and Rothstein, Raphael. *A History of the Israeli Army, 1870–1974.* San Francisco: Straight Arrow Books, 1974.

Schueller, George K. *The Politburo.* Stanford, Calif.: Stanford University Press-Hoover Institution Studies, Series B: Elite Studies, Number 2, August 1951.

Schulz, Heinrich E., and Taylor, Stephen S. *Who's Who in the U.S.S.R., 1961–62.* London: Intercontinental Book and Publishing Company, 1962.

Schuman, Frederick L. *Soviet Politics at Home and Abroad.* New York: Alfred A. Knopf, 1953.

Schuster, Rudolf. *Deutschlands Staatliche Existenz im Widerstreit: Politische und Rechtliche Gesichtspunkte 1945–63.* Munich: R. Oldenbourg Verlag, 1963.

Seaton, Albert. *Stalin as Military Commander.* New York: Praeger Publishers, 1976.

Shannon, David A. *The Decline of American Communism.* Chatham, N.J.: The Chatham Bookseller, 1959.

Short, Anthony. *The Communist Insurrection in Malaya, 1948–60.* New York: Crane Rusak and Co., 1975.

Shulman, Marshall D. *Stalin's Foreign Policy Reappraised.* Cambridge: Harvard University Press, 1963.

Sinha, V. B. *The Red Rebel in India.* New Delhi: Associated Publishing House, 1968.

Slater, Leonard. *The Pledge.* New York: Pocket Books, 1970.

Smith, Jean Edward. *Germany Beyond the Wall.* Boston: Little, Brown and Co., 1969.

Soviet-Yugoslav Dispute. Text of the Published Correspondence. London and New York: Royal Institute of International Affairs, 1948.

Spechler, Dina. *Zhdanovism, Eurocommunism, and Cultural Reaction in the U.S.S.R.* Jerusalem: The Soviet and East European Research Center, The Hebrew University of Jerusalem, March 1979.

Stevenson, William. *A Man Called Intrepid.* New York: Ballantine Books, 1976.

Swayze, Harold. *Political Control of Literature in the U.S.S.R., 1946–1959.* Cambridge: Harvard University Press, 1962.

Swearer, Howard R. *The Politics of Succession in the U.S.S.R.* Boston: Little, Brown and Co., 1964.

Swearington, Rodger, ed. *Leaders of the Communist World.* New

York: The Free Press, 1971.

Sworakowski, Witold S., ed. *World Communism: A Handbook.* Stanford, Calif.: Hoover Institution Press, 1973.

Tiersky, Ronald. *French Communism, 1920–72.* New York and London: Columbia University Press, 1974.

Ulam, Adam. *Titoism and the Cominform.* Cambridge: Harvard University Press, 1952.

_____. *Expansion and Coexistence.* New York: Frederick A. Praeger Press, 1968.

_____. *The Rivals.* New York: Viking Press, 1971.

_____. *Stalin.* New York: Viking Press, 1973.

United Nations Official Records. General Assembly. First Special Session, 1947, vol. 1. Second Session, 1947, vols. 1–5.

United Nations Special Committee on Palestine. *Report to the General Assembly.* Annexes, Appendices and Maps to the Report of August 31, 1947. London: His Majesty's Stationery Office.

United States Central Intelligence Agency. *Membership of U.S.S.R. Academy of Sciences.* Washington, D.C.: March 1977 (Cr-77-11360).

United States House of Representatives. Select Committee on Communist Aggression. "Communist Takeover of Estonia." Special Report Number 3. Washington, D.C.: U.S. Government Printing Office, 1954.

_____. Committee on Foreign Affairs. *Strategy and Tactics of World Communism.* Washington, D.C.: U.S. Government Printing Office, 1960.

_____. Committee on Un-American Activities. *Facts on Communism, Volume II: The Soviet Union, from Lenin to Khrushchev.* Washington, D.C.: U.S. Government Printing Office, 1960.

Upton, A. F. *Communism in Scandinavia and Finland.* New York: Anchor Books, 1973.

Utechin, S. V. *Everyman's Concise Encyclopedia of Russia.* London: J. M. Dent & Sons Ltd., 1961.

Vali, Ferenc A. *Rift and Revolt in Hungary.* Cambridge: Harvard University Press, 1966.

_____. *The Quest for a United Germany.* Baltimore: Johns Hopkins Press, 1967.

Van Creveld, Martin. *Hitler's Strategy, 1940–41: The Balkan Clue.* London: Cambridge University Press, 1973.

Van der Kroef, Justus M. *The Communist Party of Indonesia.* Vancouver: The University of British Columbia Press, 1965.

Werth, Alexander. *Russia at War, 1941–45.* New York: E. P. Dutton and Co., 1964.

_____. *Russia: Hopes and Fears*. Harmondsworth, England: Penguin Books, 1969.

_____. *Russia: The Post-War Years*. New York: Taplinger Publishing Co., 1971.

Wolfe, Thomas. *Soviet Power and Europe, 1945–1970*. Baltimore and London: Johns Hopkins Press, 1970.

Wolin, Simon, and Slusser, Robert M., eds. *The Soviet Secret Police*. Westport, Conn.: Greenwood Press Publishers, 1957.

Woodehouse, C. M. *The Struggle for Greece, 1941–49*. London: Hart-Davis, MacGibbon, 1976.

Wright, Gordon. *The Ordeal of Total War, 1939–1945*. New York: Harper and Row, 1968.

Yarmolinsky, Avraham. *Literature under Communism*. Russian and East European Studies, vol. 20. Bloomington: Russian and East European Institute, Indiana University, 1960.

Ypsilon (Pseudonym). *Pattern of World Revolution*. New York: Ziff-Davis, 1947.

Zagoria, Janet D., ed. *Power and the Soviet Elite: "The Letter of an Old Bolshevik" and Other Essays by Boris I. Nicolaevsky*. New York: Frederick A. Praeger Press, 1965.

Western Sources: Articles

Antic, Zdenko. "Kardelj Describes Clashes with Stalin over Federation with Bulgaria." *Radio Free Europe-Radio Liberty*, RAD Background Report/28 (Yugoslavia), February 7, 1980.

Associated Press. "Bulgaria Stands by Yugoslav Ties," *New York Times*, July 1, 1948, p. 8.

_____. "End to Split Held Possible." *New York Times*, September 2, 1948.

_____. "Finnish Newspapers Accused." *New York Times*, September 9, 1948.

_____. "Finnish Reds Admit Blunders." *New York Times*, September 9, 1948.

_____. "Public Trial in Syria Alleges Some Had Been Bribed." *New York Times*, March 23, 1949.

_____. "Russia 'Scoops' Reporter Who Questioned Premier." *New York Times*, September 25, 1946, p. 3.

_____. "Soviet Calls Text of Stassen Wrong." *New York Times*, May 9, 1947, p. 3.

_____. "Stassen Praises Press." *New York Times*, May 9, 1947, p. 3.

_____. "Vishinsky Named as Molotoff Aid." *New York Times*, September 8, 1940, p. 28.

_____. "Yugoslav Reds Mourn." *New York Times*, September 2, 1948.

Atkinson, Brooks. "Stalin's Unexplained Absence Hushes Big Moscow Parade." *New York Times*, November 8, 1945, p. 1.

Barghoorn, Frederick C. "The Varga Discussion and Its Significance." *American Slavic and Eastern European Review*, vol. 8, October 1948, pp. 214–36.

Bulletin de l'Association d'Etudes et d'Informations Politiques Internationales. "Georges Alexandrov n'est plus ministre." Vol. 7, no. 129, April 16–30, 1955, pp. 10–11. "A propos du 'conflict' Jdanov-Malenkov." Vol. 5, no. 92, July 1–15, 1953, pp. 13–14.

Burin, Frederic S. "The Communist Doctrine of the Inevitability of War." *The American Political Science Review*, vol. 57, no. 2, June 1963, pp. 334–54.

Corbett, Percy E. "The Aleksandrov Story." *World Politics*, vol. 1, no. 2, January 1949, pp. 161–74.

Dallin, David J. "Kremlin Spies on Trial." *New Leader*, vol. 36, no. 11, March 16, 1953, pp. 9–10.

Duevel, Christian. "M. A. Suslov's Role in Postwar Soviet Politics." *Radio Liberation*, Central Research Department. Munich: August 4, 1958.

_____. "The Purge of N. A. Voznesensky." *Radio Liberty Research*. Munich: December 2, 1963, no. 1648.

_____. "The Soviet Press Falsifies the Biography of Purge Victim N. A. Voznesenskii." *Radio Liberty Research*. Munich: December 3, 1973, RL 381/73.

East Europe (London), vol. 3, no. 152, October 16, 1947. "Conflict of the Antipodes," pp. 1–2.

The Economist, vol. 152, no. 5413, May 24, 1947. "The Russians and Palestine," pp. 801–03.

The Economist, vol. 151, no. 5386, November 16, 1946. "Soviet Anniversary," p. 784.

Griffin, Charles. "Chile Links 2 Ousted Yugoslavs to Comintern Plot on Americas." *New York Times*, October 10, 1947, p. 1.

Halperin, Ernst. "Between Belgrade and Moscow." *Swiss Review of World Affairs*, vol. 5, no. 4, July 1955, pp. 14–17.

Harris, Jonathan. "The Origins of the Conflict between Malenkov and Zhdanov: 1939–41." *Slavic Review*, vol. 35, no. 2, June 1976, pp. 287–303.

Lazitch, Branko. "Tito et Moscou pendant la Deuxième Guerre

Mondiale, 1939–1945." *Bulletin de l'Association d'Etudes et d'Informations Politiques Internationales,* June 1–15, 1954, supplément du numéro 111, pp. 1–12.

Lissan, Maury. "Stalin the Appeaser." *Survey,* Summer 1970, no. 76, pp. 53–63.

Ma'ariv (Israeli afternoon daily), January 4–5, 1979, weekly illustrated section. "The Lost Weapons List," p. 5.

McNeill, Terry. "The Specter of Voznesensky Stalks Suslov." *Radio Liberty Research,* October 11, 1974, RL 338/74.

Marantz, Paul. "Soviet Foreign Policy Factionalism under Stalin: A Case Study on the Inevitability of War Controversy." *Soviet Union,* vol. 3, part 1, 1976, pp. 91–107.

Mathews, Herbert L. "Stalin Applauds British Socialism." *New York Times,* May 10, 1947, p. 4.

Mavris, N. G. "Dodecanese Seek Rights." Letter from the President of the Dodecanese National Council to the Editor. *New York Times,* August 8, 1945, p. 22.

Middleton, Drew. "Soviet 'Unafraid' Zhdanov Asserts: Stalin Order Urges Preparedness." *New York Times,* November 7, 1946, p. 1.

_____. "Malenkov's Star Rises in Kremlin Since Death of His Rival, Zhdanov." *New York Times,* November 22, 1948.

Miller, J. "Prof. Kedrov on Philosophy and National Self-Assertion." *Soviet Studies,* vol. 1, no. 1, June 1949, pp. 84–91.

Miller, J., and Miller, M., "Voprosy Filosofii (Problems of Philosophy), 3 (1948)." *Soviet Studies,* vol. 1, no. 2, October 1949, pp. 210–30.

Moore, Patrick, with G. S. "The Macedonian Polemic Rides Again: Tsola Dragoycheva's Memoirs." *Radio Free Europe-Radio Liberty,* vol. 4, no. 5, January 25–31, 1979. RAD Background Report/26 (Bulgaria), January 31, 1979.

New York Times.

"Transcript of Interview between Stalin and Stassen on World Cooperation." May 4, 1947, p. 50

"Communism in Chile." Editorial. October 11, 1947, p. 16.

"Yugoslavs Cut Chilean Ties: Hint Santiago is U.S. Puppet." October 12, 1947, p. 1.

"Reds in Bulgaria Decree Self-Purge." July 10, 1948, p. 15.

"Zhdanov Loomed as Heir to Stalin." September 1, 1948.

"Zhdanov Dies at 52, Cominform Head, In 'Inner Cabinet.'" September 1, 1948.

Nicolaevsky, Boris. "Palace Revolution in the Kremlin." *New Leader,* vol. 32, no. 12, March 19, 1949, pp. 8–9.

_____. "The Coming Soviet Purge." *New Leader,* vol. 33, no. 7,

February 18, 1950, p. 3.

_____. "Malenkov—His Rise and His Policy." *New Leader*, vol. 36, no. 12, March 23, 1953, pp. 2–6.

_____. "How Did Stalin Die?" *New Leader*, vol. 36, no. 16, April 20, 1953, pp. 2–7.

_____. "Russia Purges the Purgers." *New Leader*, vol. 36, no. 52, December 28, 1953, pp. 3–5.

_____. "The Abakumov Case." *New Leader*, vol. 38, no. 2, January 10, 1955, pp. 14–15.

Pierre, André. "Quand Staline Garde le Silence." *Le Monde*, December 3, 1946, p. 1.

_____. "André Jdanov est Mort à Moscou." *Le Monde*, September 2, 1948, p. 2.

Pistrak, Lazar M. "Malenkov: The Man and Myth." *New Leader*, vol. 36, no. 11, March 16, 1953, pp. 6–8.

"G. M. Popov, Prominent Survivor of the 'Leningrad Affair,' Dies." *Radio Liberty Research*, January 22, 1968, CRD 37/68.

Reston, James B. "Big Three Snarled on Italian Empire, Iran, Dardenelles." *New York Times*, August 5, 1945, p. 1.

Rigby, T. H. "How the Obkom Secretary Was Tempererd." *Problems of Communism*, vol. 29, no. 2, March–April, 1980, pp. 58–61. See Patolilchev, N.S.

Rosa, Ruth Amende. "The Soviet Theory of 'People's Democracy.' " *World Politics*, no. 4, July 1949, pp. 489–510.

Salisbury, Harrison E. "Close Stalin Aide Rebukes High Red." *New York Times*, December 25, 1952, p. 11.

_____. "Trofim L. Lysenko is Dead at 78: Was Science Overlord Under Stalin?" *New York Times*, November 24, 1976.

Schlesinger, R. J. A. "Some Materials on the Recent Attacks Against Cosmopolitanism." *Soviet Studies*, vol. 1, no. 2, October 1949, pp. 178–88.

Schwartz, Harry. "Rare Open Fight for Power." *New York Times*, December 25, 1952, p. 11.

Schwarz, Solomon. "The Eclipse of a Soviet Economist." *New Leader*, vol. 31, no. 7, February 14, 1948, p. 4.

Souvarine, Boris. "Confidences d'un diplomate Communiste." *Est et Oeust*, vol, 10, no. 190, March 1–15, 1954, pp. 1–4.

Soviet Analyst.

"Promoting Old Comrades." Vol. 6, no. 20, October 13, 1977, pp. 3–4.

"Soviet Leaders: A Time for Decisions (2)." Vol. 7, no. 13, June 29, 1978, pp. 4–6.

Stankovic, Slobodan. "Memoirs of Yugoslavia's Former Ambassador in Moscow—Part II." *Radio Free Europe-Radio Liberty*, vol. 3, no. 3, January 18–25, 1978. RAD Background Report/9 (Yugoslavia), January 20, 1978, p. 11.

_____. "Yugoslavia Commemorates Anniversary of Dimitrov's Death." *Radio Free Europe-Radio Liberty*, vol. 4, no. 28, July 11–17, 1979. RAD Background Report/159 (Yugoslavia), July 17, 1979.

Sulzberger, C. L. "Balkan Elections to Ignore Allies, Regimes Backed by Reds to Stay." *New York Times*, October 25, 1945, p. 1.

_____. "Question of a Successor for Stalin is Unanswered." *New York Times*, October 28, 1945.

_____. "Stalin is Believed Quitting Some Jobs." *New York Times*, November 8, 1945.

_____. "Shake-up in Kremlin Council Linked to Stalin's Successor." *New York Times*, March 18, 1949.

_____. "Quiet Soviet Purge Taking Place—Thousands Ousted." *New York Times*, June 6, 1949.

_____. "Two More Leaders Reported Victims of Purge in Russia." *New York Times*, June 19, 1949.

_____. "Malenkov's Rise to Power is Key Soviet Development." *New York Times*, June 23, 1949.

_____. "Malenkov Faction Climbing in Russia." *New York Times*, October 11, 1949.

_____. "Purge of Backers of Zhdanov at End." *New York Times*, November 26, 1949.

Survey, no. 63, April 1967. "Extracts from the Book by A. M. Nekrich, 22 June 1941," and "Discussion of the Book," pp. 170–80.

Szenfeld, Ignacy. "The Metamorphosis of a Biography." *Radio Liberty Research*, August 30, 1974, RL 274/74. (Deals with official Soviet biographies of N. A. Voznesenskii.)

Tikos, Laszlo M. "Eugene Varga: A Reluctant Conformist." *Problems of Communism*, vol. 14, no. 1, pp. 71–74.

The Times (London).
"Soviet Ties with America—Mr. Stalin's Talk to Mr. Stassen." May 5, 1947, p. 4.
"The Stalin-Stassen Interview—Puzzling Accusation by Moscow," May 9, 1947, p. 3.
"Soviet Tactics in Germany." January 28, 1949, p. 3.

Vishniak, Mark. "The Red Terror." *New Leader*, vol. 32, no. 22, May 28, 1949, p. 10

Voigt, F. A. "Is Tito Worth Saving?" *New Leader*, vol. 33, no. 48, December 4, 1950, pp. 2–4.

Whitney, Craig R. "Lev Kopolev, A Soviet Dissident, Who Does Not Want to Emigrate, Speaks Out." *New York Times*, July 29, 1979, p. 2.

U.S. Government Sources (General)

ANNUAL REPORTS:

United States Department of State: *Foreign Relations of the United States* (FRUS), annual collected volumes on the Soviet Union and Eastern Europe, 1940–1953. Washington: U.S. Government Printing Office.

DECLASSIFIED DOCUMENTS

Carrollton Press. *The Declassified Documents Series, Retrospective Collection* (on microfilm).

Foreign Broadcast Information Service. Series for Eastern Europe and the U.S.S.R., 1945–1948.

MICROFICHE

United States Central Intelligence Agency. "Who's Who in the Soviet Government, January 1948." CIACR 76-12971, Collected D.S.O.'s 1948–1966, unclassified, 1, 2 of 39.

"Party and Government Officials in the U.S.S.R., March, 1950," CIACR 76-12971, Collected D.S.O.'s 1948–1966, unclassified, 3, 4, 5, of 39.

INDEX

Yudin, Pavel F., 114, 165
Yugoslavia, 42–53, 75–79; Albania
and, 46–47, 137; Britain and,
77–79; Bulgaria and, 138,
139; Calcutta conference and,
111–15; Chile and, 114;
Churchill-Stalin deal, 44, 45;
delegates at the founding
meeting of the Cominform,
103, 104–5, 109–10; expulsion from the Cominform, 42,
50, 104, 143; Greece and,
47–52; international policy of,
44, 45; Middle East and, 83;
"new democracies," 54, 64,
75, 76, 84; Palestine and, 80,
81, 82; Partisans of, 44;
Russia and, 42–53, 66, 76,
82, 135, 137; socialist
economy in the F.P.R.Y.,
75–76; on the United States
and, 104–5; Vardar
Macedonia, 140; Voznesenskii
popular in, 76. See also Tito
Yugoslav People's Youth, 97

Zakhariadis, Nicholas, 48–49, 50
Zhdanov, Andreii Alexandrovich,
1, 8, 10; Aleksandrov and,
12n, 17, 58, 87, 173–76;
Allied Control Commission
and, 22; antidismantlement
sentiment of, 93; anti-
Zhdanov front, 20; attack on
artists, 58; attack on Leningrad literature, 56–57; Beria
and, 151; Britain and, 105–6;
Central Committee and the
death of, 149; chairman of the
Supreme Soviet's Foreign Affairs Committee, 13, 25; chief
of Department of Propaganda,
17; Cominform and, 101,
105–6, 143; Committee on
Liberated Areas and, 25; as
"Crown Prince," 132–34;
death of, 134, 149, 150–51,
166, 167; director of Agitprop, 12; economics and,
40–41; Eighteenth Party Congress and, 13; Estonia and,

15; evacuation of Leningrad
and, 20, 22; Finland and, 14,
132–33, 148; "Ghost Com-
intern" and, 21; head of the
Foreign Department of C.C.,
25; India and, 112; intellig-
gentsia and, 38; international
policy of, 25, 26, 27, 39, 40,
46, 96; Leningrad Party and,
13; Leningrad Purges and, 28,
33, 56–57; Lysenko and, 59,
60; Manuilskii and, 22;
Palestine and, 81; post-
Zhdanov, 153–60; pro-
German, 18, 19, 86, 87, 96,
100; Ribbentrop-Molotov Pact
and, 14; science and, 59;
secretary of the Central Committee, 12; Shcherbakov and,
14n*; Stalin and, 136–37;
Supreme Naval Council and,
14, 14n†; Tito and, 3, 52–53;
Tuil'panov and, 88; United
States and, 105–6; Yezhov
and, 171–72; Zhukov and,
32n, 133
Zhdanovites, 25–41;
antidismantlement sentiment
of, 93; Budenny, 34;
Bulganin, 33–34; Cominform
and the, 101; decline of the,
135–52; flag for the *Freies
Deutschland*, and, 96–97;
Germany and, 85, 89, 96;
Govorov, 31; international
policy of, 46, 96; Khrulev,
30; Konev, 31; Kosygin,
28–29, 151; Kuznetsov, A.
A., 29, 149; Kuznetsov, N.
G., 29–30; Kuznetsov, V. V.,
34; Leningrad Affair and, 28,
29, 30; "Parade of the
Victors," 36; Patolichev,
30–31; Popkov, 66, 149–50;
Popov, 30, 150; Rodionov,
150; Shikin, 85, 150;
Shkiriatov, 33; Shvernik,
34–35; Tito and, 48, 50,
52–53; Tiul'panov, 85;
Vasilevskii, 34; Vershinin, 34;
Voprosy Filosofii, 60;

65864